Letters
from the Mountains

Between the Years 1773 and 1803

VOLUME 2

ANNE MACVICAR GRANT
EDITED BY J.P. GRANT

CAMBRIDGE
UNIVERSITY PRESS

CAMBRIDGE UNIVERSITY PRESS

Cambridge, New York, Melbourne, Madrid, Cape Town,
Singapore, São Paolo, Delhi, Tokyo, Mexico City

Published in the United States of America by Cambridge University Press, New York

www.cambridge.org
Information on this title: www.cambridge.org/9781108033497

© in this compilation Cambridge University Press 2011

This edition first published 1845
This digitally printed version 2011

ISBN 978-1-108-03349-7 Paperback

CAMBRIDGE LIBRARY COLLECTION

Books of enduring scholarly value

Women's Writing

The later twentieth century saw a huge wave of academic interest in women's writing, which led to the rediscovery of neglected works from a wide range of genres, periods and languages. Many books that were immensely popular and influential in their own day are now studied again, both for their own sake and for what they reveal about the social, political and cultural conditions of their time. A pioneering resource in this area is Orlando: Women's Writing in the British Isles from the Beginnings to the Present (http://orlando.cambridge.org), which provides entries on authors' lives and writing careers, contextual material, timelines, sets of internal links, and bibliographies. Its editors have made a major contribution to the selection of the works reissued in this series within the Cambridge Library Collection, which focuses on non-fiction publications by women on a wide range of subjects from astronomy to biography, music to political economy, and education to prison reform.

Letters from the Mountains

First published in 1806, and revised and edited by her son for this 1845 sixth edition, this collection of letters by Anne Grant (1755–1838) tells her story of thirty years' residence in the Scottish Highlands. Described by the author as 'sketches of a life spent in the most remote obscurity', it was one of the first works to acquaint the public with the romantic scenery of the Highlands. Anne Grant's lyrical descriptions of the landscape and characters of the rural parish of Laggan caught the imagination of a generation captivated by the poetry of Scott and Burns. Volume 2 includes engaging descriptions of the pleasures of rural life alongside frank and emotional accounts of personal tragedies. The work is an important example of a woman's literary contribution to the Romantic movement. For more information on this author, see http://orlando.cambridge.org/public/svPeople?formname=r&person_id=granan.

Cambridge University Press has long been a pioneer in the reissuing of out-of-print titles from its own backlist, producing digital reprints of books that are still sought after by scholars and students but could not be reprinted economically using traditional technology. The Cambridge Library Collection extends this activity to a wider range of books which are still of importance to researchers and professionals, either for the source material they contain, or as landmarks in the history of their academic discipline.

Drawing from the world-renowned collections in the Cambridge University Library, and guided by the advice of experts in each subject area, Cambridge University Press is using state-of-the-art scanning machines in its own Printing House to capture the content of each book selected for inclusion. The files are processed to give a consistently clear, crisp image, and the books finished to the high quality standard for which the Press is recognised around the world. The latest print-on-demand technology ensures that the books will remain available indefinitely, and that orders for single or multiple copies can quickly be supplied.

The Cambridge Library Collection will bring back to life books of enduring scholarly value (including out-of-copyright works originally issued by other publishers) across a wide range of disciplines in the humanities and social sciences and in science and technology.

LETTERS

FROM

THE MOUNTAINS;

BEING THE CORRESPONDENCE WITH HER FRIENDS,

BETWEEN THE YEARS 1773 AND 1803,

OF

MRS. GRANT OF LAGGAN.

EDITED, WITH NOTES AND ADDITIONS, BY HER SON,

J. P. GRANT, ESQ.

IN TWO VOLUMES.

VOL. II.

THE SIXTH EDITION.

LONDON:

PRINTED FOR

LONGMAN, BROWN, GREEN, AND LONGMANS,

PATERNOSTER-ROW.

1845.

CONTENTS

OF

THE SECOND VOLUME.

LETTERS.

APPENDIX.

LETTERS

FROM

THE MOUNTAINS.

LETTER I.

TO MISS OURRY.

Laggan, February 5, 1791.

My ever dear Friend,

I own it; our correspondence did, for a while, languish on my side. But what has not this interruption cost me, and how various and painful were the causes of it! I have written, and inquired again and again, without success.* I shall, however, make this last effort to discover whether my dearest Anne is still a fellow-traveller through this vale of shadows; or whether I am to consider her as one of those separated spirits, whom tremulous hope and fond imagination flatter us with recognizing, at some future period, in holier, happier regions; for I will not, cannot suppose you capable of neglecting, slighting, or even forgetting me.

* Miss Ourry was at this time in England; an interval of twelve years had occurred in the correspondence of the two friends.—ED.

Had my last letter reached you, I am certain you would have answered it. Even my unavailing friendship was worth gratitude; because it was very warm and very true, and pure from every selfish motive, except the vanity of being esteemed by a person of superior merit; which was certainly very pardonable. However, as you are a human creature, and, as such, liable to change, I shall admit the bare possibility of your having received and neglected my letter; and shall, therefore, suspend giving any account of my concerns till I have it under your hand, that you are desirous to hear of them.

I will not regale you with an account of the fine children which it has pleased God to bestow on me; of the still finer ones whom He has thought fit to resume to Himself; or of the tranquillity and comparative happiness I have enjoyed since I saw you; no, nor of the health and prosperity of my parents, or the great and wonderful vicissitudes that have happened in the circle of our acquaintance. I must not only be desired, but entreated, before I make any of these communications. I will tell you, however, that nothing shall ever abate that tender regard, which I shall carry to my grave for you. Mr. Grant, who is your great admirer, longs also to hear of you. Do not mind postage; mind only what you owe on the score of friendship to your unaltered,

ANNE GRANT.

Letter II.

Laggan, March 27, 1791.

My dearest Nancy,

The sight of your well known dear-loved hand filled my heart with a pleasure to which I knew nothing comparable, unless what the woman of Zarepta might have felt, on receiving her lamented son alive from the hands of the prophet. Alas! I have a sad reason for too deeply feeling the force of that allusion; but I will not cloud our first meeting with a detail of sorrows; as little will I take up your time with a tedious recital of the ways and means I have used to hear of you. I had not Mr. Malliet's address, but endeavoured to point him out by the circumstances of his being a Fellow of the Royal Society, and having held a place at court.* By your having formerly taught me to address you under Lord Kinsale's cover, I was led to discover you in the manner which has proved so gratifying to us both. May my benedictions rest and remain with this good Lord! I wish it were as honourable to him, as the privilege of wearing his hat where he pleases.

Why should I tell why I was so much concerned and afflicted at the melancholy detail of what you have lost, and what you have suffered? I can but too easily conceive what you must have felt at the

---

* Mr. Malliet, the father of Miss Ourry's friend, Miss Malliet, then held an office about the Palace, and lived in Westminster.

final parting with your worthy parents. You all lived
so much, and so entirely with each other, and loved
each other so *exclusively* as well as tenderly. You
can better judge why Young was so great a favourite
with me, now that you know, by sad experience,

> " There is no pang, like that of bosom torn
> From bosom bleeding o'er the sacred dead."

The depredations which fraud and villany have made
on your little store I sincerely regret. Yet, when I
consider that your mind was always superior to trappings and tinsel, and that sorrow and sickness must
have long since dissolved the charm that attaches us
to the mere exterior forms of life; when I consider,
too, that you appear to have gathered much more than
would have been expected from the wreck of your
father's property, and that you are now cherished in
the tender bosom of friendship and true sympathy; I
would fain hope your pecuniary resources are equal to
your wants, though not to your spirits and past expec-
tations.

I shall give you the desired detail of past transactions
in a future letter, which will be sent under the cover
of Fingal,* who is a Cornish Member, and having
contrived, like Orpheus, by the power of his lyre,
to build a house in this country, is our neighbour
and acquaintance. I hope the musical manes of the
said Orpheus will forgive my blunder, in imputing to
him what was done by Amphion, who, on better
recollection, built the Theban walls; and, though I

---

* The late James Macpherson, Esq. of Belleville, the translator
of Ossian; who was our neighbour in the country, and used to frank
covers for us.—(1807.)

know you dearly love a little hit at me, I hope you will have so much respect for my classical recollections, as to resist the temptation of comparing me to one of those savages who danced to the said plastic strains; I lie the more open to this, from my singular delight in long descended song. Receive, meantime, an abridged, but faithful description of the present state of my family and affairs.

We live on the banks of the Spey (would, for your sake, it were the Tweed); Mr. Grant possesses, one way or other, an income of . . . . . . We occupy a comfortable cottage, consisting of four rooms, light closets, and a nursery, and kitchen built out by way of addition. It is situated in a southern aspect, at the foot of an arable hill, behind which stretches an extensive moss, once a forest, and still abounding in fuel, which is surmounted by a lofty mountain, the top of which is often lost in the clouds, while its bosom, hollow and verdant, is a reservoir of copious springs, and abounds in early pasturage, and berries peculiar to these regions. Our little domain, to which the church-lands are added, stretches about a quarter of a mile over a meadowy, I might well add, flowery valley; through which the river turns and returns again like the Links of Forth, which its waters far excel in purity. At the end of the house is a brook, which often reminds me of Franky's purling brooks, for it purls abundantly through summer, babbles in harvest, and brawls, like a termagant, all winter. In the meadows below, it assumes a new character, and winds, in a deep channel, through richly decorated banks, with a murmur so dulcet, so softly plaintive, that one is almost tempted to ask what ails it. I should have told you that at one end of our cottage is a garden, in which we have planted a variety of trees, and where small fruit abounds. At our door is a stone porch, with seats; this rural portico is so covered with honeysuckle, that you would take it for a bower; we have a little green court inclosed before, which, in fine weather, forms a supplement to the nursery. I should have begun by telling you that we hold a farm at a very easy rent, which supports a dozen milk cows, and a couple of hundred sheep, with a range of summer pasture on the mountains for our young stock, horses, &c. This farm supplies us with everything absolutely necessary; even the wool and flax, which our handmaids manufacture to clothe the children, are our own growth. But it is time to introduce you within doors, where you will find the master of the dwelling in the midst of the circle he most delights in, and in that home where he appears to most advantage; because his hospitality and warmth of heart here shine through that cloud of reserve and diffidence, which conceals him everywhere else. Singularly domestic, a fond husband, and tenderly indulgent father, he delights in his children from their birth, without nursing them like an old woman; judicious and attentive to what regards out-door management, but totally unconcerned as to what passes within; considering, like a true Highlander, household affairs as entirely the female province, and the duties of his sacred function as the only object, beyond his family, deserving of serious regard. Next, his mate, very little altered in sentiment and principle since you saw her, yet having the wings of romantic elevation somewhat clipt by increasing years and cares, and the fervour of enthusiasm a little abated; with that matronly cast of manners, which the constant exercise of authority, mingled with affection, naturally produces.

You will not think my taste improved when I tell you it is, if possible, more primitive than ever; and that all my pastoral, popular, and American prejudices, have " grown with my growth, and strengthened with my strength." How will all this agree with your " prejudice against prejudices?" But we shall agree in the long run, as we ever did. Our minds, indeed, must have had a strong predisposition to unite, when they surmounted so many differences in what with common minds is everything, early habits and education. My children I shall characterize at more leisure. At present, I shall only say, the first is said to be like her mother, the second like her father, and the third like—a ewe lamb.* Now, to form a more precise idea, you must consider these resemblances, as not only literal, but characteristic of my sons. Charlotte and Petrina are twins, perfect contrasts, one being dark haired, quick and lively; the other, fair, soft, and delicate. . . . . . . Here is the family-piece drawn, and the landscape; I have not yet shaded my drawing, but I shall throw in the shades in my next. I had more sons; but Heaven has resumed its own, and I ought silently to bow to its decrees. Expect in my next the eventful history of our friends at Fort-Augustus, most of whom have

* Mary, Catherine, and Isabella.—ED.

already set out before us, to explore the wide ocean of
eternity. Meantime, dear friend, briefly adieu!

LETTER III.

TO MISS OURRY, COLFORD, GLOUCESTERSHIRE.

Laggan, June 4, 1791.

My dear Friend,

What a history would it make, were I to relate all
the little family occurrences, which, in rapid succession, have hurried on the time since I wrote my last.
I carried down my second daughter, who had a threat-
ening illness, to my father's, at Fort-George, for sea
air. You cannot think how the good old people rejoiced to hear that I had found you again :—their
lively feelings on this occasion delighted me. I love
to see the evening of life warmed by the gentle flame
of kindly affections. Of all the evils that wait on the
decline of life, there is none I shrink from so much as
that chilling torpor of the soul, which contributes more
than all our infirmities to make old age unlovely. I
returned home from Fort-George through Strathspey,
where all Mr. Grant's relations live, and was unavoid-
ably detained some days with visits. Mr. G. came
some miles to meet me. I had Catherine and Isabella
with me in a little open carriage, which we keep for
these journeys. He presented your letter, which I
snatched with avidity, and read over with delight.
I shall defer any reference to its contents till I go
through my promised narrative.

For some years after you went away from Fort-

Augustus, my letters furnished you with an unbroken series, of which take this succinct and pithy sequel.*

* * * * * * * *

I had been all this while projecting a visit to Glasgow, but had deferred it from time to time, out of sympathy for Mrs. Newmarch, who hoped for her lord's return, and would feel most forlorn without me ; but the marriage of her father, the Governor, and the crowd of company which succeeded, leaving her no room to complain of solitude, I went southwards in the summer of 1777, to Glasgow, where my visit, only meant for a month, was drawn out to near a year, which was most agreeably spent. I look back upon it, indeed, as one of the most pleasant periods of my life ; not being passed in a perpetual flutter of idle visits, but in confirming and strengthening the friendships of my earlier years, and making new and valuable additions to them, which have been ever since a source of great comfort and pleasure to me. Leaving the excellent family, with whom I spent this year of felicity, I returned home through Perth, where I had the high gratification of meeting some of my distant relations, who were people of distinguished merit, and whose taste and manners were so suited to my own, that my heart adopted them to a nearer connexion than those distant ties can form. Those lovely sisters,† who lived in this world with all their views directed to another, and meekly sheltered in the shade of retirement qualities

---

* Here followed a detail of events at Fort-Augustus for some years previous to the Author's marriage, in 1779.—Ed.

† The late Mrs. Young, of Perth ; and Mrs. Bonar, married to the Minister of Cramond.—(1807.)—See Vol. I., Letter XXX.

entitled to universal esteem and admiration, lived only long enough to prove that they could fulfil every duty, and grace every department of life. In the bloom of youth, tenderly beloved by the worthiest of husbands, blessed with everything their regulated and modest wishes could aspire to, they obeyed the irresistible summons. The youngest, who was the most beautiful, departed in her twenty-second year, in the high triumphs of faith, taking not only a serene but joyful leave of friends whom she loved with unusual tenderness. Her sister, in whose arms she died, was immediately seized with the same disorder, and met death with the same well-grounded heroism.

" Surely to blissful realms those souls are flown,
That never flatter'd, censur'd, envied, strove."

My dear, you will excuse this digressive tribute to departed excellence. What havoc has been lately made in the little circle of those I loved!

" Yes, even here, amidst those secret shades,
The simple scenes of unreproved delight,
Affliction's iron hand my breast invades,
And death's dread dart is ever in my sight."

Indeed my meditations hover so constantly about the confines of the world unknown, where my aching eyes are continually exploring the departing footsteps of those who still live in my remembrance, that I now see this world and all its vanities, as the apostle says we do futurity, " through a glass darkly." These frequent excursions of the mind into the trackless ocean of vast eternity, contribute not a little to throw a dim shade over everything that dazzles and attracts, in

this valley of vision.—Unwillingly must I return to
my Fort-Augustus narrative, though no motive less
potent than a desire to gratify you, would induce me
to retrace such a series of crime, folly, and misfortune.
Hear then, and be, if not amused, at least instructed.
. . . . All this happened in 1779, when Mrs.
Newmarch, Curtis the surgeon, and I, as by common
consent, took our final leave of the place in the space
of one month. He took shelter in the East Indies,
she at Inverness, and I in Laggan and matrimony.
We left the demons of discord and deceit to rule their
votaries; none of us would have liked to have out-
stayed the other. My year's residence in Clydesdale
had revived and cherished the love of peace, virtue,
and decorum in my heart. The disorders of that
most beautiful, but most unhappy place, Fort-Augustus, had shown me vice and folly in their ugliest
aspect. Judge, then, whether, in the midst of tranquillity, mutual affection, domestic harmony, and the
esteem and good-will of a decent neighbourhood, I
did not enjoy my situation, without repining after languid idleness, insipid chit-chat, artificial wants, poor
attempts at finery, and all the mortifications which
result from the feeble efforts of inferior people to grasp
that fleeting phantom, fashion. I am a wretched nar-
rator, and miserable chronologer; I write fluently
from my heart, but very lamely from my memory.
Two marriages, however, not of the number said to
be made in heaven, I will detail; and let Desdemona
heedfully attend, for it is no small plague to me to
rake up my recollections. . . . .
My father removed from Fort-Augustus to Fort-

George some years ago,* where he lives very happily, and derives much pleasure from his grandchildren. Different friends from Glasgow and Edinburgh have visited us in this retreat.—By the death of my third son, a charming infant, who lived not many days, I was convinced of what I could not have easily believed, that the death of such an infant could produce severe feelings of sorrow for the time; a thing both sinful and unaccountable. I had, however, another son remaining, in whom all my delight was centered, and who was, indeed, an extraordinary child, spoke, walked, and showed tokens of sensibility and understanding long before the usual period. Strong, robust, and manly, we looked on him as the future pillar of our family, and never dreaded that stroke which we bore so ill when it came. In the fatal May of 1789 our children were seized with the measles, and had it favourably, all but the darling and pride of our hearts; who being seized at the same time with a worm fever, which we were not aware of, and knew not how to manage, made his escape from the troubles of life, and left us overwhelmed with the most sinful and extravagant sorrow. But you are no novice in distress, and I will not awaken your griefs, by opening afresh the wounds of mine. My constitution, enfeebled by the rapid increase of my family, was greatly impaired by this shock, but I have had better health since the birth of my twins, who, I hope, will continue to be the youngest. My spirits are pretty equal, though that sad event has added to my habits of musing.

* In 1783.

The soil here is very rich, though the climate is cold and gloomy. I am very fond of the lower class of people; they have sentiment, serious habits, and a kind of natural courtesy; in short, they are not mob, an animal which Smollet most emphatically says he detests in its head, midriff, and members; and, in this point, I do not greatly differ with him. You would wonder how many of the genteeler class live here. They are not rich to be sure; so much the better for us. For,

> "Where no contiguous palace rears its head,
> To shame the meanness of the humble shed,"

people do very well, and keep each other in countenance. They have been mostly in the army, are socially and kindly disposed, and have more both of spirit and good-breeding than is usually met with in people of their pitch; and, as for an inclination to gaiety and hospitality, you may judge of them by what you have seen among your quondam neighbours in Ireland. If they have foibles, why should I expatiate on them? They have treated us with uniform kindness and civility, and shown us as much friendship as, in their idea, it becomes them to show to such as are not kindred, the sole measure of affection here. I shall quit the ungrateful topic of censure with observing, that, after all, they have more dignity in their pride, and less absurdity in their vanity, than your Hibernian friends, for whom, too, I still retain a sort of kindness, after all; but indeed I saw an excellent sample of them.

I have made a great acquisition of late; a fine young creature, a relation of Mr. Grant's, who is under his protection, and passes the winter with her friends in town, and the rest of the year here.* At more leisure I will tell you her story, but am now as tired of narrative as I have made you. Mr. Grant has been at Edinburgh, attending the General Assembly, which answers to your poor dead, or rather dumb Convocation. I meet him next week at Kenmore, in Perthshire, where he is to come with some of my Glasgow friends.

When I hear from you again I shall acquaint you with the result, and give my ideas coolly and distinctly on the subject of your letter, and your present mode of living. I can now only congratulate you on enjoying the society of your Louisa,† to whose superior mind yours must be a higher gratification than any that wealth can procure. What, indeed, can wealth procure that the vulgarest wretch may not equally taste and enjoy, except that first of intellectual joys, which wealth so rarely attains, the society of an elegant mind, purified by virtue and endeared by friendship. I long to hear of your crossing the mountains on a goat, and how Wales agrees with you. I shall mark the geographical bearing of my dwelling minutely in my next letter. We live about fifty miles from both Inverness and Perth, which are the nearest towns; yet, in spite of distance and obscurity, my sworn foe, fashion, pursues, overtakes, and surrounds me. Do not wait for a frank; one who despises all other luxuries as I do, may well claim this single in-

* Miss Charlotte Grant, afterwards Mrs. Smith, and already referred to.
† Miss Malliet, mentioned in a former letter, as a friend of Miss Ourry.

dulgence. Adieu, my beloved friend. I am, unalterably, your own

A. G.

LETTER IV.

TO MRS. SMITH OF JORDANHILL, GLASGOW.

Laggan, October 4, 1791.

My dear Friend,

I had a hurried letter from you more than a month ago. Lest I forget again to tell you, I have heard twice from Miss Ourry since she went into Gloucestershire, where she is very happy with her aunt, Mrs. Dessolles, to whom she must be a great comfort. The health and freedom she enjoys in that peaceful retreat seem to have given a new turn to her spirits; she is evidently more cheerful, and makes reflections on her situation similar to your own. Her invaluable friend, Miss Malliet, has, I hope, by this time, received her at London. I always forgot to tell you Mr. Grant's answer to your query, "Whether he had changed his mind about never more going from home?" He bids me say he has been kissing his door-posts ever since his return, and always finds his devotion to his household gods much increased by any suspension of the usual worship. Yet I doubt not, the inducement of being able to carry these teraphim with him, might induce him to travel a good way in a given direction.

What a stroller I have been this summer! When children came one at a time, I staid at home, and attended to them with great care; now they come in pairs, I scamper away like a hen ostrich, or a fine lady. I began my career by going to my father's in spring; that was on business, and I only staid two days. You know where we met in June.* When I returned, I was obliged, in consequence of an old engagement, to visit some friends in the lower part of the country, at a most beautiful place about ten miles distance. I left Charlotte in the house of the pastor there, whom you have heard me mention as a person of fine taste, superior abilities, and extensive information.† I should have told you, how I happened, at this time, to go to Fort-Augustus. I have a cousin, who succeeded my father in his office of Barrack-Master there, and possesses a large farm in the neighbourhood. He had a most promising family growing up, and was very prosperous in the world, having fallen into the succession of a small estate since he came there. But, lately, they met with the deepest affliction, in consequence of having lost, at one time, their favourite son and daughter, the one about eighteen, the other nineteen, years old. Their father, always infirm and delicate, fell into a dangerous illness soon after, from which he is now slowly recovering. Mr. Grant had to go over to attend a church court, to be held there last week, and I accompanied him. We took an odd fancy, for grave people twelve years wedded; and what was most to be wondered at, the proposal was

* Alluding to a meeting with her friend at Kenmore, in Perthshire, that summer.

† The late Rev. John Anderson of Fochabers, then Minister of Kingussie, near Laggan.—ED.

not mine, to whom you would most readily impute it. It was, to leave the vehicle and Angus at the foot of Corryarick, to go the circuitous road which you may remember, while we took the shepherd's footpath from the bridge, which, leading down a steep, where no carriage can venture, led into the long-known, dear-loved recesses on the borders of the Tarffe, where the hazelwoods, the echoing Drimen Duie, and the charming waterfall that I have so often described to you, lay in our path. Now you are not to suppose that we were so much of a Corydon and Pastora, as to go there for the mere purpose of enjoying sylvan beauties, and reviving tender recollections. It was humane, for it saved the poor horse; it was prudent, for it saved near two miles; it was civil, for it managed our time and road so as to put it in our power to visit our friends at Culachy, to whose abode this pathway was a short cut. But you have no idea of the wild beauties of this walk; their shades, sacred so often to contemplation and to friendship, have improved in solemnity and variety in the ten years' inter-regnum. When the triad* used to find such pleasure in haunting these deep retreats, the trees were not nearly so lofty, the incursions of hunters were more frequent, the country was more populous; but now the coppice is become a grove, whose tenants have increased, conscious of their safety. Oh, that you could see those hazel bowers, and the light festoons of wild honeysuckle pendent from their topmost branches; that

* The Author and her two friends, who used to explore these scenes together when living at Fort-Augustus, as mentioned in the early Letters.

you could hear the sweet responses of native music,
the deep murmur of the dark and secret stream, and
the mysterious echo of Drimen Duie!*   These are,
indeed, like sounds

> " Sent by spirits to mortals good,
>   Or th' unseen genius of the wood."

Do you think we could pass by the beautiful rocky basin
I have so often told you of, where a little tributary
stream falls in broken rills down a steep rock, decked
with fantastic tufts of flowers and nodding plants?
We did not pass it by, but stood a while on the brink,
recollecting the associate of our wild wanderings, and
the unequalled melody of the richest and mellowest
wood-notes that ever met my ear.   For here we used
to rest and listen to " songs divine to hear;" either
such plaintive notes as the " voice of Cona sung,"
given in his native language, or our own sweetest
pastoral lays, sung with simplicity, taste, and expression, that will never meet again in these days of
artifice.

> " O, lost Ophelia, sweetly flow'd the day,
>   To feel thy music with my soul agree;
> To taste the beauties of thy heartfelt lay,
>   To taste, and fancy it was dear to thee!"

I could not help saying this to my companion, here,
where her image seemed to hover.   We paid the due
tribute of tenderness to the memory of our hard-fated
friend;† tenderness unmingled with regret; for we

---

* See a particular account of this picturesque eminence, in the
note subjoined to the Letter of 10th August, 1778, p. 162.

† Miss Christina Macpherson of Culachy, frequently referred to
in the earlier Letters of this collection.—*See* Letter LI., Vol. I.

were pleased to think she had escaped from a world, where she, in particular, had so much to suffer, and so little to enjoy. Full of her remembrance, we followed the course of the stream which led to Culachy, the house of her favourite brother. He was not at home; but his pretty little wife welcomed us with a grace and cordiality that made us regret having only a single hour to spend with her. When we emerged from " the valley of vision," and saw Loch Ness from the eminence on which the house stands, I felt as if time had run back; but that was a mere momentary sensation.

I will not tell you how glad my relations at Fort-Augustus were to see me, or how the villagers flocked about me, to tell all their intervening history. But, finding it vain to hope for solitude and quiet to perform one of my customary *acts of recollection*, I rose one morning at five, and went round the boundaries of our old domain and the Fort; then crossed the bridge of Oich, and, from the rocks of Inchnacardach, took a wide survey of the lake, then a perfect mirror, and the noble steep of Sigchurman, decked with fantastic wreaths of rolling mist, that changed their form every moment as the sun broke out upon them. I retired towards Inchnacardach, where I mused, undisturbed, till fancy had her fill. I felt like a person transplanted to the poetical shades, who wanders among myrtle groves and Elysian vales in pensive contemplation, and sees the shadowy forms of those beloved in life, and mourned in death, glide silent by him. The sweet recesses, and sequestered scenes, in the vicinity, are become more beautiful than ever. I took a kind of solemn

c 2

delight in thus retracing my wonted paths among them; and, you may well believe, fancy peopled them with the shades of the departed. The gentle spirit of poor Mrs. Newmarch was not absent. Her death, or rather her release from life, I could think of with serenity, when I recollected how much she deserved, and how little she obtained in this state of probation.* Her father, the Governor, whom I have so often looked on with indifference, I regarded with unmixed compassion; anything so forlorn and helpless I have not seen. He seemed pleased to see me for her sake, and tried, in trembling accents, to speak of her. My cousins seemed gratified by our visit, and I was glad we made it. I saw several people to whom I wish well, whom I shall probably never see again. Then my mind was so easy with regard to the family, and the little gemini, as Charlotte had the entire charge of them, who is the very best deputy-matron I ever knew. You see I have made the most of this summer, being the first, since I was married, that I was not *very particularly* engaged at home.

It will refresh you, after all this tragi-pastoral, to hear that Gwynn† is married quite to his mind, and is the happiest of human beings. Though no one had more the habits and notions of a confirmed bachelor, yet, formed only for domestic life, he languished in tasteless apathy, wanting he knew not what, for he was carefully taught to despise matrimony. He has

* This interesting lady died in England soon after the death of her last surviving child.
† The late Captain Mark Gwynn, Commander of the King's galley at Fort-Augustus. His son is now a surgeon there.—(1845.)

got a very good little woman, with an easy temper, and just as much intellect as he would wish for, who loves him, and has brought him a fine child, in which he takes great pleasure. All this fills the void in his heart, and the vacancy in his time that made him formerly most deplorably listless, though the best hearted creature imaginable. A brother of his wife, who died abroad, has left her a pretty little fortune ; so he has, every way, drawn a prize in the lottery of marriage. Good connexions are not wanting, for the lady is one of Mr. Grant's hundred kinswomen, and, consequently, Mark Gwynn is now allied to us. What a privilege !

Now, that I have given you no brief abstract of my summer campaign since I saw you at our assignation at Kenmore, you must needs do justice to my diligence in recording important transactions. Though you should not hear from me for half-a-year to come, these commentaries will bear witness of my unshaken fidelity. In return for these reveries of solitude, you owe me something from the busy haunts of men. Retirement at the Fairlie is a mere pretence ; you go to be merry, and at ease, among your intimates, and then call it retiring.

We found all well at home, and the little *gemini* the finest and most amusing creatures. How lucky for you that I am near the end of my paper, or they might

" Live in description, and look *squat* in song;"

for squat they both are, this moment, on the floor. But I cannot " paint, ere they change, the Cynthia of

the minute," though you should take an interest in them
as the favourite playthings of your affectionate friend,

A. G.

LETTER V.

Laggan, April 2, 1792.

My dear Friend,

I know it will give you concern to hear that my
silence, for most part of this winter, was owing to
illness. This, though not dangerous or alarming, was
of such a nature as to throw the most oppressive gloom
upon my spirits. I am none of those querulous beings
who delight in brooding over evils, and oppressing
their friends with all that troubles them. That sanguine turn of mind which you early remarked in me,
has accompanied me through all the vicissitudes of
health and sickness, all the quick shifting scenes of
joy and sorrow, that have occupied the intervening
period. I have often, as now, waited months for an
interval of health and cheerfulness, to visit an absent
friend with the breathings of a mind in some degree
composed and cheerful.

Since I have set out so hopefully with egotism, I
will even give you the detail of my winter's confinement, and have done with it. All my transactions,
nay, my very ideas, are so blended and interwoven
with the dear branches that sprout and depend from
me, that you must extend the toleration of friendship
beyond its usual bounds, before you can truly relish

my correspondence. You must not only indulge
egotism in the first person, but you must have patience
with egotism once removed, and hear me speak of my
children as diffusely as I do of myself. Did I ever
tell you of another *daughter* I have, who, though not
born to me, is as dear, and has cost me much dearer
than any of the rest? This daughter of my affection
is called Charlotte Grant; she is nearly related to Mr.
Grant, was left motherless in her tenth year, and
cruelly treated by a near relation, whose hand,

> " Like the base Indian, threw a pearl away
> More worth than all his tribe."

The history of her early and uncommon sorrows, from
its singularity, is very deserving of a recital, and would
do more than amuse you ; it would deeply interest
and affect you; but it is so complicated, and requires
such a detail of minutiæ and delineation of character
to make you thoroughly understand it, that I really
have not spirits or resolution to enter into the detail at
present, and must defer it to sometime when I have
more leisure and am capable of more exertion. Suffice it for the present, that, in the sixteenth year of
her age, she was separated from her family, and placed
by some relations under Mr. Grant's guardianship;
that we then brought her to our family, when I had
the pleasure to observe, that though in a great measure
neglected and uncultivated, she possessed a strength
of intellect, a purity of sentiment and rectitude of
principle, that afforded the best foundation for the
embellishments which instruction might add to the
rich gifts of nature. It was evident that this disposition would richly reward the labour of any one who

should, by a little culture, unfold the beauties of a mind, which, though untainted with vice and undebased by folly, had been so crushed by harshness and severity, and clouded by seclusion, and so shut up by reserve, that it required some penetration to discover of what it was capable.

Thus forlorn, neglected, and pierced with many sorrows, it was the will of Providence to throw her under our protection, as those relations who made such a provision for her as to secure her from want, could not, from various circumstances, receive her into their own family. When we thought of bringing her to ours, we had the general voice of all the impertinent, the ill-natured, and the coolly prudent against us. My very friends were all against me; they were sure my anxious tenderness for this amiable sufferer, and the trouble I should take about her, would be a fresh source of painful solicitude to a mind already enfeebled with many cares. But I was resolute. Why should I renew my own sorrows, by telling you what difficulties and embarrassments attended the outset of my plan, what weeding and pruning I had to go through, and how I sacrificed everything to the one favourite object of making this child of sorrow appear to the world that lovely and estimable object for which nature designed her. I will rather invite your gratulation, by telling you how amply my cares have been repaid, and how richly her warm gratitude, her rapid improvement, and the justice which even the selfish world now does to her distinguished merit, have recompensed me for all I have done and suffered. Her mother's relations, who are people of the first consideration, now pay her every attention. It is four years since she came under our roof; the first year she spent entirely with ourselves. She has spent the two last winters in Glasgow and Edinburgh, where she is very much admired and caressed. The other seasons she passes with us, and is as sedulous in her endeavours to share and soften the many cares incident to my large family and bustling manner of life, as the most dutiful child could possibly be. I find her now a most pleasing and rational companion, possessed of genuine sentiment without romantic extravagance. She joins to the open and generous spirit of youth, a depth and solidity of reflection, which is the natural result of early affliction in a strong and well principled mind. She is admired for beauty more by others than by me; but she confessedly excels in grace and elegance. Her countenance is certainly most singularly interesting; and her manner, her air, her figure, and her motions, have all a mingled softness and dignity peculiar to herself. I have said a great deal too much, but indeed, my dear, I am very proud of her.

My eldest daughter lives constantly at Fort-George with my father and mother, who are very happy in their new establishment. She shows a taste for letters, and a retentive memory; her temper is even and placid. I have her here just now, and propose sending her to town, where I hope she will not only derive benefit from the schools she is to attend, but from the society and example of a lady of genuine worth, an old and true friend of mine, with whom she is to reside.

I must not repine at the very long interval you have placed between us and the meeting, on my side so ardently desired. You must allow me to have been very modest on this subject : the favour comes so entirely from your side, the fatiguing length of the journey, the homely rusticity of the accommodation, so much the reverse of what you now enjoy, make me mention my very wishes on this subject with fear and trembling. Yet, could I invite you to share in the perfection of rural elegance,—could I send my carriage to transport you,—with what eager importunity would I urge you ! We all know him to be the Man of Wisdom, but you must also allow him to be a man of *feeling*, who said, " Hope deferred makes the heart sick."

You gratify me beyond expression by your ideas, so different from those of the rest of the world, and so consonant to my own, regarding the views and notions with which I ought to inspire my children. On a subject which thrills through the deepest recesses of the heart, and awakens all the ardour of enthusiasm, to find in a kindred bosom the image of our own reflections and sensations, affords a pleasure like that of hearing unexpectedly the sweetest music in perfect unison with the awakened sensibility of the moment. Soon may you see those children whom I have been endeavouring to train to the exercise of humble and patient virtue ! You will see, that, like the Laplanders,

> " They love their mountains, and enjoy their storms;
> No false desires, no pride-created wants,
> Disturb the peaceful current of their time."

Our manner of living here is, in some degree, patriarchal. The large family of artless, primitive people
we are obliged to keep about us, and the number of
our children, who look up to us as the only object of
love and veneration, occasion our lives to be spent in
alternate acts of power and beneficence. Now what
more have kings but trappings and pageantry!

When shall I hear of your appearing at the bar of
the National Assembly,* to claim the rights you inherit
as representative of the eldest branch of your family?
for so you seem entitled to do by their late liberal
edicts. Pray, has Miss Malliet caught the Galloma-
nia? The energy of mind, which I admire in that
lady, would naturally lead her to be warm in the
cause of liberty; but whether this be truly liberty,
time will show. Yet its infection spreads widely.
Now I conjure and entreat you, by all that is sweet
in sympathy or sacred in friendship, to write instantly
before your heart cools after perusing this affectionate
though desultory scroll. Should my present illness
terminate fatally, it will be the last you will receive
from one who loves and esteems you with cordial
warmth and truth. Believe me ever affectionately
yours,

A. G.

* Of France.

LETTER VI.

TO MRS. MACINTOSH, OF DUNCHATTAN, GLASGOW.

Laggan, April 27, 1792.

Dear Madam,

Once more returned from the limits of that undiscovered country,* on whose dim-seen confines our hopes and fears are continually hovering, I devote one of the first efforts of my pen to you, who are so well entitled to every mark of grateful attention on my part, on my own account, as well as that of others, who engross my tenderest cares, and occasion me perpetual anxiety. For, though I am satisfied that they are much happier and more attended to than they could be with me, even the scenes of gaiety and pleasure, that I know them to be engaged in, are a source of inquietude to my fond apprehensions. "Perfect love," we are told, "casteth out fear." That may be the case when it is fixed on the All-perfect Object, who is alone worthy to excite and engross it; but when our weak human affections are engaged by beings as imperfect as ourselves, fear and doubt continually mingle with them.

When my young travellers return to the cottage, their allotted home, it will require more than common reflection and solidity to reconcile them to still life, frugality, and homely habits; though, after all, I sincerely believe it is the state most akin to safety

---

* Alluding to a late dangerous illness of the Author, after the birth of her daughter, Anne, 11th April, 1792.—ED.

and comfort.—Charlotte says, she has been at a ball lately, which concludes her public exhibitions for the season. I am glad of it; for, though I must own my vanity is much flattered by the admiration which her person and manners have excited, and that I am gratified by the pleasure she receives, my judgment and my fears militate against her growing familiar to the public eye. Her situation is too peculiar and delicate, to make it safe for her to attract so much attention; this will not fail to turn the jealous and scrutinizing eye of female envy upon her. Public admiration is a thing that soon dies of itself; a person who might never have had a wish for it, will feel forlorn at its departure. Besides, one admired solely for beauty will be always considered as a mere pretty girl; her merit will never be thought of. My young daughter, by the by, has as much merit as any lady of her age can have; for she is very quiet, and never disobeys me. Having few good things to bestow on her, we resolved to begin with giving her a good name, and have called her Anne Ourry. Let me not be forgotten on the *Dune;* and believe me incapable of forgetting its inhabitants. Believe me, &c.,

A. G.

Letter VII.

TO MRS. SMITH, GLASGOW.

Laggan, May 10, 1792.

My dear Friend,

I have now to thank you for your two kind letters

that you wrote soon after Mary's arrival, and mostly on her subjects, and the other you so considerately wrote on the same sheet with her. No doubt the correspondent numbers of eightpence and eight children would occur to you. Self-denial stands in place of economy to me; many have more the skill of the purse and the little habits of cautious frugality which watchful self-love dictates. Yet these I see often led bound to the triumphal car of vanity or some other passion, and occasionally scattering with profusion the fruits of their watchful care. But I being troubled with no violent desires, no irresistible craving for dress, for company, or any of the enjoyments that betray people into extravagance, am under no violent temptation to any expenses but expenses of the heart. To you, who have a heart, I need not explain that certain postages come under this class. Charity here ranks among these expenses; but we have increased and multiplied so fast, that we are in a fair way to consider charity as beginning at home. Yet, though philosophically indifferent to all other luxuries, I have still a hankering after this one; so that though you and Mary had filled separate sheets, I should not have grudged it.

I am astonished beyond measure at your being all so partial to Mary's looks. She was so pretty a child, and about two years ago promised so much grace and sweetness in her countenance, that, when she appeared last winter, I was perfectly shocked to see her so overgrown, and her features become so large. It is really hard, though she be still tolerably decent, to hear her raised above myself—my former self too.

For you know people generally take delight in magnifying their departed beauty. The only thing I fear, with regard to her, is indolence, which, after all, I hope is curable. It is not a selfish reluctance to act, but a kind of musing abstraction or thoughtful indolence, which proceeds partly from not setting the due value on things which, though trifling themselves, become useful and necessary from their connexion in the chain of indispensables. Young people of reflection and sensibility greatly require to be taught that useful lesson,

"That little things are great to little man."

None ever more needed this caution than myself.

I see you preserve the same style of gratulation which my other friends make use of.* They all congratulate me, it is true, but their congratulation has greatly the air of condolence. In the Highlands, particularly, a daughter to a poor gentleman, who has a moderate stock of that kind already, is considered, at best, as a *blessing in disguise*. Yet, if they could be kept about one, and bred up in habits of humble industry, I think it is easier to keep a watch on the morals of girls than of boys, who, of necessity, must ramble from one; and I think the great affair, after all, is, how many rational creatures one can be the means of preparing for usefulness in this world, and happiness in another. There being a number of them together in a family where strict frugality is necessary for getting them reared, will, perhaps, be eventually

* On the recent addition to her family of a daughter (Anne).

much to their advantage.　The other week a gentleman sent us the Review for 1789,—the first thing that
opened was the following specimen of a curate's address to Fortune:—

> "And art thou come, ere zephyr mild
> 　Has waked the blackbird's vernal strain;
> And art thou come, my beauteous child,
> 　Where Poverty her iron reign
> Extends more bleak and cruel far
> Than winter or the northern star?
> Yet cease these cries, that all my pity move;
> Though cold the hearth, my bosom burns with love."

I forget the prayer that follows, but the exquisite
pathos of the first stanza imprinted it on my memory.

Mary inquires anxiously for the name, complexion,
&c., of her young sister; will you tell her that her
hair is very dark, her complexion very fair, and her
eyes the darkest shade of blue, and that she is so stout
I fear she will be as big as herself, and so quiet that
I sometimes forget I have her.　Mary's letters please
me greatly; they are perfectly free from the presumption and petulance to be dreaded from one so soon
brought forward, quite unconstrained, and betray no
ambition of shining.　Little Robert Brown and King
William at the Cross are the only gentlemen she mentions; in all her letters to different people who know
nothing of either of you, she never fails to tell that
Mrs. Brown and Mrs. Smith are very good to her,
and that Mrs. Smith gave her a ticket to a concert,
and another to a play.　She raves about the plays,
and says she was never so delighted.　She would not
give a single scene for the dancing-school ball, which
she renounced most cheerfully.　Mrs. Brown in this,
as in all other things, acted most judiciously.

How shall I speak of the prospect I so fondly cherished of passing the remainder of my days near you.* I see I must give it up; yet I cannot do this without unspeakable regret. Had this scheme succeeded, no doubt the flesh-pots must needs be abandoned. The *leeks* and the *onions* would not follow us, nor could we expect to enjoy the same plenty of many conveniences of life. But there are so many and such strong motives for making the preference; it is so totally impossible, amid the cares and endless avocations which surround us here, to pay due attention to our children, which I consider as everything. But I will not dwell on subjects the recollection of which aggravates my pain, and will not lessen yours, for I take it for granted that you feel as I do on this occasion. Mr. Grant was far from thinking coldly of a change that flattered him with a prospect of bringing up his children about him, which, next to his beloved tranquillity, he considers as the first earthly felicity. I will not add to all the plagues I have given Mrs. Brown, that of writing her now. With best regards to those you love, I am yours,

A. G.

* Alluding to a plan that had been under consideration by Mr. Grant's friends, to have him transferred from Laggan to a clerical charge in Glasgow.—Ed.

LETTER VIII.

TO MRS. MACINTOSH.

Dear Madam,   Laggan, August 21, 1792.

The deep sense I feel of the kindness expressed in
your much-valued letter, and the consolation which
the acquisition of regard, from a character so estimable, affords, even under the pressure of my present
affliction,* encourages me to write to you, even now,
when I am very unfit to communicate my ideas, except where they will be received with the most partial
indulgence. I know it is unbecoming, nay, almost
unchristianly for me, to use the emphatic language of
sorrow, in speaking of an infant's happy transition
from the dangers and snares of this chequered scene
to a state of stable felicity. She is departed before
she has known sin or sorrow, and before we could
have room to judge whether those beautiful blossoms
of sprightliness, generosity, and tenderness, which
charmed us so much in her enticing little ways,
would ever ripen into the expected fruit. My reason
not only acquiesces in the justice of the dispensation,
but my heart so far acknowledges its mercy, that,
could a wish bring my darling back to my bosom, I
think I would not form that wish. She was so un-
usually strong and healthy, that we dreamt not of

---

* The death of her infant daughter, Petrina, which had taken
place about a week previously, in the third year of her age.

fear till it became too late. She spoke to me in a
clear, distinct voice, showing tokens of the fondest
affection, three hours before her death. Thus, you
see, the stroke was very sudden. Then we had such
delight in her; not only for her own sake, but for
the great resemblance she bore to her dear departed
brother, whose every look and gesture was restored
in her; so that her death was just like losing him
over again. It is also so melancholy to see the poor
thing that remains, wandering like a ghost, and constantly bewailing her sister.

There are few things that could gratify me more
than to find you so cordially interested in poor Charlotte. I am not a little pleased to find your sentiments and mine concerning her, coincide so entirely.
Her integrity of heart, her sincerity, and general rectitude of intention, are such as, to one that knows
her intimately, suffice to ensure esteem, and even
affection, beyond all that shines, and all that pleases
in those, whom happier fortunes, and a more finished
education have set in a fairer point of view. I am
very well satisfied to find that she is going to stay for
some time at Mr. Douglas's. I hope she will take
particular care to please those who are so well worth
pleasing. I conclude, from her thorough confidence
in you, from whom no thought of her heart is concealed, that you know of a visitor whom she daily
expects. This visitor is certainly an object of compassion; and the attachment, from the beginning so
singular and romantic, seems daily increasing. I
have so very good an opinion of the person in question, and so very bad an opinion of the safety or

stability of such premature engagements, that what to judge or determine I am utterly at a loss. I leave her, then, entirely to your direction, who, with equal warmth of good-will towards her, have more judgment, experience, and knowledge of the world.

I have received Mr. Macintosh's friendly letter, and feel the full force of his judicious and affectionate consolation. The hope of seeing you here at no very distant period, pleases me even now, when very few things, indeed, have power to interest your obliged and faithful, &c.,

A. G.

LETTER IX.

TO MISS OURRY, LONDON.

Laggan, September 3, 1792.

Never did a cordial come more opportunely to a poor creature fainting with weakness, than my dearest Anne's kind letter, to soothe my agonizing heart, and divert, for a little, my attention from one sad object, which fixes and engrosses it, in spite of my prayers and endeavours. Petrina, my lovely Petrina, the sweet image of my dear lamented Peter, is no more. This is a wound very near the heart, and yet I must own the justice of it. I had a darling before, on whose animated and sensible countenance I gazed with un-bounded rapture, and whom I always regarded with unwarrantable partiality. Yet I might well have judged, from his dissimilarity to ourselves, and the rest of the family, that he would not remain with us. After having dazzled and charmed us for four years and a few months, he returned to Him from whom he came, leaving us overwhelmed with excessive and sinful anguish. About a year after his death, those twins were born. The eldest I instantly recognized to be the exact resemblance of my sweet boy, whose memory is twisted with the fibres of my heart. As she grew older, her vivacity, her open, generous temper, her robust appearance and quick growth, everything renewed him to us, as well as the expressive and animated countenance that seized the eye of every stranger, and the heart of every one of the family. Indeed she was too lovely, and, till a week before her death, was the very picture of health and vigour. What a profusion of love was heaped upon her, during the period of her short life! Her brothers and sisters, her father, all doted upon her. But her heavenly Father has now vindicated his right, and punished our presumptuous partiality. When I am abler, I shall tax your patience with a recital of the aggravating circumstances of her death. I can now only tell you, that on Sunday, the 12th August, she made her way, through the keenest agonies, to everlasting felicity;

" Ye that e'er lost an angel, pity me!"

Never child gave so little trouble and so much pleasure to parents. I well know how rich I am in remaining blessings, and how both reason and religion forbid repining, because He who has bestowed so

many good gifts, sees fit in his own manner to resume
them. When the prayers I daily offer have the
desired effect, I may bow patiently to the Divine
decree; but now, my dearest friend, a cup can only
hold its fill, and mine is filled to the very brim. Were
all my earthly comforts removed, I could only grieve,
as I do now, as much as my nature can sustain,
though I might mourn longer and more excusably.
Farewell. Be charitable, for you do not know how
you could bear this.

LETTER X.

TO MISS (ADDRESSED MRS.) OURRY.

My dear Friend,   Laggan, September 18, 1792.

My last sombre epistle has, by this time, reached
you, and awakened all your sympathy. It affords a
ray of comfort to me at this distance, to think you feel
with and for me. Those who are immersed, as most
people around you are, in eager pursuits of pleasure
and ambition, can have no idea of distress like mine.
They have not the simplicity of taste which enjoys and
feels the attractive charm of infant innocence. Can
those who grasp at a thousand shadows which render
the mind both callous and fastidious, by their empti-
ness and variety, contemplate with stedfast gaze and
ever new delight, the dawning of sensibility, the unfolding blooms of intelligence and affection ? It is in
the shady vales, the obscure retreats of life, far from

the noise of turbulent passions, and the parade of
splendid vanities, that the soft and kindly affections
root deep, and flourish fair. There, all the pleasures
they afford are tasted in perfection; but it is there,
when these tender ties are broken, that anguish is
most pungent. The twin sister of my Petrina has
been very unwell. I regarded her danger with composure that excited my own wonder; perhaps, like
Burns,

> " With firm, resolved, despairing eye
> I view each aimed dart,
> Since one has cut my dearest tie,
> And quivers in my heart."

O, may I be forgiven for these effusions of despondency, and enabled to fix my thoughts on that awful
day when I fondly hope to recognize my children
among the blessed heirs of immortality. Oh! if this
hope be sinful, I am indeed a great sinner; it feeds
my imagination, and cherishes my heart, and, at intervals, soothes my woe-worn spirits into a sublime
tranquillity. Sure, we shall not forget our fellow-
travellers in this vale of mortality, in the bright regions
of blest futurity. We cannot retain a partial recollection of past events; that is, we cannot separate the
retrospection of them from the remembrance of those
who have enjoyed and suffered with us in this transient
state of probation. How can we remember the numberless mercies received, the many dangers escaped,
and temptations resisted, which will furnish themes
for praise, at least during our noviciate in bliss; how,
I say, can we remember these, without, at the sametime, calling back those who were our associates in

suffering, those who lived in our bosoms, and were to us the objects of an innocent and pure affection, such as helps to preserve us from the contagion of the world, and keeps the heart warm, and open to the best impressions? . . . .

Mean, obsure, and dull as everything must appear to you here, I have so made up my mind, and so forewarned and forearmed you, that I look forward to your arrival here next May as the time that is to relieve my mind of its burden. I am in no pain about finding out a tolerable travelling companion for you; I shall set inquirers on foot very early, and will engage that you shall not find yourself a stranger while in Edinburgh; at any rate, you shall not sojourn there without benefit of *clergy*.

I was not much surprised to hear of the conduct of your Devonshire friends. You well remember a time when the *amor patriæ* burned with uncommon and imprudent ardour in the breast of your friend. Now, though I used to fight "tooth and nail" for Scotland, and had not then reflection enough to discriminate in my defensive operations, there were two or three causes equally dear to me blended with my defence of Mother Meg—virtuous and dignified poverty, elegance of sentiment that lives in the heart and conduct, and subsists independent of local and transitory modes; a degree of amiable simplicity among the middle ranks of life, and of modest decorum, resulting from pious impressions, in the lower, not often to be met with in that class. For the ease of our social intercourse, and our general good-will towards strangers, we are certainly indebted to our former connexion with France.

Our national pride and poverty, so well known, and so generally stigmatized, is, notwithstanding, of great advantage to us. From the one we derive a certain dignity, which, when joined with our ordinary sense of integrity, preserves us from mean and unworthy actions. Our poverty, again, produces frugality and temperance, for which, I hear you observe, we are not much to be thanked. I have wandered from my subject; but I meant to observe that, with all the pride with which we are so justly charged, there is no instance on record of any person, however wealthy, treating a near relation, respectable in all things, purse excepted, with such gross neglect as your Devonshire friends did their respectable relative. Clanship, doubtless, narrows the affections, and produces many absurd and unpleasing associations; yet, it is better to love forty or fifty people warmly and exclusively on absurd grounds, than to love nobody at all, and then pretend to love all the world (which does not care a straw for you); as the Parisian philosophers do, on whom the demons of scepticism and discord will soon visit all the mischiefs they are doing, and the far greater mischiefs they occasion. My poor dear Odyssey tells a fine story of Æolus having the winds in a bag, and what havoc followed when they were unskilfully let out. Now, I think popular writers possess bags, in which those winds are contained that blow the embers of discontent into flames of destruction. What a dreadful account is to be rendered for the use of power so unlimited! No despotism is like that practised by the rulers of opinion. But I believe it is become customary to have no settled opinion, but to keep the

mind open for the reception of experimental whimsies.
But I feel the water getting deeper every moment,
and shall return, to avoid drowning. Shallow streams
are safest, therefore I bid you farewell; and believe
me, in all circumstances, yours invariably,

A. G.

P. S.—You see I have at length brought myself to
call you *Mrs.* Ourry; but it was with a struggle.
The solemn renunciation of youth, and all that there-
unto pertains, may be very prudent, very heroic, &c.,
but it is, in the meantime, very grating to my feelings.
It gave me the same sensation I feel annually when
one tells me the night begins to lengthen; it always
frets me.

LETTER XI.

TO MRS. MACINTOSH, GLASGOW.

Laggan, Monday morn, 2 o'clock,
October 7, 1792.

Dear Madam,

I had the pleasure of your letter, and you may
judge of my willingness to answer it, by my sitting up
the past night to watch the dawn of Monday morn,
that I might write without infringing on a better day.
Do not smile; it is not superstition, but self-distrust ·
I make resolutions, and try to hold them inviolable.
I should be satisfied with your good-will, but would
fain preserve a *deference* for myself. On this past day,

the most solemn ordinance of religion* has been celebrated here. Many of the congregation live at such
distances, and the service continues so long without
interval, that we find it proper to bring down a good
many people to a slight refreshment through the day.
The assisting clergy sleep here, and three other visitors; so you may judge what bustle and fatigue all
this must occasion to me, and how unfit I am to write;
but you will make all allowances.

I am very glad that same visit is over; and, though
I have the very best opinion of the heart and understanding of your visitor, it is, perhaps, as well the affair
is over; for, I suppose, we shall hear no more of it.
I felt exceedingly for the person in question. Yet we
must consider how very particular her situation is, and
how very dangerous it would be for her to incur the
imputation of even a pardonable deviation from strict
prudence. I startle at the thought of her being led to
favour anything so vague at present, and which might
prove dangerous in future. She has too much good
sense, and too much dependence on those whose faithful friendship she has experienced, to form any connexion (for what less is a correspondence), with any
one in a precarious situation, who might incur blame
on her account. Of this person's delicacy of sentiment I have not the smallest doubt; but that very
delicacy, youth, and natural shyness, preclude him
from that knowledge of the world, and, perhaps, of
exact propriety, that would render the consequences
which might result to her, obvious to his view. People

* The administration of the Sacrament.

of the character I suppose him to possess, are more
likely to conciliate esteem and respect, in the sphere
of their particular acquaintance, than to push their
way through a hard, unfeeling world. . . . .
Will you also tell Charlotte I shall write to her very
soon, and inform her of many particulars which, I
know, she would wish to be acquainted with. I wrote
her a long melancholy letter, with the narrative of
dear Petrina's loss, and all my distresses, which wore
me out so, that I left off abruptly. I told her, however, how much I was satisfied with all she did. Tell
her * * * has been talking very loud all the time I
write; so you may be thankful you have escaped his
incoherences. I have a profusion of complimentary
messages to send you, but entreat you will imagine
them. Adieu, dear madam ! I am, in all humours,
and at all times, much yours,

A. G.

LETTER XII.

TO MISS OURRY.

Laggan, December 1, 1792.

You cannot conceive, indeed you cannot, how reviving the cordial warmth of your last letter was to my
drooping heart—a heart from which all the cares and
all the tenderness arising out of a family, so large, so
helpless, so loving and beloved, cannot exclude you.
For the years I thought you dead, and when you were

dead to me, your image would very often recur with a
short, quick pang, like that which now accompanies
the angelic form of my dear, lost Petrina, when it
beams across my fancy ; for, indeed, I do not sit down
to grieve, but endeavour to pay the best tribute to her
memory, by a sedulous discharge of my various and
complicated duties to those who loved her so tenderly
while she was lent to us.

I think of everything I see with reference to how you
will like it, when we shall have the happiness of seeing
you here on the long expected visit. I foolishly think
that you will be as much pleased as I am with all the
budding virtues and graces with which my sanguine
fancy decorates my children ; little considering that,
from the external elegance to which you have been
accustomed, they must, at best, appear to you, at first,
a parcel of awkward cubs, unformed and overgrown.
The culture of the heart is our great object ; we let
the acquisition of knowledge, manners, &c., go on
piano till we make sure of the main point. Where
the natural temper is mild and generous,—and theirs
appears very much so, deep impressions of integrity
and early habits of benevolence must communicate to
the manners the unconstrained air of open rectitude,
and that animated softness which a disinterested wish
to please always produces. Indeed, we have few maxims ; one of those few is, that it is easier to be than to
seem.

Mrs. Macintosh* is a singularly respectable woman,
of strong intellect, who possesses a masculine energy

* Mrs. Macintosh of Dunchattan, with whose brother, Dr. John
Moore, Miss Ourry was well acquainted.

both of understanding and virtue. She inquired about you of her brother, who spoke so highly of you, that she was quite delighted with the thoughts of making such an addition to the stock of living merit, within the circle of, her personal knowledge, and pleases herself with the thoughts of bringing you here herself, and setting you down at our little gate, where she hopes to meet yet another—*white crow*,—to express it elegantly; yet I should not conclude without telling you that Mr. Macintosh is a man worth taking a journey to see, not of active benevolence only, but of restless impetuous benevolence. I will teach you to venerate him at more leisure, having now no time to do him justice. Yet I am by no means reconciled to your going so far out of the way as Glasgow, even to receive or pay the homage that superior minds owe each other, and is more frankly paid than any other, even than that which the Scots pay to " Influence and Dundas." But this will lead me into the maze of politics, in which I will not bewilder myself, being sufficiently occupied with the care of our limited (very limited) monarchy at home, in which I participate, by turns, the legislative and executive powers, and though I never aim at despotism, try to keep firm to my *veto*.

Our tumults in the north appear aggravated and formidable to you in London, which is the region of political panics. Honest John Bull is very liable to the vapours; and the Stocks

> " Turn at the touch of joy or woe,
> But, turning, tremble too;"

of which those who live by feeling their pulse take the advantage. The only cause of complaint in Scotland is the rage for sheep-farming. The families removed on that account are often as numerous as our own. The poor people have neither language, money, nor education, to push their way anywhere else; though they often possess feelings and principles that might almost rescue human nature from the reproach which false philosophy and false refinement have brought upon it. Though the poor Ross-shire people were driven to desperation by the iron hand of oppression, they even then acted under a sense of rectitude, touched no property, and injured no creature. As for the mobs in towns, they are mere ebullitions of ignorance and wantonness in a people who were never so rich before, and to whom wealth and freedom are such novelties that they know not the true use or bounds of either.

I got your letters regularly, and wrote to you by the Fingalian cover. Tell Miss Malliet I respect her for her own sake, and love her for yours. Adieu, my dearest Nancy! Affectionately yours,

A. G.

LETTER XIII.

TO MISS OURRY, LONDON.

Laggan, January 12, 1793.

My dear Friend,

You may believe I received with very great pleasure an assurance of what before I greatly doubted, that you will once more breathe the pure mountain gales, impregnated with wholesome heath, and diffusive of the spirit of wholesome poverty; the train of rigid, sinewy, and hard-featured virtues superadded. You see, notwithstanding your good-humoured irony, the hypothesis of situation continues to be a favourite one with me, and I despair not of making you, on rational grounds, a proselyte to my opinion. When France was the land of wit and refinement, if not of wisdom, it was a maxim of one of its best authors, that we are all, in some degree, *les animaux d' habitude;* that, in short, forms of life tincture our virtues with their peculiar dye, and not only often produce, but in some measure palliate our vices. This is no flattering hypothesis for me. It always humbles me in my own eyes, by reminding me, that, from the examples I have seen, from the pure precepts and safe obscurity under the influence of which I was educated, far from all that corrupts the heart and dazzles the imagination; I say, when I reflect on all these collateral aids to the propensities of a warm heart, in which the seeds of truth were early sown, I must, in common honesty, disclaim your compliments. So circumstanced, I must have been a monster of depravity, had I acted through life with less practical reverence for virtue than I have done. Though I have all the abhorrence of vice natural to a person of strong feeling, living much out of its reach; yet, when I see, as it often happens, strong flashes of generosity, probity, and humanity, breaking through the gloom of mental sloth and ignorance, and casting a transient lustre over characters debased by habitual vices, which too early intercourse with a bad world have produced, my heart melts to think how amiable those persons might have been had they gone out into the world, fortified with good principles, and acquainted with sublimer pleasures than the world has to bestow. . . . . . . Now, here are two marked instances of virtue so modified, that have had no small influence on your own mind.

I see you have greatly mistaken my political creed, which is borrowed from a much sounder judgment than my own, and much nearer your own than you are aware of. The only real grievance Scotland labours under, originates with landholders : perhaps, more remotely, in commerce, since the tide of wealth, which commerce has poured into the northern part of the island, has led our trading people to contend with our gentry, in all the exterior elegancies of life. The latter seem stung with a jealous solicitude to preserve their wonted ascendancy over their new rivals. This pre-eminence can only be kept up by heightening at all hazards the rents of their land. Thus the ancient adherents of their families are displaced. These, having been accustomed to a life of devotion, simplicity, and frugality, and being bred to endure hunger, fatigue, and hardship, while following their cattle over the mountains, or navigating the stormy seas that surround their islands, form the best resource of the state, when difficulties, such as the inhabitants of a happier region are strangers to, must be encountered for its service. When we consider this world as merely a passing scene, at the conclusion of which the question will not be, who has supported the most consequential character, but who has acted best the part allotted, we must look upon that as the best destination, which affords the widest scope for the exercise and effects of various virtues. In civilized society, wealth does, and must give influence; but it would be a wretched state indeed, in which wealth should be the only distinction. A man whose ancestors have rendered themselves for a course of time eminent in the state, has generally some among them to whom he looks back for example, and whose virtues and abilities reflect lustre on his descendants. Though the depravity of our nature appears but too conspicuously among the higher classes of mankind, yet among these, too, talents and merit appear with greater splendour, and are of more ornament and service to mankind, than the same qualities in their inferiors. Condescension and affability, for instance, would vanish if we were all equal. The charity and hospitality of a nobleman will be more admired and imitated than the same qualities in a wealthy tradesman :

"A saint in crape, is twice a saint in lawn."

In short, everything that decorates, or enlightens, is best seen from an eminence. Nothing but pure patriotism, great poverty, and perfect equality, an assemblage we shall never see combined, could make a republic on a large scale at all supportable. Believe me, I have no prejudice against monarchy mildly exercised, or duly limited; I consider it as an institution naturally growing out of that patriarchal sovereignty, which, in the primitive ages, the parent, doubly revered for his many years and great experience, was wont to exercise over his numerous and obedient offspring. In a state where no unalloyed good is indulged to us, we often show our best wisdom, when of many evils we choose the least. For my own part, though I were so French and so new-fangled as to consider all legal governments as monsters let loose to eat up liberty, I should still prefer the three-headed Cerberus, whose salutary terrors prevent the condemned from entering the regions of bliss, like our threefold government, whose terrors only affect the wicked; even this, I say, I should prefer to the many-headed hydra, who, breathing death and contagion indiscriminately, may represent the barbarous genius of mob government.

Now that I am got into classical allusions, permit me to *Burkify* aTittle longer, and to assure you that I should be very much grieved to see that good old lady, or gentleman (I know not which to call it), the Constitution, cut up and dismembered because it has a few wrinkles or grey hairs; or to see Medea's old kettle put on again, while Mr. —— and Lord L. stood chief cooks, and Tom Paine scullion. I think I see Mary W—— and so many more public-spirited ladies bringing aprons-full of herbs, like witches, to the magic cauldron. The ways of the Almighty baffle our penetration. This temporary triumph of irreligion and false philosophy will tear the mask off the monster, who, wrapt in the specious disguise of moderation, and speaking the language of sentiment and liberality, has, for near a century past, been undermining the foundations of religion and morality. What pains have been taken to promulgate that profound discovery, "that bigotry and religious zeal have done more hurt in society, than scepticism and all the mere

E 2

speculative evils of philosophy." The reason is plain. Great bodies of people were confederated together, under the influence of bigotry and superstition. The crafty and ambitious few made the passions of the well-meaning though ignorant many, subservient to their cruelty and avarice, and thus produced those tragedies which deform the face of history. But hitherto these enlightened philosophers have been dispersed here and there, without numbers or cohesion to enable them to begin their practical operations. We have never, till now, seen a nation of refined enlightened infidels governed by the dictates of philosophy; and it is to be hoped that the world will be terrified and warned by the dreadful spectacle. I here dedicate to you the first fruits of my pen upon the arduous and intricate subject of politics; and as I am pretty much of opinion it will also be my last excursion into those unexplored regions, pray regard it with some fellow-feeling, it being like yourself, an only child.

Mr. Grant has not yet conquered his astonishment at your growing fat. "Bless me, Miss Ourry fat! it is impossible:" his fancy had formed you a mere skeleton. A few grey hairs begin already to adorn my temples; the small portion which fell to my share of "celestial rosy red," has most ambitiously forsaken its native station, and mounted up to my "lack-lustre eyes." Constant solicitude and the cares of the nursery have made me

"Like a meagre mope, adust and thin,
In a loose night-gown of my own wan skin."

I will describe no longer. Come, see, and conquer.

Receive numberless loves from those I best love, and believe me yours from her heart, and unaltered,

A. G.

LETTER XIV.

TO MISS OURRY.

Laggan, January 26, 1793.

You will not let me alone, nor will I give up my point. In spite of your raillery, I insist that the ties of blood bind stronger, and the duties of relationship are better understood, in the Highlands, than anywhere else. I by no means except the Low country of Scotland. This, too, is not a reflected moral sense of duty, but the mere effect of honest habits and salutary prejudices. It is a singular instance of the Almighty's goodness, that, in these poor barren countries, from which he has withheld so many of the blessings he bestows on others, the few who possess any portion of wealth should be stimulated by those kindly propensities to diffuse it among their remote relations. These last, besides the habitual pride and indolence attending imagined high birth, have not, from education or situation, the means of procuring a livelihood, as in wealthy and commercial countries. This, no doubt, forms no pleasant chain of dependence; but in this, as in many other instances,

" What happier nature shrinks at with affright,
The hard inhabitants contend is right."

Though I applaud this reverence for kindred, I do

not benefit by it; but, on the contrary, though I regard my neighbours with the utmost esteem and good-will, I cannot give away anything so precious as friendship to any one who, after all, would prefer the most insignificant of her third cousins to me.

Believe me, my children, though prepared to love and admire you, are neither taught to expect a beauty, wit, or fine lady; but one who has no small merit in disclaiming pretensions to all those envied characters, and associating, by a rare combination, softness of manners with strength of mind, vivacity with reflection, and that common useful sense which hourly discerns the proper and expedient in ordinary life, with that delicacy of perception which apprehends and tastes all that enlightens the understanding, and enlarges the heart, in knowledge or sentiment. If, as you say, no wandering rivulet renovates your powers, you are surely, like the Leeward Islands, visited by frequent water-spouts, that is, inspirations, that fertilize your intellects. I certainly have an ample cistern which retains all I acquire. This, common observers mistake for a fountain.

Tell Miss Malliet that I love her as well as one can love a rival. Mr. Grant sends you his benediction, and rejoices to think your portly figure will do credit to his housekeeping, which the present appearance of his spouse has rather brought into discredit. Adieu, dearest. Write very soon to your tenderly affectionate,

A. G.

LETTER XV.

TO MRS. SMITH, GLASGOW.

My dear Friend,   Laggan, February 11, 1793.

I am just recovering from an indisposition so severe, that it would have robbed you of a correspondent if it had continued much longer. This is a sickly season even amidst these mountains, where the keen atmosphere is so often agitated by storms, as well as by the dashing torrents, that it seldom stagnates into impurity. This, with the temperance and exercise which wholesome poverty produces, is the reason that death confines his ravages to infancy and declining age. There are very few instances here of people dying in early youth; and when they do happen, they seem objects of general concern and speculation. Mr. Grant had a relation, a young lady, remarkable for nothing but singular mildness, piety, and prudence. Having been from her earliest youth subject to nervous affections, she became last winter quite emaciated and enfeebled, and at last died of a mismanaged rose fever, like my sweet Petrina. Yet every one insisted that her death was caused by grief for the loss of her brother. Another young creature, who has languished all this winter with similar complaints, is pronounced to be dying of love, though no mortal can say of whom. Thus primitive and romantic are the notions of our mountaineers.

I am now to notify to you a removal, in which you

will, for my sake, be interested; it is that of my father
from Fort-George to Glasgow, which you know was
matter of doubtful speculation, but is now decided. I
feel the increased distance very painfully; yet there
are many considerations, which at more leisure I will
explain to you, that reconcile me to it. I have lived
so long entirely for others, that self-denial becomes
with me rather a habit than a virtue; and whatever
is proposed or thought of, it is not my own gratification, but the manner in which it affects the various
branches of my individual self, that occurs first to me.
I have likewise to inform you that Miss Ourry comes
to us, positively, about the beginning of May. Glasgow is out of her way, and she will grudge every hour
she is absent from us, after she enters Scotland. She
cannot stand a Highland winter, and Miss Malliet will
not be happy if she does not return at the appointed
time. When that comes, I shall probably accompany
her to Glasgow, and see my father's family, including
some of my own, settled. I hope you do not think I
had the confidence to urge my friend to come to such
a place, and such humble accommodation. She invited
herself most cordially, and I received her proffered
visit with grateful joy; but I have most pathetically
represented how like our *peat reek*, &c., are to the
comforts of Quilca and Cavan, immortalized by Swift.
Yet she is unalterable, and I rejoice thereat. The
ancestors of this lady and her friend both left France,
for conscience' sake, on the repeal of the edict of
Nantz, and they have no doubt many relations there.
Judge how they must be affected by the state of that
unhappy country, and what their feelings must be in

consequence of the last fatal catastrophe. It was but last night we heard it: news reaches us but slowly. Would you think, after being so long engrossed by domestic cares and anxieties, and drinking so lately the bitter draught of private and particular sorrow, that I should weep for a king?* I wonder at it myself; and yet I wept abundantly, and was disturbed and agitated all night. I am still under a dead weight of sadness: the recent wound of my heart, which is but skinned over, seeks only a pretence to bleed anew. Do you feel thus? Pray get Home's tragedy of Agis, and read it for my sake and that of the French King. I remember, when I was very young, and felt deep impressions from what I read, I was charmed with the choruses in that tragedy. I am as usual haunted with an apposite quotation :—

> When Jove decrees a nation's doom,
> He calls their *worthies* to the tomb,
> Fearless they fall, immortal rise,
> And claim the freedom of the skies.
> He fell not as the warrior falls,
> Whose breast defends his native walls;
> To treason Agis bow'd his head,
> And by his guilty subjects bled.

I have altered one word, to make it the better apply to the benign Louis. I have observed in the history of all nations, that when the women became impudent and licentious, and the sacred bond of marriage was made light of, that nation's downfall was near. We are very consequential beings, believe me; the purity of female manners is the basis on which, morally speaking, all the order and virtue of society are

---

* Louis XVI., who was executed at Paris on 21st January, 1793, a few weeks before this letter was written.

founded. Who cares for his country, but in consequence of first loving the relations who attach him to
it? And who can care much for parents, brothers,
and children, where relationship is dubious? It is an
abominable state of society; even setting the great
cordial of life, the hope of futurity, out of the question!
May you and I never live to see our dear country
tainted with this infectious depravity! I am, in joy
and sorrow, yours unalterably,

A. G.

LETTER XVI.

TO MRS. MACINTOSH, OF DUNCHATTAN, GLASGOW.

Laggan, March 20, 1793.
Dear Madam,

I have been for some days tortured with a most
outrageous toothache. I now snatch a lucid interval,
which I fear will be but a short one, to enjoy and
acknowledge the lively and sincere pleasure I feel
from your intimation through Charlotte, I mean of
your intention of coming in June. I hope your jaunt
will be favoured with good weather, and that you will
see the harsh features of nature around us softened
into their mildest aspect. I flatter myself novelty will
make you as partial to these wild and solitary scenes,
as habit has made me. You shall have one of the
warmest corners both in our cottage, and in our
hearts. If you come while Miss Ourry stays, each of
you, I am sure, will put up with a little crowding, to
share these apartments, or rather compartments, with

the other. If you set out as soon as I wish and hope, I dare say you will get the start of her, and be first in possession. She was detained in London three weeks beyond her intention, settling the affairs of an old granduncle. That intricate piece of business is now, I hope, satisfactorily concluded. Not hearing of her this fortnight, I take for granted that she has begun her journey. By letters from Edinburgh, I find our friends there are very willing to do her the honours of the good town most completely. Their politeness, and the fatigues of the former journey, may perhaps detain her there for some days. Among the various obligations I owe to you, the interest I am told you take in this highly-valued friend is not the least. The affection that subsists between her and me is too old, and too mellow, for the little jealousies and mono-polies of little girlish attachments. It is like a deep-rooted tree, which, far from requiring to be fenced or propped up, extends its shelter to younger plants around it. By loving each other so long and so well, our hearts are more fitted to pay the warm tribute of esteem to merit wherever it exists; and by recip-rocal sympathy, we feel as if engaged for each other in debts of gratitude and kindness.

Here you have a rhapsody, a simile, and I know not what. People, at my time of day, seldom deck out common objects with the vivid hues of enthusiasm. But you have only to account for this natural cu-riosity of a latter spring in the imagination, by sup-posing that, in the toothache, as in the gout, the intervals of ease are distinguished by an uncommon flow of spirits. As I take it for granted, you come

rather with a pious intention to hermitize and contemplate, than with any view to amusement, I shall
be in no pain for the sameness that awaits you here.
Being a lover of nature, and a mother, perhaps it will
afford you some pleasure to see a family of young
creatures as happy as health, good-nature, and perfect
liberty, can make them; who never knew what it was
to form an artificial wish, or to have a natural one
ungratified, unless it were for a little gilt book, whose
wondrous assemblage of rare portraitures had excited
their admiration. Your arrival will, I am sure, greatly
revive Charlotte, who has mourned immoderately for
the great loss we have all sustained in Mrs. Macpherson of Ralia.* I am happy to hear your daughter
has recovered, and has a prospect of passing the summer so agreeably, with the worthy family at Ardmore,
of whom I have been taught to think very highly
indeed. Mr. G. joins in every good wish towards
the dwellers on the Dune, and rejoices with me at
the nearer prospect of seeing the lord of the said Dune

"Once more on the borders of the brawling brook."

Believe me, my dear madam, with warmest regard,
&c., &c.

A. G.

* This lady was married to a near relation, and intimate friend,
of the Minister of Laggan. She was distinguished for beauty and
understanding, and died about her thirtieth year, on the birth of her
youngest son, leaving eleven children to lament her irreparable loss.

LETTER XVII.

TO MISS OURRY, LONDON.*

Laggan, April 8, 1793.

My dear Friend,

Your last was a downright reprieve to me. I conjectured, feared, and at last dreamed, most powerfully, of every possible evil that could befall you; but, indeed, I never dreamed or supposed that such an evil had befallen me, as being forgotten or neglected by you. If I had, I should have certainly grown *mice-and-throw-puss.*†

But I must now proceed to business. It seems you have not only revived the humour of pilgrimages, but are determined to carry it through by loading the shrine with offerings. You do not consider the expense of so long a journey. To you, who are but poor in England, though you will be thought very rich when you cross the Tay, the expense, I say, of your journey is, of itself, a lavish offering on the shrine of Saint Friendship, who, by the by, though I verge on forty, is the first saint in my calendar. Your other proposed liberalities go beyond devotion; they are downright bigotry and enthusiasm. I do not, however, disclaim your kindness; for if you could easily

---

* Who had offered, on her intended visit to the Author's family, to bring some little presents for the children, and requested Mrs. Grant to suggest what would be most suitable for their different ages.—ED.

† Misanthrope. A playful allusion to an incident in their early correspondence.

afford it, I could owe obligations to you, I think, more easily than to any one of your sex. I do not reflect on the sex, but allude to a worthy man whom I shall teach you to admire hereafter. You cannot imagine how plainly people of the mid lling rank educate their children here. Families are generally numerous in this prolific northern hive; and Edinburgh, the only place that affords a genteel education, is both dear and distant. French, music, and drawing, are confined to people of rank or wealth. The genius for music is very prevalent in this country; but I see those that are taught languages and drawing, merely burlesque them. Mary is so steady, and has such memory and application, that I dare say she would do more in a quarter, under your occasional tuition in French, than others do in two seasons, while distracted with the hundred nothings they learn at once in a boarding-school. She has been a twelvemonth in a friend's house in Glasgow, attending day-schools; she has sewed pictures on satin, fire-screens, &c. I mean to get her to work a great woollen shawl for my rheumatic shoulders. You will bring her a set of worsteds to sew it, and a pattern; also a copy of Paradise Lost, with engravings, which, though nominally her's, will instruct and delight the whole race.

Will you be surprised to hear that, except Catherine's learning to dance for a short time, none of the other girls ever set foot in a public school, and you may well believe we could ill afford the expense of a private governess for them. This delay in their education was partly owing to our balancing some time on removing to Glasgow, merely for their sakes; for I hate a town life. Yet they read, write, and do plain work tolerably; and their sentiments and manners are much above what you would expect from their utter seclusion. Catherine is more lively, petulant, and headstrong than Mary. She has a voice and exquisite ear for music,—is so clever that she would learn anything with the least instruction,—has a turn for works of ingenuity, and a taste for letters. Her heart is warm and generous, and she is, to the last degree, charitable and compassionate; yet requires more curbing and reining than the rest. She is a lace worker;—you will bring her a little fine thread, a few plain, narrow patterns, and some small bobbins. Isabella, the gentle, amiable Isabella, who, though no great headpiece, is goodness in the abstract, and lives only to please and serve her brothers and sisters, is ten years old. Her capacity, though moderate, and clouded with extreme diffidence, is not despicable: she is most industrious in obliging, and has an absolute genius for tending young children, which has tempted me to employ her much in that way, and thrown her very much back in other things. She has just finished her sampler;—you will bring a very few silks for her fine sampler,—sombre colours,—for the design is a monument and cypress, with a few mottoes: she will want very little, for she has the leavings of Catherine's sampler. She is very fond of a pretty book: pray bring her one,—a school collection, or some pretty thing with engravings.

A Map of Scotland will be a fit present for John. He is learning Latin. He is very good-natured,—has sound, plain intellects, and a good deal of humour: he would be music-mad if indulged, and has a rage for whistles, fifes, &c., which we discourage. Duncan is a fine, manly creature, and a very good scholar : he reads the Bible distinctly, and is just five years of age. It is only two days since he came from Fort-George, and I am giddy with joy at getting him out of the hands of my worthy parents. They made a business of softening and feminizing him; but we will make him a hardy Highlander before we part. As all his wants are well supplied, bring him some very trifling toy,—as a child's book, with pictures, or a little horse : he has a fine voice, and is constantly sketching drawings. The young children only remain, who have not sense for books, and for whom we buy nothing but shoes, for they are dressed out of their sisters' old wardrobes. Little Miss Anne Ourry has a violent passion for a doll, and nurses one most tenderly ;—bring her such a one as you get for a shilling,—a dearer one would be thrown away ; for once she sets eyes on it, she will never part with it. You may also bring a pair of shoes, such as will fit a child of two years old,—for her feet and herself are frightfully big ;—have them coarse, like the maid that wears them, and the ground she goes on. To prevent disputes, you must bring a little doll to Charlotte the Younger. She is rather pretty after all, but over-sized.

When you arrive at Edinburgh, send word first to Dr. Gregory Grant, physician, and then to the Rev. Mr. Kemp; they are both people whom every one knows, and who are well worth your knowing. I have directed some others, too, to call and assist in doing you the honours of the good town. If you hear of one coming to Glasgow, take that road, for I think it is shorter than the one by Edinburgh, since it was opened through Lanarkshire. If that be your route, send, on your arrival, to my friend, Mr. Archibald Smith's, George Square, where you will find people who have admired you for many years, and will rejoice much over you. Mr. Macintosh lives a little out of town, at Dunchattan, but will wait on you directly. Whatever road you take, let us know the very day you leave London, that Mr. Grant may attend you at Perth. If possible let your next letter be so dated as to reach Edinburgh on Saturday, for the post comes to these antipodes but once a-week. Give my best love to Miss Malliet, if she will cheerfully lend you to me. Committing you to the protection of St. Andrew, I remain yours tenderly,

A. G.

LETTER XVIII.

TO MISS OURRY.*

Glasgow, January 2, 1794.

My dear Friend,

I am far from imputing neglect to you after your two spirited efforts from Ferrybridge and London, when fatigue might have pleaded your excuse, and the other very pleasing testimonies of attention to my dear friends at Laggan, of which I heard as they passed through the town. After this elegant exor-

---

* Miss Ourry had spent the summer and part of the autumn of 1793 at Laggan, and Mrs. Grant afterwards accompanied her friend to Glasgow on her return to England.—ED.

dium, with which you must be greatly edified, it remains for me to account for staying so long here, contrary to my mate's tender injunction and your entreaties. First, then, my father has been very ill, and had I been much inclined, which I honestly confess was not the case, I could not, till now, have thought of returning. Then I have not put Isabella to school, or done half what I meant.

I have seen Mary Wollstonecraft's book,* which is much run after here. It has produced no other conviction in my mind, but that of the author's possessing considerable abilities, and greatly misapplying them. To refute her arguments would be to write another and a larger book; for there is more pains and skill required to refute ill-founded assertions, than to make them. Nothing can be more specious and plausible, for nothing can delight Misses more than to tell them they are as wise as their masters. Though, after all, they will in every emergency be like Trinculo in the storm, when he crept under Caliban's gaberdine for shelter. I consider this work as every way dangerous; first, because the author, to considerable powers adds feeling, and I dare say a degree of rectitude of intention: she speaks from conviction on her own part, and has completely imposed on herself before she attempts to mislead you. Then she writes in such a strain of seeming piety, and quotes Scripture in a manner so applicable and emphatic, that you are thrown off your guard, and surprised into partial acquiescence, before you observe that the deduction to

---

* A Vindication of the Rights of Woman.—1792.

be drawn from her position is in direct contradiction not only to Scripture, reason, the common sense and universal custom of the world, but even to parts of her own system, and many of her own assertions.

Some women of a good capacity, with the advantage of superior education, have no doubt acted and reasoned more consequentially and judiciously than some weak men; but, take the whole sex through, this seldom happens; and were the principal departments, where strong thinking and acting become necessary, allotted to females, it would evidently happen so much the more rarely, that there would be little room for triumph, and less for inverting the common order of things, to give room for the exercise of female intellect. It sometimes occurs, especially in our climate, that a gloomy, dismal winter day, when all without and within is comfortless, is succeeded by a beautiful starlight evening, embellished with aurora borealis, as quick, as splendid, and as transient, as the play of the brightest female imagination. Of these bad days, succeeded by good nights, there may, perhaps, be a dozen in the season. Now what should we think of a projector, that, to enjoy the benefit of the one, and avoid the oppression of the other, should insist that people should sleep all day, and work all night, the whole year round? I think the great advantage that women, taken upon the whole, have over men, is, that they are more gentle, benevolent, and virtuous. Much of this only superiority they owe to living secure and protected in the shade. Let them loose, to go impudently through all the justling paths of politics and business, and they will encounter all the corruptions that men are subject to, without the same powers either of resistance or recovery; for the delicacy of the female mind is like other fine things; in attempting to rub out a stain, you destroy the texture. I am sorry to tell you, *in a very low whisper,* that this intellectual equality that the Misses make such a rout about, has no real existence. The ladies of talents would not feel so overburdened, and at a loss what to do with them, if they were not quite out of the common course of things. Mary Wollstonecraft and some others put me in mind of a kitten we had last winter, who, finding a small tea-pot without a lid, put in its head, but not finding it so easy to take it out again, she broke the pot in the struggle; her head, however, still remained in the opening, and she retained as much of the broken utensil round her neck, as made a kind of moveable pillory. She ran about the house in alarm and astonishment; she did not know what was the matter, felt she was not like other cats, but had acquired a greater power of making disturbance, which she was resolved to use to the very utmost, and so would neither be quiet herself, or suffer any one else to remain so. I leave the application to you.

Our powers are extremely well adapted to the purposes for which they are intended; and if now and then faculties of a superior order are bestowed upon us females, they too are, no doubt, given for good and wise purposes, and we have as good a right to use them as a linnet has to sing; but this so seldom happens, and it is of so little consequence whether it happens or not, that there is no reason why Scripture, custom, and nature, should be set at defiance, to rear up a system of education for qualifying women to act parts which Providence has not assigned to the sex. Where a woman has those superior powers of mind to which we give the name of genius, she will exert them under all disadvantages: Jean Jacques says truly, that genius will educate itself, and, like flame, burst through all obstructions. Certainly, in the present state of society, when knowledge is so very attainable, a strong and vigorous intellect may soon find its level. Creating hot-beds for female genius, is merely another way of forcing exotic productions, which, after all, are mere luxuries, indifferent in their kind, and cost more time and expense than they are worth. As to superiority of mental powers, Mrs. W. is doubtless the empress of female philosophers; yet what has she done for philosophy, or for the sex, but closed a ditch, to open a gulf! There is a degree of boldness in her conceptions, and masculine energy in her style, that is very imposing. There is a gloomy grandeur in her imagination, while she explores the regions of intellect without chart or compass, which gives one the idea of genius wandering through chaos. Yet her continual self-contradiction, and quoting, with such seeming reverence, that very Scripture, one of whose first and clearest principles it is the avowed object of her work to controvert: her considering religion as an adjunct to virtue, so far and no farther than suits her hypothesis; the taking up and laying down of Revelation with the same facility; make me think of a line in an old song,

" One foot on sea and one on shore,
To one thing constant never."

What, as I said before, has she done? She has shown

us all the miseries of our condition ; robbed us of the only sure remedy for the evils of life, the sure hope of a blessed immortality ; and left for our comfort the rudiments of crude, unfinished systems, that crumble to nothing whenever you begin to examine the materials of which they are constructed.

Come, let us for a moment shut the Bible, and listen to Mary. Let us suppose intellect equally divided between the sexes. We may deceive the understanding, but it would be a very bold effort of sophistry to attempt to impose on the senses ; we know too well that our imaginations are more awake, our senses more acute, our feelings more delicate, than those of our *tyrants*. Say, then, we are otherwise equal. These qualities or defects would still leave the advantage on their side : we should much oftener resolve and act, before we called reason to counsel, than they would. Besides, I foresee that the balance will go in the old-fashioned way at last, if Mary carries her point. When the desired revolution is brought about, will not the most sanguine advocates of equality be satisfied, in the first national council, with having an equal number of each sex elected ? Now, I foresee that when this is done, (as girls, or very old women will not be eligible for the duties of legislation, and mothers have certainly a greater stake in the commonwealth), a third of the female members will be lying-in, recovering, or nursing ; for you can never admit the idea of a female philosopher giving her child to be nursed. Whatever other changes may be found proper, I hope they will retain the wool-sack in the upper house, and add some more. The membresses, of course, will bring their infants into the house; this will interrupt no debate: for children that suck in philosophy with their milk, will not cry like the vulgar brats under the old regime, but they may possibly sleep during a long debate, and then the wool-sacks will be very convenient to lay them upon. There is no end either of reasoning or ridicule on this truly ridiculous subject. If the powers of a very superior female mind prove so inadequate to its own purposes, when thus absurdly exerted, what will become of those who adopt her vanity and scepticism, without her knowledge and genius to support them?

To conclude this subject: I see it is a great custom now for people to dabble in scepticism and speculative impiety, keeping all the while a slight hold of their original principles, that they may return when they please, as if *thus far and no farther* belonged to finite natures. Yet these same people would be very unhappy, if they saw their young children going out of their depth into a current, trusting to a slight hold of a twig on the brink; though the worst that could happen in this latter case were only drowning. In fact, the Bible is or is not the charter of our salvation; it is necessary both for our peace of mind and consistency of conduct, that we should either believe or not believe it. The nature of the subject admits no wavering; it is all true, or all false. Let us, then, seriously regard the most important object that can ever be presented to our view. These truths must be either wedded or renounced; if we mingle daring innovations and unwarranted practices with a feeble and dubious belief, haunted with pungent remorse or gloomy uncertainty, we shall not enjoy even the fleeting day that is passing from us. Let us then grasp hard our principles, or let them go. As the reformers manage, they have the fears without the hopes that religion inspires. Let us, at any rate, in these important concerns, be guided by the common sense that directs us in ordinary bargains. Let us examine well what we are to get, before we part with what we have.

My poor brains could never support the rotation of opinions which seems to delight some people in this city ; they remind me of Hotspur, when he talks of living in a windmill. What a pleasing transition I am about to make from those who believe too little, to those who believe rather too much. With what delight and reverence I shall listen to dear Moome's* awe-compelling tales, after all this farrago. Adieu! dear friend. May you reap the fruits of steady principle, and consistent conduct, both here and hereafter. Farewell, kindly,

A. G.

LETTER XIX.

TO MRS. MACINTOSH, GLASGOW.

Dear Madam,   Laggan, July 2, 1794.

We begin now to be very impatient for the confirmation of the glad tidings of your coming north. It

---

* Moome, an endearing Gaelic term, applied to Mrs. Macpherson, a humble neighbour of the Author's family. See afterwards, Letter of 3d October, 1796.

was wrong to mention it, unless you mean to carry it
through ; the prospect having so much elated the
young family. Isabella is particularly so ; even her
meek spirit is occupied in premeditating chicken
slaughter, for the poultry are in her department ; and
then she is so engrossed with considering what fruits
and vegetables will be in season. My principal fear
is, that our stock of good weather will be exhausted
before you arrive ; for, as the man says of his Italian
wash balls, we have really had Italian sunshine for six
weeks past, which, with the addition of tranquillity,
and an easy, regular progression of family and farming,
has been a great source of enjoyment to us ; so that,
were it not for the French and the caterpillars, we
should be quite happy ; but the former disturb our
peace, and the latter destroy our gooseberries.   I
should not speak plurally, for my sovereign is not so
much the sport of petty contingencies.

  You see, thus, in the midst of innocent pleasures
and laudable employments, I remain a perturbed example of that great moral truth, that there is no unmixed felicity here ;—at least out of Plymouth, for
there the orb of joy shines round and bright in the
beatified dwelling of Captain Furzer and his mate,
without being obscured by clouds, or waning into
diminution.   In short, Mrs. F. seems highly pleased
with the change of state, and delighted with the character of her mate.*   No wonder, if he be all she
thinks ; and I do not doubt of her judgment or veracity in this or any other instance.   Such mildness of

  * Alluding to the recent marriage of Miss Ourry to Captain Furzer, an officer of the Royal Marine Force.

disposition, rectitude of principle, and singular delicacy of sentiment, as she ascribes to him, must enchant a person of her taste and feeling. The porch, like our own, is often the most decorated and pleasant part of the dwelling; yet, I flatter myself, my dear friend's case will not confirm this observation, but that she will find herself just as happy at the close of this century. Her great fear at present is, that her lord should be called out to Channel service; but, I hope, now that Lord Howe has so completely established our superiority there, it will no longer be accounted a post of danger. You never tell me a word about your son John, which you ought to do, in common charity, to afford me a pretext for saying something about mine. When did you hear from him, from St. Helena? I have used all means to get Charlotte home, for near a month past, and am now likely to succeed.

*　　*　　*　　*　　*

I see Robespierre, too, has been lately the object of a young lady's enthusiasm. I hope he will meet some enthusiast soon, who will send him on a journey he is little prepared for. Mr. Grant is still ideal chaplain, for the choice is not declared; but we think the same appointment in an old regiment would be better.* With kind love to you all, in which the pastor joins, I am, very gratefully, yours,

A. G.

* Referring to a proposal to procure a military chaplaincy for Mr. Grant.—Ed.

LETTER XX.

TO MRS. BROWN, GLASGOW.

Laggan, August 17, 1794.

My dear Mrs. Brown,

I am very tired and very stupid, yet the recollection of you, and all your kindness and goodness, comes so strong on my mind, that I cannot omit this opportunity of writing to you. I do not believe I owe you anything on the writing score, for I have not only written most meritoriously through a thousand obstacles, but have so sung and celebrated you, that both sides of the Tweed have resounded with your praise, and all the Grampians have re-echoed it. So you see it is you that are in my debt. Besides, as Falstaff most judiciously said to Prince Hal, "Thou owest me thy love ; and thy love is worth a million, *Jean.*"

If my hand, which is at present nearly disabled by an accident, would let me, I would tell you how I spent the brightest and finest summer I ever saw in these Northern regions ; but I have not time to enlarge, nor have I acquired the said Falstaff's happy knack of imitating the honourable Romans in brevity. Suffice it, that the first part was delightfully serene and tranquil, and the latter part agitated and melancholy on poor Isabella's account, who, you will be glad to hear, is now recovering from a dangerous illness : you would hear of her wonderful adventure in Drumochter, which, I dare say, increased, if not produced, her indisposition.

Since Mrs. Macintosh and her spouse came here, I

have accompanied them to Moy Hall,* for a short visit, the lady of which mansion has the honour to be related to the lord of this august dwelling. Were I at leisure to exert all my narrative and descriptive powers, you, too, should accompany me there, to share the lady's superlative civility, admire the Laird's superior urbanity, and traverse the lake in a pleasure-boat, as I did, to visit the ruins on the Island, and explore the wooded shores ; not to mention the garden gay with flowers, rich in fruits, and abundant in wasps, one of which stung my hand, which has since been inflamed, and procured much idleness and sympathy.

I have not room for half the compliments and good wishes my family send to yours. When W. C. returns to Glasgow, I will pay my epistolary debt to your sister, who, by the by, has " said the thing that was not" about writing by said W. I am your very true but drowsy

A. G.

LETTER XXI.

TO MRS. MACINTOSH, GLASGOW.

My dear Madam,   Laggan, August 30, 1794.

Though I had not received your letter, inclination would prompt me to write to you without the stimulus of having anything important to say; but if you expect me to be punctual, you must give ample license

* The ancient seat of the Chief of Mackintosh, near Inverness.

for dullness and absurdity, besides a full allowance to
my happy talent of digression, my rare felicity in
parenthesis, and my peculiar knack at circumlocution.
Do not let the solemnity of my parting with you* too
deeply impress you; it was merely the effect of a
momentary impulse, which I could not control; I am
sorry it saddened so much of your journey. I, too,
consumed the time at home in sympathetic dejection; for the impression did not wear off so soon as
these bursts of tenderness and melancholy generally
do. The acuteness of my feelings, and the horror
with which I shrink from the evils of life, are but
short-lived in my mind, by reason of a happy facility
in rousing up images of joy and comfort, and catching
at the bright side of every object, and every prospect.
To a projector or adventurer, this might prove a dangerous faculty; but to one whose fate it is to walk
peaceably (though sometimes pensively) through the
obscure bye-paths of life, it is an advantage to have
a quickness in discovering every violet that springs
up among brambles, and every rainbow that smiles
through the tears of the sky.

I think the soft melancholy produced in your mind
by the music of your Irish piper, would have a sweet
accordance with the sensations which those " sympathetic glooms" about Dunkeld are so well fitted to inspire.
I, for my part, though a stranger to the art of music,
am well acquainted with its power, and subject to its
influence, in its rudest forms; particularly when it
breathes the spirit of that sentiment which, for the

* Mr. and Mrs. Macintosh had lately made a visit of some weeks
at Laggan.

time, predominates in my mind, or wakes some tender remembrance with which accident has connected it. When my dearest little boy was in the last stage of that illness which proved fatal to him, we had three maids who had all good voices; one was afraid to sit up alone to attend my calls, on which the nurse-maid agreed to sit with her, and lull the infant beside her. The solitary maid was then afraid to stay alone in her attic abode. The result was, that the three Syrens sung in concert a great part of the night, which seemed to soothe the dear sufferer so much, that when they ceased, he often desired they would begin again. He listened to it three hours before he expired. I never hear the most imperfect note of *Cro Challin** since, without feeling my heart-strings accord with it:

> " It gives a very echo from the seat,
>   Where grief is throned :"

and were I to hear those moving sounds which, we are told, " drew iron tears down Pluto's cheek," they could not open every source of anguish more effectually. You have it now in your power to taste the pathos of music in its full extent, Mr. Balfour, I am told, having unrivalled power in doing justice to our old plaintive melodies. We were consoled for your short stay by knowing you found his family at Dunchattan.

Charlotte is, and looks much better than when you saw her. This has been a day of joyful quiet to her, and no less joyful bustle to every one else. The servants, tenants, and children, are all busy making our

* Cro Challin is a sweet and very popular strain of pastoral music, invariably sung in every Highland fold.

great hay-stack; John and the men drive carts; the
rest trample down the top, and the two little ones are
handed back and forward, or driven up and down in
the carts, to their great delectation. Being Saturday,
the stack must needs be closed to-night; so they have
no time to come down to dress the dinner; but a cold
collation has been conveyed to the top of the stack
with great glee, and devoured with alacrity. This is
what I account one of the pleasures of a country life,
to see so many people usefully busy and innocently
happy.

Mr. Grant rejoiced to hear the 90th regiment belonged to so good a man as Balgowan;* he is much
better of late, not at all the worse, perhaps, for the
prospect of being appointed chaplain to the regiment
aforesaid. . . . . Robespierre's fall has had all
deserved aggravations; imagination shrinks from the
images that such a death suggests. Of whom was
it said that " Hell grew darker at his frown?" I
wonder if the modern philanthropists, whose affections
comprehend all but those who might be the better for
them—I wonder, I say, if they have found out a cool
place for this minister of vengeance, or wrapped him
in a corner of the wide mantle of everlasting sleep.
Adieu, tenderly.

* Colonel Graham of Balgowan possesses a great landed property in Perthshire; and represents one of the most ancient and
considerable families in Scotland. For his taste, his talents, his
courage, and his virtues, he is justly considered as one of the
greatest ornaments of his country.—(1807.) Colonel Graham became afterwards celebrated, first as Sir Thomas Graham, and afterwards as Lord Lynedoch, and the companion in arms of Wellington.
(1845.)—ED.

Letter XXII.

TO MRS. MACINTOSH.

Dear Madam,   Laggan, September 9, 1794.

I knew, some years ago, a good-natured worthy
creature, a great simpleton nevertheless, at Inverness.
He, to his great delectation, prevailed on a fine, sweet-
looking girl, who had more sense than himself, and
of whom he was dotingly fond, to take him for better
and worse.   To be sure he was half mad with exulta-
tion, when he had gained his point; and when their
friends came to visit them, without waiting for their
congratulations, he used to start up, embrace them,
and wish them much joy.   A clever little boy, the
same whom Clan sent out to Antigua the other day,
happening to be in the house, was quite scandalized
at his want of propriety, and told him those people
had no share of his pleasure, and that he had better
be quiet and let them wish *him* joy.   Now, I feel
much inclined to follow my wise friend Frank's example, and wish you joy of the chaplaincy's being
obtained for Mr. Grant, because I am convinced that
you feel as much joy on the occasion as I possibly
can.   Nothing less than the power of procuring an
essential benefit to a family we love and esteem, could
indeed exceed our present satisfaction.   Before I quit
the subject of benefits conferred, let me detail to you
the late arrival from our friend, Miss Ourry that was,
now Mrs. Furzer. . . . .

Though the transition from this to potatoes is sudden, and rather violent, yet as you know little things are great to me, you will be pleased to hear, that we have a crop of that useful root, far superior in quantity and quality to any former, and that our corn also is excellent. The cheerfulness of our work-people, and the soft serenity of the air, during these tepid gleams that Thomson speaks of so feelingly, have almost made us, this autumn, " taste the rural life in all its joy and elegance." Never, never can the rural life be tasted or enjoyed by those who are too rich to enter into rural employments, or who lead, that most insipid of all lives, a town life in the country. Those whose anxious views are confined to mere profit, who have their bodies worn by labour, and their souls by care, have neither leisure nor discernment to admire the face of nature with ardour. In this, indeed, the lower class of Highlanders excel all other low classes, being possessed of a superior degree both of fancy and feeling, and their pastoral cares including more, both of leisure and variety, than falls to the lot of other peasants; but, geographically speaking, numberless peculiar blessings are attached to the temperate zone of life, that middle state, which Agur prayed for.

Charlotte the elder is well, cheerful, and means to be very eloquent on the subject of *drapery* one of these days. Mr. Grant means to be equally eloquent on a more dignified subject. Now, you are not to be surprised or over-dazzled, when I have thus announced the blaze that is about to break forth from these worthies. Adieu!

LETTER XXIII.

Dear Madam,   Laggan, September 21, 1794.

My last was to Mr. M.   Since then, indolence and
indisposition have induced me to seize the pretext of
not hearing from you, as an excuse to delay writing.
My better judgment, however, tells me I have no
right to be ceremonious with you; and past experience
convinces me, that writing easily and fully to a real
friend, will exhilarate my spirits, if once I could whip
myself up to it.   I have been just discharging a painful
task of duty; it is that of writing a long monitory
epistle to poor Mary, whom I have a long while unpar-
donably neglected.   I know she is cherished with the
tenderest care, and has the advantage of having her
moral and religious duties inculcated in the most forcible manner. . . . . . .

Did I tell you what pleasure it gave me to find
your friend and favourite, Dr. Maclean, had given up
that wild scheme of going to America?   I was fond
of that country to enthusiasm, and spent the most
delightful and fanciful period of my life in it; for mine
was a very premature childhood.   The place where I
resided* was the most desirable in the whole continent;
there my first perceptions of pleasure, and there my
earliest habits of thinking were formed; and from

---

* Albany, on the Hudson river, and its neighbourhood.

thence I drew that high relish for the sublime simplicity of nature which has ever accompanied me. This has been the means of preserving a certain humble dignity in all the difficulties I have had to struggle through. Yet, from what I know of the alterations which the last twenty years have brought about in that country, and the still greater difference which other views and associations have made on myself, though I had it now in my power to return, my judgment would check my inclination. The paths that lead from nature and simplicity, towards elegance and false refinement in manners, and artificial modes of living, do not indeed tend to happiness, but they slope with our inclinations and wind with our caprices; though, when too far pursued, they lead directly to selfishness and depravity. These paths can never be retrodden. When tired of the idle and frivolous bustle, and the vain empty pursuits that fill up, I can scarcely say diversify, fashionable life, we languish under the burden of ceremony. The multiplied elegancies and conveniencies, the various and mixed society which at first delighted, begin now to encumber us. Those pleasures lose the force of novelty, and our riper judgment undervalues what we once thought essential to felicity. We now retrace our first and purest ideas of happiness—the rural ease that dwells in the pastoral valley, the soothing quiet and artless innocence of the cottage, the solemn gloom of the forest in which we wish to meditate undisturbed, and the sublime solitude of the mountain, from whose elevation we wish to look down on low pursuits, and give a kind of repose to the wearied mind. We forget that nature presents us with no unmixed cup of enjoyment. Habituated to the profusion of art which accumulates pleasures till they grow vapid and tasteless, we do not easily reconcile ourselves to the parsimony of nature, which preserves its relish by a frugal distribution. We endeavour to return to those habits which long distant recollection has endeared, which poetical description has decked with beauties innumerable, but which are incapable of being combined and enjoyed together. Estranged from nature, enervated by luxury, and softened by false delicacy, we set about the experiment; we find the cottage quiet, indeed, but smoky, confined, and deficient in a thousand things on which we are become too dependent. The narrow bounds imprison us, the low roof crushes, and scanty light which struggles in through the little casement, bewilders us. The inhabitants we find innocent, hospitable, and willing to please; but we are shocked with their vulgar language, disgusted with their uncouth manners, and tired with the sameness to which their narrow circle of ideas confines their conversation; and we are unable either to descend to their topics, or bring them up to ours. We find dull uniformity and listless languor in the valley, whose culture does not employ, and whose produce does not enrich us. The forest walks are damp and intricate, and its gloom melancholy and oppressive to us who have not accustomed ourselves to reflect, but to observe and to find continual employment for that faculty among the busy haunts of men. In vain we climb the mountain in search of more extended prospects, and more exalted serenity:

fatigue follows, and chagrin overtakes us; the wind
pierces, and the cold benumbs us; the prospects are
perhaps obscured by mist, or lost in dim confusion,
and we hasten back, weary and unsatisfied, from scenes
that expand the soul, and tranquillise the spirit of that
faithful lover of nature, who has never admitted into
her bosom artificial joys, or wandered in the vain
search of happiness not meant for this threshold of
existence. It is indeed a singular effort of a vigorous
superior mind to preserve through life the love of
artless manners and cheap pleasures. Your unequalled
steadiness in this respect is one of the strongest ties
that hold me to you. Do not call this flattery. I
cannot even flatter you so far as to say, that the disquisition I have just wandered into was meant for
your amusement. Truly, I have amused myself by
unburdening my mind, and arranging my ideas. If
you, too, are amused, I shall not be sorry; and if, on
the contrary, you are wearied, I shall not be angry.

I have received your letter, and Mr. M.'s: more of
them anon. I am glad that Charlotte thinks I look
so well; I do not think so myself. Languor and
thoughtfulness grow upon me, and I become less able
and willing to take exercise. I rather think I resemble
grandmother Eve, of whom we are told that

> " So much of death her thoughts had entertained,
>   As dyed her cheek with pale."

Yet you must not think me vapourish. That change
in the mode of our existence which is before us all,
has become familiar to my mind from frequent perils.
I can bear to look at it, and wish not to be surprised
by it. I am not so ignorant of the nature and import-

ance of preparation for futurity, as to wear myself out in fervors of forced devotion, during this short period of suspended fear and expectation, in hopes of blotting out the errors of a negligent and self-gratifying life, by the feeble struggles produced, not by rational and vital piety, but mere selfish terror. I endeavour to repose my hopes on a nobler and surer foundation. The dim and tremulous light that comes in short glimpses to my mind, beams forth from merits far transcending what human duties can pretend to, or human efforts arrive at. I do not think I have a worse chance for passing through the approaching crisis, than any other person, worn out by many similar risks. And, if it be the Divine will to preserve me amidst my family, will it lessen my after usefulness or enjoyment, to have endeavoured to resign my mind to what must inevitably happen at some future period?—I am glad you were so pleased with the "Nymph of the Fountain,"* whom I have endeavoured to recommend to your attention, by making her both a Highlander and a moralist. Those light excursions of fancy, where " soft description holds the place of sense," are merely the relaxation and play of the mind. Were I to dilate my awakened powers towards greater objects, and give vent to my feelings on subjects still more serious and impressive, where there is abundant scope for pathetic painting among the sad realities of life, I should require to be more self-possessed and freed from the

* Some poetical verses bearing this title, addressed to Miss Charlotte Grant, and included in the Author's volume of Poems, published in 1803.—Ed.

pressure of the present exigencies; but that time may
come. I can now only add that I am always yours,

A. G.

LETTER XXIV.

TO MRS. MACINTOSH, GLASGOW.

Laggan, December 20, 1794.
Dear Madam,

Angus Mackay comes so sudden, and stays so short
a time, that I have barely an opportunity to acknowledge your two last favours. Your attention in the
writing way, in this time of need, is very considerate;
it gives a necessary fillip to the drooping spirits, to
know that one is of consequence enough to be pitied
and remembered by one's absent friends; and there is
no one living more conscious of the efficacy of such a
cordial. I shall not attempt to answer your letters in
detail, being scarce able to answer them at all. All
this day I am much indisposed, but am so used to
these preparatory alarms, that I am not alarmed at
them. We are much gratified by your favourable
opinion of Mary. There is nothing more natural than
for a parent to be vain of the real or imputed excel-
lencies of children. Yet with me, much reflection,
and some observation have so far conquered that propensity, that I am not sure whether I should not be
sorry to discover those tendencies to genius that some
imagine to exist. Distinguished abilities are attended,
especially in the *undistinguished sex*, with much risk,
and much envy. Second rate talents, again, afford a

pretence for imaginary superiority, which flatters and intoxicates the mind more than what is real. In fact, I think pretenders are far more liable to self-opinion and affectation, than minds of a truly superior order. Mary has reflection, taste, and an excellent memory, but has neither energy of mind, nor sprightliness of fancy for any great effort of intellect. Whatever capacity she may possess, I have the comfort of knowing she will never use it invidiously or ostentatiously. Now that I am forced on thinking back on what I have done, and forward to the probable consequences, amidst the regrets I feel at not having it in my power, through constant hurry, occasional depression, and, perhaps, negligence, to bring my children as forward as some others, in diligence, exactness, &c.; amidst these regrets, I say, I feel a ray of comfort in retracing the unwearied pains I have taken in the cultivation of their hearts; and impressing upon them such just notions of the dispensations of Providence, and of their own peculiar state, as may prevent their looking down on any one with contempt; while the same regulated views make them regard their superiors with a respect free from envy or servility. In short, I have laboured, I flatter myself, not in vain, without having often recourse to formal precepts, to make my children love virtue, and despise and detest every instance of meanness and malignity. I have so far felt the advantage of this culture, that, whatever childish faults they may commit, covetousness, envy, or strife have not, as yet, been known amongst them; and they live united by a bond of the most disinterested affection. Forgive this, and consider it merely as a soliloquy, with which

I am comforting myself, when I feel much need of all earthly comforts, to go no higher.

It would be both ungrateful and unjust to quit this subject of my children and my comforts, without owning, that I have great reason to account our joint charge, Charlotte, one of the chief of them ; and should this be the last letter I ever write, I will not close it without making it a faint memorial of her faithful friendship, ardent gratitude, inflexible integrity, unexampled tenderness, and diligence of attention to all my cares and infirmities ; of a character, in short, which every day rises, even upon me, who know her so intimately, and breaks, with double lustre, through the gloom of adversity. I meant to say very little, yet I have said too much. I depend on your indulgence, and shall be, while I live, with the purest truth of affection, yours most sincerely,

A. G.

Letter XXV.

TO MRS. MACINTOSH.

Laggan, March 6, 1795.

Dear Madam,

Yesterday, and not till then, I received your letter, with the account of your poor George's departure ; which, as far as the change affected himself, was, I am sure, matter of gratulation. Well might he say with the patriarch, that " few and evil had been the days of his pilgrimage." Doubtless, from the felicity of that new state of being, which, through the Divine mercy,

he has now attained, he looks back on his past sufferings, as we do on a dream of misery that disturbed
our sickly slumbers, when we awake to peace and
comfort.

I do not wonder you should feel the pang of separation very severely, in spite of all that reason offers to
reconcile you to the stroke. However eagerly we may
grasp at delusive pleasures, we have but to examine
our own undepraved feelings, to be convinced, that
even the most painful exertions, arising from a virtuous sentiment, afford a secret, unspeakable enjoyment. Even the sadly-pleasing recollection of friends
long since mingled with the dust, is endeared to us by
the worth that sweetens their remembrance ; though
the thought of them opens afresh the wounds that time
has closed, yet we love to indulge it. When such are
removed from us, we follow them with regret, though
certain of their happiness. No doubt we feel a sad
vacuity in our hearts ; yet, I believe, we miss full as
much the innate consciousness of exercising a benevolence so exalted, so utterly disinterested. Your
merit of this kind has been great and exemplary ; yet
not unprecedented, or singular. Cynic philosophers
delight to represent all our views as terminating in
self. Yet, without having recourse to the annals of
heroism, the domestic history of families affords so
many instances of the virtue which I have been so
long describing, and you so long practising, as may
serve to overturn their frozen system. I understand
too well the self-reproach you feel at what you think
omissions in duty. My maternal tenderness was never
put to so long and so severe a trial ; yet a conscious-

ness of a failure in duty to a beloved and lamented child, will wring my heart, and oppress my mind, as long as I can feel, or remember.

LETTER XXVI.

TO MRS. FURZER, (FORMERLY MISS OURRY.)

Laggan, April 11, 1795.

My dearest Friend,

I had your kind, welcome letter from Goodamere in course; and you would think your attention well bestowed, if you were present, invisible, to see the joy and pride the whole family derived from your remembrance. I am charmed to find the oblivious matrimonial gulf, so fatal in general to female friendships, has not swallowed up the image of your old unaltered friend. After ascribing abundant merit to you, I begin to take a little to myself for holding, so long, a place in such a heart. Mr. Grant observes, that I have told every one that comes to the house the wonder of your being as punctual since marriage as before. Your description of the present state of matters at your uncle, the Admiral's, is very striking and impressive indeed. It requires much worth and wisdom to act the concluding scene decently, when there are no tender connexions to keep the heart warm and open. Your account of your aunt, too, and poor Miss Malliet's forlorn and uncomfortable situation, for such I am sure it is since you left her, has made me very thoughtful, and very thankful. Those who must needs tug through difficulties, such as I have always been environed with, are very apt to think, whatever face they put on the matter, that there is but one impediment to their felicity. Blest with comforts which wealth cannot purchase, they think the means of procuring some convenient elegancies, and extending their charity and hospitality a little, would make them completely happy. Even the gay social winter I spent in Glasgow* was a most forcible lesson of instruction to me, in this respect; all the friends I most value, except Lady Clan,† who is wise enough to neglect forms and live as she pleases, are slaves to the world, and to a world they contemn, and have been long disgusted with. For some reason or other of form, of policy, or convenience, elegant leisure, the nurse of fancy and of friendship, is sacrificed; life seems to glide from them like a dream, in pursuits which their reason despises, and among people against whom their hearts are closed up.

> " O why, since life can little more supply
> Than just to look about us, and to die,"

should the few among us who understand its value, squander it so lavishly, and leave so little for active benevolence, social comfort, or elegant pleasures ? besides the great object of endeavouring to qualify ourselves for that exalted society, to which we aspire in an hereafter, divided as we are from that hereafter by so slight a barrier.

Do not think I am preaching like a cynic from my

---

* 1793-94.

† Lady Clan, *i. e.*, the Lady of Clan.—Clan was a favourite appellation given to Mr. Macintosh by his intimates, on account of his Highland enthusiasm.

tub either. Though I endeavour to be satisfied with the
station allotted to me, and feel I have many blessings
which are withheld from those who have more visible
sources of enjoyment; yet I do not deny that I feel
the privation of some for which I have a keen relish—
elegant society, for instance, after which I should languish, were I at leisure to languish for anything. But
my consolation is, that my time is passed usefully; I
enjoy the peace and quiet of the evening exceedingly,
when my hour of leisure is sweetened by reflecting,
that I have all day been doing some service, or procuring some pleasure for those I dearly love. Even
the unvaried self-same circle I move in, though confined and obscure, is interesting, because everything
in it connects with those branches of myself, in which
I live and feel. I have no room for *ennui;* my occupations so crowd upon me, that I find every day too
short for its allotted task. Thank God, my tasks of
every kind are grown much lighter; my elder daughters are becoming assistants and companions to me;
the younger are now no trouble, this blessed sewing
school, lately established here, is such a relief. Their
improvement is inconceivable. Your little namesake,
who is now well, sits as quiet in school as the oldest
scholar there; you cannot think what a quick, sensible creature it is, and how bewitching in her little
ways. When I look grave or displeased, or reprove
her for anything, she looks wistfully in my face, then
clasps me about the neck and kisses me, so that
there is no resisting her. So much for egotism once
removed.

After all the sacrifices you have made, methinks it

would be a very meritorious one, could you bring yourself to stay with your infirm relation, who has so little comfort, while your beloved is destined to wander on the ocean. There, for your comfort, he may now wander in security, and have little to do but to sing "Rule Britannia;" for those vile French seem destined to do all their mischief on one element; like our witches, who, when in pursuit of a devoted object of vengeance, dare not cross a running water, that being a boundary by the laws of magic irremeable; a very comfortable regulation this for good nautical Christians. I know you have a strong plea against what I hinted to you about staying with your aunt. You answer as the man did, who, being invited to some high party of pleasure, said, he had spent three quarters of his constitution for his friends, and was resolved to keep the fourth for himself. You have certainly been rather too long acting the part of Noah's dove, and I do not greatly wonder that you should not wish to return a second time to the ark. It is rather hard that you should have been so long the victim of caprice, and such successive and oddly varied caprice; all the worse, that the inflictors were people you loved, and who loved you as far as they were capable of loving anybody; and meaning, forsooth, no harm. Yet daily experience will convince you of what I have often told you, that the state of a woman living alone is forlorn and unprotected.

This fatal war must of necessity end soon; it seems indeed drawing fast to a conclusion. Then you may hope for halcyon days, in the bosom of affection and tranquillity, with your best friend, whom I truly love for deserving you so well. It is indeed time your storm-beaten vessel should come into port; but as this interim will be a period of disquiet and anxiety at any rate, what you cannot give to comfort, you may even give to virtue and self-denial, as you have done so great a portion of the time past. I should be sorry that your relative left this world without a representative bearing the family name of Ourry. I *do* love old prejudices, especially those which affinity and affection have entwined with the heart-strings. I hate innovations, detest the new light of philosophy, abhor the Rights of Man, and abominate those of Woman. Think then how I am prepared to receive your friend Helen Maria Williams' new publication: though I admire her style, and confess that nobody embellishes absurdity more ingeniously. I am greatly inclined, too, to respect the purity of her religious principles; yet when I recollect the associates with whom her political bigotry has connected her, I think I hear the Syrian leper entreating the prophet's permission to bow a little occasionally in the house of their god Rimmon.

Do you know that your pupil, Mary's, French is much approved, and she is said to translate with purity and elegance. She passes this summer at home, great part of which I mean to devote to the task of forming a mind that appears to me possessed of solidity and stamina, which make it capable of culture and worth the pains. Accept a thousand compliments, delivered in various forms, but you must be content with the aggregate. I have not room for a literary curiosity composed for your sole emolument;

it is an epistle in French, which will go under the next cover. Farewell, cordially,

A. G.

LETTER XXVII.

TO MRS. BROWN, GLASGOW.

My dear Mrs. Brown,   Laggan, July 23d, 1795.

If I had not been dying all winter, and half killed with fatigue all summer, in consequence of the number of things neglected which I was unable to overtake, it would have been unpardonable in me to have been thus long silent to you, on whose friendship I set so great and just a value. Mrs. Smith says you had a sick child in your arms. This, I take for granted, was William, whom I know to be as fine a child as Mary described. I think if there was any danger, she would have mentioned it more seriously. I am charmed to hear you are so well pleased with our Catherine, nor do I much wonder at it, considering that there are many *you-isms* about her; though she wants that spirit of accuracy by which you were so early distinguished. She is active, lively, and has an ardent, generous disposition. This does not evaporate in profession, but labours rather to serve, than to please. For all your partiality, I still think she has many of the awkwardnesses which distinguish an unbred girl. Yet I willingly allow, it is not quite a vulgar awkwardness; for, as I formerly observed to you, where there is mind, there is always, to a certain degree, manner. Miss Ourry and I used to call that embarrassment which results from much feeling and spirit, joined with little usage of the world, elegant awkwardness. I believe a certain portion of indifference must go towards the composition of perfect fashionable ease; you must be fully satisfied with yourself, before you can be fully convinced that every one else is satisfied with you, and the contrary idea is painful and embarrassing.

I give you joy of the nephew or niece you are about to acquire. Your sister is astonished at my calling this a joyful event; no wonder, considering how I am worried and worn out with such acquisitions. Yet people here, though they should be at the utmost loss how to support their children, still continue to rejoice at every addition, and consider the loss of offspring as the greatest misfortune that can possibly befall a family. Those who live in towns and highly civilized societies, where such numberless little somethings become necessary to make up the sum total of felicity, have no idea how strong the great simple outlines of what constitutes happiness in a state of nature, are drawn on the untutored heart. Without reasoning or reflecting, such hearts find the strongest and most pleasurable emotions excited, merely by the exercise of tender and laudable affections. Strangers to false refinement, and incapable, from want of cultivation, of that exalted enjoyment that arises from sentimental attachment grounded on intellectual excellence, the ties of nature, the " charities" of life, are the great sources of their comfort, and sweeten all their hardships. Since bad seasons, and new modes of farming, have impoverished

the peasantry, I do not think there is a poor tenant in
this parish but what is in some measure supported by
his children. And there is no instance of one failing
in this tender retribution. Brought up with generous
sentiments, but frugal and self-denying habits, they
are not like the children of luxury and indulgence,
whose desires go always beyond their acquisitions, and
leave nothing for bounty or for gratitude. Neither
are they like the grovelling offspring of callous vulgarity, who are taught to glean and hoard and think
for self only.

I have rambled as usual; but I believe I, at first,
meant to remark how insensibly, in course of time,
we, in some degree, adopt the habits and prejudices
of those about us, even while we pity their ignorance,
and fancy ourselves more enlightened. For my part,
I have learned to rejoice at the birth of people's
fifteenth child, and to listen to stories of apparitions
and predictions with as much indulgence, though with
less credulity, than N. B. Halhed exercises towards
Brothers. For instance, the other day my dairy-maid,
who has been above seven years in the house, and is
a pious maiden, and a perfect treasury of local and
traditionary anecdote, told me a story, which I am
going to translate literally for your behoof, and which
I was forced to hear with a face of belief, for fear of
being thought an infidel. I must premise that our
dairy-maids always speak very wisely to the cows,
though it is only in rare instances, like this, that the
cows answer them. " Yesterday fortnight (I am sure
it is very true, for I saw a man with these eyes that
saw the dairy-maid), the minister of Moulin, in Athol,

you know—well, his dairy-maid went into the byre and put out all the cows but one, who lay down and would not move. ' Get up,' says the dairy-maid; ' I will not get up,' says the cow; ' But you shall,' replied the damsel, a little startled. ' Go to your master, and bid him come here,' says the cow. So the girl went, and her master came to the byre. ' Get up,' said he to the cow; ' No, I will not,' said she,' I want to speak to you.' ' Say on,' said her master, ' since you are permitted.' The cow began—' Expect a summer of famine, a harvest of blood, and a winter of tears.' So, then the cow went about her business." Now, this fine story gains ample credit, and it would be thought impiety to doubt it.

Could you have believed that there existed manners and opinions so primitive as those which are still preserved in the parish of Laggan? Will you condemn or laugh at my singularity, when I tell you that I am so wearied and disgusted with seeing ignorant, conceited, and irreligious coxcombs form absurd pretensions to reason and philosophy (by affecting to despise all that Newton, Boyle, Locke, and other lights and ornaments of their species believed, and all that inspiration and piety have taught), that I begin to think my poor Anne's credulity more tolerable than such cold-hearted scepticism? I would, at any rate, sooner listen to the sad predictions either of Achilles' horse, or the minister of Moulin's cow, than to many " dreamers of gay dreams," who imagine themselves " wit's oracles." No doubt, the true line lies between credulity and scepticism; but if I quit that line, let me go where I am led by the imagination and the heart. Did you but know how very, very busy I have been all day, having twenty people at work, cutting our winter fuel in the moss, and only one servant at home to provide food for all these, with little aid, you would think my writing all this stuff, now that everybody is asleep, as great an exertion as that of the minister of Moulin's cow. I bid you drowsily adieu, for the first lark is warning me to bed like an owl, as I am.

A. G.

Letter XXVIII.

TO MRS. FURZER, PLYMOUTH.

My dear Friend, Laggan, Aug. 15, 1795.

Do you know that, by Mrs. Macintosh's friendly interference, John Lauchlan* is an Ensign; not that we, by any means, intend him for the army. He will have leave to recruit, friends will recruit for him, and his education will proceed in the meantime. This is a Fencible Regiment, and will, I trust, be sent to graze before he is fit to kill or be killed. About ten days since we made a great hay-stack, which brought you very fresh to memory, as treading on it last year in the fulness of rural glee. But before I tell my sad story, I must inform you that, while the rest of

---

* The Author's eldest son.

Scotland, and England's own self were pinched with scarcity, we had last year, in this corner, the best crop ever remembered, and this year's is at least equal. Judge of our distress when, after driving a cart all day, John was brought in bleeding and torn, in consequence of Paddy's being startled, and going off with the cart. You never beheld such a scene, all the maids were in tears, the young children crying, and Mary fainting; but John behaved like a hero, comforting his sisters, and assuring them he would soon be better. The muscles and sinews, I trust, are not materially injured, and he will not, I hope, be lame. The spirit and manliness he has shown in this exigence have greatly endeared him to us.

Give a little of your leisure to writing to me a few lines soon. Yet, why a *few* lines? If you habituate yourself in your solitude (for I do not hope for it when your spouse returns), to pour out your thoughts to me without restraint or arrangement, this employment of time will answer many good purposes. While it steals us a while from wearing cares and trivial occupations, it will perform half a miracle; it will recal the fleeting phantom, youth, and arrest the worst effects of time's silent progress. Yes, it will preserve the kindly propensities and tender confidence that are scattered fresh and sweet, like early dew in the delightful morning of life. Yet a while we may thus preserve the sunshine of the breast, and repel the unkindly frosts of cold suspicion and distrust, and the bleak sharp blasts of caprice and peevishness, " that make loved life unlovely," and force the callous and the crafty to say, at last,

> " The yellow leaf,
> And that which should accompany old age,
> As honour, love, obedience, troops of friends,
> I must not look to have."

I grasp with avidity the wish, the hope you express
of our meeting once more. It were, indeed, a con-
summation devoutly to be wished, and I have seen
too many strange things to despair of this. I think
with you, that I should love your husband; so much
probity and tranquillity of temper would suit me
who detest art and *finesse* in all its shapes, and sicken
at restless turbulent people, who are for ever in a
bustle about they know not what. I do love a little
constitutional philosophy. Farewell, dear friend, affectionately yours,

A. G.

LETTER XXIX.

TO MRS. MACINTOSH, GLASGOW.

Laggan, Feb. 20, 1796.

" Why dost thou build the tower, son of the winged
days?* Soon wilt thou depart with thy fathers. The
blast from the desert shall rush through thy hall,
and sound upon thy bossy shield." Do you recollect,
dear Madam, when I stopped with you at the gate of
Belleville, I repeated those lines, and observed what
a suitable inscription they might prove for the front

---

* The subject of this letter was a celebrated and well-known translator of ancient Scottish poetry.—(1807.) The late James Macpherson, Esq. of Belleville, and M.P., the Translator of Ossian.—(1845.)

of poor James Macpherson's new house. It would appear I was moved by a prophetic impulse when I predicted that he never would see it finished. Friday last, R. dined there; James had been indisposed since the great storm, yet received his guests with much kindness, seeming, however, languid and dispirited; and towards evening he sunk much, and retired early. Next morning he appeared, but did not eat, and looked ill; R. begged he would frank a letter for Charlotte; he did so, and never more held a pen. When they left the house, he was taken extremely ill, unable to move or receive nourishment, though perfectly sensible. Before this attack, finding some inward symptoms of his approaching dissolution, he sent for a consultation, the result of which arrived the day after his confinement. He was perfectly sensible and collected, yet refused to take anything prescribed to him to the last, and that on the principle that his time was come, and it did not avail. He felt the approaches of death, and hoped no relief from medicine, though his life was not such as one should like to look back on at that awful period: indeed whose is? It pleased the Almighty to render his last scene most affecting and exemplary. He died last Tuesday evening; and, from the minute he was confined, till a very little before he expired, never ceased imploring the Divine mercy in the most earnest and pathetic manner. People about him were overawed and melted by the fervour and bitterness of his penitence; he frequently and earnestly entreated the prayers of good serious people of the lower class who were admitted. He was a very good-natured man; and now, that he had got all his schemes of interest and ambition fulfilled, he seemed to reflect and grow domestic, and showed, of late, a great inclination to be an indulgent landlord, and very liberal to the poor; of which I could relate various instances, more tender and interesting than flashy or ostentatious. His heart and temper were originally good; his religious principles were, I fear, unfixed and fluctuating. But the primary cause that so much genius, taste, benevolence, and prosperity, did not produce or diffuse more happiness, was his living a stranger to the comforts of domestic life, from which unhappy connexions excluded him. Tavern company, and bachelor circles, make men gross, callous, and awkward; in short, disqualify them for superior female society. The more heart old bachelors of this class have, the more absurd and insignificant they grow in the long run; for when infirmity comes on, and fame and business lose their attractions, they must needs have somebody to love and trust, and they then become the dupes of wretched toad-eaters, and slaves to designing housekeepers.

Such was poor James Macpherson, who certainly was worthy of a better fate. His death and the circumstances of it, have impressed my mind in a manner I could not have believed. I think we are somehow shrunk, and our consequence diminished, by losing the only person of eminence among us. It is like extinguishing a light. His Will, which was made sometime before this period of anguish, was, alas, too strongly marked with that vanity and ostentation which threw a deep shade over many good qualities he really possessed. The parade of going to Westminster Abbey marks him out as the first man in the annals of time that, dying in the very spot where he was born, and where all his ancestors were buried, desired to have his bones carried out of his native country. There is a sum of £500 appointed to be laid out on a monument at Belleville. So lived, so died James Bellavill, for that is the true Highland name of the place. I have been diffuse, perhaps tedious, in what concerns the exit of this extraordinary man; because I thought you might, like me, be anxious to know how people quit the world who have made any noise or figure in it. His death found me sad, and has made me sadder. The sudden death of two poor men, our tenants, who have left young, helpless families, which happened last week, also threw a great damp over us. But I will no longer croak my funereal note: though death is ever present to my thoughts, not in his mildest form, I will "give it its wholesome empire; let it reign." Adieu, dear madam,

A. G.

LETTER XXX.

TO MRS. SMITH OF JORDANHILL, GLASGOW.

Laggan, May 30, 1796.

My dear Friend,

I have of late been a good deal indisposed, and, as Mary leaves us immediately, Mr. Grant proposes, by way of making an economical jaunt for my restoration to my wonted easy irregularity, that I should accompany him to Blair-Athol, where he will leave me to wander quietly and solitarily through that sweet place till he returns from Stirling, when he is to take me up and bring me home. I could ill afford to leave home so long, were it not for the entire dependence I can place on poor Isabella, whose steady, prudent care of the house, and unequalled love and care of the children, is beyond anything you can have an idea of. All her little endeavours are directed to one object, that of making every one about her as easy and happy as possible. Every day discovers some new charms in Anne. Do not suppose I talk of beauty; yet she is much better in that respect than you could have expected—the purest white, and most cheerful, healthy, yet delicate bloom enlivens a countenance marked with such traces of understanding, chastened by extreme softness and timidity, that no person of feeling and discernment can look at her without expecting some of that inward loveliness which beams out through everything she says and does. The excelling sweetness of this blossom makes me sometimes think she will not ripen with us,

> " But bloom,
> Where seraphs gather immortality,
> On life's fair tree."

I must now conclude, referring you for all farther intelligence to Mary, whom I part with very reluctantly, and whom, I flatter myself, with having greatly improved since she came home. A large family living in affectionate harmony, and under perfect subordination, far from the seats of corruption and artificial necessaries, and informed of everything that human happiness is promoted by knowing, is certainly one of the best schools both for morals and economics. She leaves us with a reluctance which I consider as no unfavourable sign of her disposition, and would not leave us at all, were I not unwilling to deprive my dear mother of her society. I hear the most flattering accounts of your little boy, and feel gratified every time I think that there is such a new source of happiness opened to you. May we be thankful to the Author of all goodness for the many blessings we possess. With love to you, I am, very affectionately yours,

A. G.

Letter XXXI.

TO MRS. MACINTOSH.

Blair-Athol, June 19, 1796.

Dear Madam,

I have passed three charming days here, during which I have been soothed by the novelty of ease and leisure; so immersed in the luxury of embowering groves, flowery walks, solemn shades of dark larches with drooping branches, that seem to weep over the wanderers that muse or mourn beneath them, or soft glades along the murmuring Tilt, where every vegetable beauty blooms in full luxuriance, safe from the nipping frost or chilling blast;—so lost I say in a dream of pensive musing, which I have enjoyed at full leisure, free from the restraints of form, and the disturbance of intrusion, that, like other people given wholly up to pleasure, I seemed to forget my friends, my duty, and myself. Nay, I began to consider whether it was most eligible to turn hermitess or hamadryad. When the fair form of the virgin huntress of the woods, which adorns one of these sweet walks, drew my attention, I thought of sheltering in her haunts as a hamadryad; but when the opening of a long vista disclosed the Gothic form of the old church of St. Bridget, my intentions took a more orthodox turn, and I began to adjust the dimensions of my cell, and think of cold vigils and midnight prayers. My head is now cooled; my visions are vanished, and I am considering how I shall get home to make frocks and mend petticoats. Mary would tell you why Mr. Grant brought and left me here, till his return from Stirling. If I could spend some days in this sweet place with you, one of my first *little* wishes would be gratified; for I am now grown too wise to form many great wishes. I am just going; his Reverence hurries me, yet sends you all many good wishes. Farewell.

Letter XXXII.

TO MRS. MACINTOSH, GLASGOW.

Dear Madam, 　　　　　　　Laggan, June 25, 1796.

Your very kind letter by Mr. Mackay, gave me great ease of mind. His Reverence, who delights in teasing me, and loves to hear the quick things I say when angry, would have it, you forgot me, was tired, &c. I am too proud, and jealous to tire any one; it is the easiest thing in the world to stop my career, either in prose or verse, particularly the latter, which

I always begin with fear and trembling. The dread of making myself ridiculous, and being laughed at as a pretender to genius, haunts and terrifies me, whenever "the light of my soul begins to rise." Yet if the occasional short excursions of my fancy can give you a moment's pleasure, I should certainly feel that a powerful motive to indulge myself; for I frankly own, that the exercise of this rhyming faculty does now and then cheer the gloom of care, and blunt the stings of anxiety. I feel the same solace, which I suppose those who possess untutored powers of musical excellence do, in warbling their "wood notes wild," merely to gratify themselves and divert their solitude. After the confinement of the winter, and the sickly languor in which I had pined away the spring, I enjoyed the return of health, ease, and leisure too much, while at Blair, to cramp myself with any set employment. Yet a ludicrous accident had very nearly set me to work. One afternoon I strolled down the approach towards the Duke's house alone, being unwilling to tax the complaisance of any of the family with attending me, and always loving a solitary ramble. I was thus deprived of the usual expedient of getting their private key to let myself into these Elysian walks, in which I delighted to wander. The family that inhabit the mansion were not at home. However, hearing the Tilt murmuring softly, and the birds singing sweetly within, I felt the true Highland impatience of bounds and inclosures, and, observing that part of the wall was formed by the bridge of the Tilt, which was then very low, I scrambled, with an agility that would do honour to one of Ralia's goats, down the parapet wall, and over the broken crags below the arch, till I got in dry and safe. My joy at outwitting the keepers, and feeling myself independent of locks and bars, broke out in a few stanzas, which I have not yet written down. As far as my pencil sketch assists memory, they begin thus ;—

> Thy jealous walls, great Duke,* in vain
>   All access would refuse;
> What bounds can Highland steps restrain,
>   What power keep out the muse?
> Where'er I go, I bring with me
> That mountain nymph, sweet Liberty.
>
> Would you engross each breathing sweet
>   Yon violet banks exhale,
> Or trees, with od'rous blooms replete,
>   That scent the enamour'd gale?
> Alike they smile for you and me,
> Like nature and sweet liberty.

There is a great deal more; but I must not fill up with trifles a paper allotted to more serious subjects. I think, however, I ought to tell you, as the moral of my little story, how the fear of detection disturbed this stolen intrusion. I was resolved to meditate a while in placid ease, as if tranquillity would come when bidden, and sought the thickest shades, but

> " Still as I went, I look'd behind,
> I heard a voice in every wind,
> And snatch'd a fearful joy."

At length I set up my rest under a broad spreading cedar, beside the statue of Diana, which seemed to protect me. I thought of Dryden's description :

* Duke of Athol.

" The graceful goddess was array'd in green,
  About her feet were little beagles seen,
  That watch'd with upward eyes the motions of their queen."

This figure was not so appropriate; it was scarcely
arrayed at all; and the crescent was the only mark
by which the sylvan goddess was distinguished. Here,
however, I composed myself, was busy with my pencil,
and forgot my fears; when, all on a sudden, a mons-
trous heron bent its heavy flight to my sheltering tree
with such noisy impetuosity, that I started up in
terror, thought of hunters and I know not what, felt
the horrors of detected guilt, and finally took a short
leave of Diana, and again committed myself to the
protection of the nymph of the Tilt. Now you are to
give this story importance, and make it instructive by
your comments. . . . . . .

C. treats his wife worse, if possible, than you could
expect. It is miserable to see so much innocence,
understanding, and good-humour, sacrificed to such a
strange compound of folly and madness, who has
neither the spirit nor manners of a gentleman to make
one tolerate his eccentricities. I hope, nay, am sure,
Charlotte will rather live, bloom, and die in single
blessedness, than throw herself away in this manner.
Now that' in her apparent merit, and the general
esteem she has obtained, I reap the fruit of all my
cares, the agonies of fear and sorrow, which I have
hitherto felt on her account, are richly paid in self-
gratulation. In trying to improve her, I have improved myself. My strenuous efforts for that purpose
have exalted my mind above follies and frivolities, to
which it might have sunk. The cruel singularity of

her fate called forth in her support all the energies of
my mind, and brought into exertion powers that I
should not otherwise have known myself to possess.
The kindness my other children receive from those
who have no relative tie to them, I consider as a
reward for my maternal tenderness to her. You see,
my good friend, what it is to confer benefits on the
superstitious ; for I do not consider even you as merely
generous and sympathizing, but as an agent impelled,
by an overruling impulse, to do what you cannot
possibly avoid doing. I write a few lines below to
Charlotte. Excuse it, and believe me very truly
yours,

A. G.

Letter XXXIII.

TO MRS. MACINTOSH OF DUNCHATTAN, GLASGOW.

Dear Madam, Laggan, July 6, 1796.

I wish to write both to you and Charlotte to-day,
but shall begin with you, having conquered some
scruples of modesty which checked my first intention.
I shall bluntly avow the purport of this, which is, to
request you would leave all the comforts and conveniences of your own pleasant and spacious dwelling,
all the beauties which summer scatters so profusely
over the Dune, and all the pleasures of refined and
elegant society, to encounter the fatigue and disgust
produced by a long journey, over dark moors and

frowning mountains, by comfortless inns and bleak blasts; and all this for what? Will you come into the wilderness, not even to people clothed in the soft garb of insinuating manners and flattering professions, but to be cooped up in a cottage, and share all its inconveniences? To share them, too, with people who have lived too long out of the world to miss a thousand things become necessary in it? To such, mutual affection, freedom, and simplicity compensate for all the advantages, of which remoteness of situation and obscurity deprive them. I only suggest this, in case of your being left alone at the Dune; but if you have the remotest desire to join the projected journey towards the south, I would not even wish to influence your determination. Only, if you are alone, permit me to remind you of your resolution to make an excursion every summer; and, preferring the Highlands for your route, what would you think of taking Fort-William and Fort-Augustus on your way?

Mr. Grant begins to recover his looks and spirits, but has had a severe shock. A succession of indispositions in the family, have made spring, and what is gone of summer, pass like an agitated dream. Mr. G. is just come in, and insists on having his sincere regards included with mine, to you and your beloved. I am, unchangeably, yours,

ANNE GRANT.

LETTER XXXIV.*

TO MRS. MACINTOSH.

Laggan, August 9, 1796.

Dear Madam,

I hope you have, ere now, safely received my letter from Blair, though it seems to have lingered on the way. I saw Mrs. Stuart put it in her drawer; if it has miscarried, your loss is great, but Miss Coates's† incalculable; for the immortality of her bandeau depended upon it, and I have preserved no copy. It would have given me pleasure to have obliged that lady in anything, because she is very obliging herself. Her frank, easy manners, and careless vivacity, together with certain emanations of goodness from the heart, had almost broken through all my outguards of pride, prejudice, and independence. In spite of all her adventitious superiorities, I began to like her. Had she been as little in the sunshine as myself, I am sure I should be fond of her; but the glitter of fortune and fashion, which has such an attraction for sycophants and imitators, repels people of spirit and

---

* This letter was written after a meeting, by appointment, which the Author and Miss Charlotte Grant had with four ladies, who came from Glasgow to Dunkeld for that purpose. These were, Mrs. Munro, her daughter, Miss Munro (now the Hon. Mrs. Henry Erskine), Mrs. Macintosh of Dunchattan, and Miss Coates.—(1807.)

† Miss Coates is a lady well known in the west of Scotland, whose character is such as it appears in these Letters. She left her bandeau unconsciously at Dunkeld, on the tomb of Fingal, a place at least said to be such; and the little poem alluded to was written on this incident.—(1807.)

delicacy, who value themselves and others only for such qualities as are innate and permanent. I allow her, and other rich people, all the merit they possess, and give them much more credit than to others for the same degree of excellence; because their manner of life is less adapted to exercise the sterner virtues, and keep the heart warm and open. I am always jealous of hazarding the only thing of value I have to give, my affection, by giving it where it may be despised, or received as the common tribute which servility pays to the prosperous. I am far from thinking myself poor, but I cannot bear others should think me so. In short, I will merely like Miss Coates, for I am not poor in spirit.

One of my first cares after my return home was to prepare for Sandy Kennedy's* wedding, which proved, in his own way, a very splendid one. The day before the marriage we had the bride's friends, with all the servants, dancing all the evening; and on the wedding-day, we had the same party at dinner, in the nursery. You are to understand that the bride served us eight years, and her swain seven, at a former period; so we could not withhold our countenance. The Sheriff is rich, according to Anne's estimate of wealth, and excels in strong sound sense; you know that he is our tenant in the glebe, which forms an additional tie. He is counted penurious, but shone on this occasion. Four fat sheep, and

---

* Alexander Kennedy, a favourite servant of Mr. Grant's, was called the Sheriff in the parish, from the deference which the neighbours had for his decisions on all occasions. His master considered him as possessing the soundest judgment and most acute discernment of any person in his station he had ever known.

abundance of game and poultry, were slain for the supper and following breakfast, which was served only in *the Chinese manner* to the inferior class. At this feast above a hundred persons assisted, three score of which consisted of our children and rustics, our tenants and servants, and the teachers of *arts* and sciences from the neighbouring hamlets. At the head of the long table was a cross one, raised higher, a humble imitation, I presume, of the dais, at which the courteous knights and noble dames sat in the days of Queen Guinever. There sat Captain Donald, his Reverence, and their ladies, with the professors of arts and sciences aforesaid, and Moome, in full glory; and Catherine, and Charlotte, and Duncan, blooming and blushing like the morning. And there were poultry, and plovers, and a roast joint, and grouse in perfection. All this was lost on Charlotte the elder, who only afforded her dignified presence at breakfast. The music and dancing were very superior to anything you could imagine ; do not whisper anything so treasonable, but both were superior to many fashionable performers in each way. Mr. Grant took a fancy to be very wise and serious; and reproved the Sheriff for killing so many sheep, and collecting so many people; and wondered at me for being so pleased. I never saw him ungracious before ; but he was not well. My versatility stood me in good stead. Every one was quiet, orderly, and happy in the extreme. I considered it was hard to grudge this one day of *glorious felicity* to those who, though doomed to struggle through a life of hardship and penury, have all the love of society, the taste for conviviality, and even the sentiment that animates and endears social intercourse, which constitutes the enviable part of enjoyment in higher circles. It would be cruel to deprive such of the single opportunity their life affords of being splendidly hospitable, and seeing all those to whom nature or affection has allied them, rejoice together, at a table of their own providing; and of seeing that table graced by such of their superiors, as they have been used to regard with a mixed sentiment of love and veneration. I myself never dance, and on those occasions join very little, outwardly, in the amusement; I rather sit rapt in reverie, or gaze in mute triumph at the collective felicity before me. The wedding was in a large barn. After breakfast, they danced a while on the green, and the scene closed with the young couple going home. The following evening we had to dress all the children for the concluding ball in our itinerant dancing-school; so you must allow for my being fatigued with festivities.

I am sure I have tired you with the history of Anne's wedding. Had it been a fine ball, such as you are used to, I should not say half so much about it; but I thought the scene would be new to you. It is such, indeed, as cannot take place but in these regions: here only you may condescend without degradation, for here only is the bond between the superior and inferior classes a kindly one. I cannot exactly say where the fault lies; but cold disdain, on the one side, and a gloomy and rancorous envy on the other, fix an icy barrier between the upper and lower classes with you. Your low people are so gross, so

sordid; but if you treated them as we do ours, they
would not be so coarse and hard; they are now, however, past recovery.   It grieves me to think that the
iron age of calculation approaches fast towards the
sacred retreats of nature and of sentiment; " the un-
bought grace of life, the cheap defence of nations," is
fast receding.   May I close my eyes in peace, before
its final departure !—Pray tell Miss Munro,* of whom
I delight to think, and could love though she were
mistress of thousands, that I recollect the night we all
spent together at Dunkeld, as an alderman does a
turtle feast; but I fear the vigil was too much for
her.   Had I been purse-bearer, I would have urged a
longer stay; but delicacy kept me silent.

On Monday next a man leaves this for Glasgow, by
whom I will inclose a pair of the Sybil's† garters for

---

* Sister to Sir Thomas Munro, Bart., late Governor of Madras,
and widow of the Honourable Henry Erskine, Lord Advocate of
Scotland.   She continued on terms of affectionate friendship with
the Author until the close of life.   Mrs. Erskine died at Edinburgh
in January 1845.—Ed.

† Mrs. Machardy, usually called the Sybil by the Author's family,
was a native of the Isle of Skye, the widow of a worthy man who had
served the Highland public fifty years in the capacity of a school-
master.   She was a person of undaunted fortitude, great industry,
and ingenuity; and was remarkable for preserving all her faculties to
the last day of her life, which was extended to a hundred and eight
years.   At ninety-six she danced reels with great spirit, and sung
the songs above mentioned when above a hundred.   She looked up
to the minister as her benefactor, because he procured her a pension
of three pounds yearly, and allowed her a cottage on his farm for
her abode.   Till the year of her death, she carried on a manufacture peculiar to the Isle of Skye.   In a small loom, of primitive construction, she wrought garters of gaudy colours and particular texture, which make a kind of ornament to the Highland dress, and are
very much sought after for that purpose: these garters she spun,
dyed, and wove; and the Author was frequently an agent in disposing
of them. Among the poems published by the Author, is one sent,
by the Sybil's request, with a pair of those garters, to the Marquis
of Huntly, on his assuming the habit of the country.—(1807.)

Miss Coates. I am grateful to that lady for encouraging the venerable Sybil's manufacture. She sang " Lochaber no more," and " Mournful Melpomene," to Charlotte yesterday, very distinctly, if not melodiously, and will assuredly contend with Old Parr. Her brother is alive, and is an hundred and four. In her I have the pleasure of an old woman's conversation, without the plague of gossiping; for, if she has any scandal, King William is the object of it. She is full of anecdote, but scorns to talk of anything that happened within the last forty years. Madame de Maintenon is the heroine of her imagination; she talks of her as if she were still living, and constantly quotes to our girls the ivory wheel with which she spun Lewis into subjection; for she considers spinning as one of the cardinal virtues, and is at this hour spinning fine wool on the distaff, of which she proposes making garters for the young Marquis of Huntly. You see I see you will not rest till you are completely LAGGANIZED; you must be interested in all my odd people, or I will have nothing to do with you. Ought you not to be so? Am I not interested in your dog " Neptune," and your great cat, and did I not commemorate your turkey hen? The least you can do in return is to venerate my Sybil. Adieu! Tell me if I have tired you.

LETTER XXXV.

Laggan, October 3, 1796.

Dear Madam,

I had the pleasure of receiving your letter, and am much consoled by finding you understand so well the motives of my grief for poor Moome,* which I feel still a weighty pressure on my spirits. I feared you would consider the excess of my sorrow on this occasion as absurd, or chimerical. Mr. Macintosh reproaches me for not letting him know of poor Moome's difficulties; her noble spirit would have been hurt if I had. She was used to difficulties, and took pleasure, not to say pride, in conquering them. I believe one reason why I did not expatiate on her singular merit to you, was a fear that you should think I wanted to awake your sympathy on her behalf. Besides her inflexible sincerity, which was to some very unwelcome, her strong attachments, and the reverence she paid to merit wherever she found it, she possessed a sturdy independent spirit, which was her chief distinction. This made her submit to work and to live harder than any one, that she might have

---

* " Moome," is an endearing appellation in the Gaelic, to which the English affords no correspondent phrase; it means a person who feels the affection, and performs the duties of a mother to children not her own. Such was Moome's love to the children of the cottage, and such their gratitnde, that our friend was always distinguished by this kindly epithet.—(1807.) The maiden name of Moome was Helen Macintosh, and at the time of her death she was the widow of Mr. James Macpherson.—ED.

it in her power to entertain her friends occasionally, and bestow charity, without giving trouble to any one; and her exertions in this way were incredible. She used to tell everybody that she owed me more than any one in the world; but I now think I was not half kind enough to her, and you would think so too, if you did but know what she did for me when there was distress in my family. She was six weeks last winter without putting off her clothes, during my alarming illness. I was killed with remorse that I had not made greater exertions to make her easy; so I attended the corpse every moment, and assisted to dress it. I never saw such deep silent grief as the poor tenants showed on the occasion. Ralia was from home in her last illness, and a letter arrived, addressed to him, which his family did not open till he returned. It proved to be from Moome's son, covering a draft for fifteen pounds, and a settlement of the same sum annually. When this was opened after her death, it renewed my grief bitterly when I thought how proud and happy it would have made her.

Thus much of the "short and simple annals of the poor" you will hear with patience. Yet is it not presumption to call Moome poor, who was so respectable, and gave so much away? Her personal wants were few, and small indeed; but her exertions, and the resources she found or made, to preserve independence and exert beneficence, were astonishing. Our children were the pleasure of her life, and pride of her heart; they were her theme wherever she went. None of the persons you ever served or obliged, could be so sensible of your kindness, as she was of your goodness to her son. Indeed, the generous are always grateful. She was as proud of Clan's* praise as the vainest of mortals could be of her own. She is buried with our children, under the shade of our evergreens; and, if ever we can afford it, we shall place a stone over her, with this inscription :

> Sacred to the memory of
> HELEN MACINTOSH,
> Relict of JAMES MACPHERSON,
> Whose integrity was unsullied,
> Whose beneficence was unbounded,
> and
> Whose fortitude was unequalled!

You must have seen the grief of her poor neighbours to form any idea of it. I perfectly agree with you, not only from the determination of my judgment, but from the sad experience of the heart, that the esteem and affection of a truly worthy person is an invaluable acquisition, and the loss a privation unspeakable. It is with the utmost difficulty that I can turn my thoughts from the painful retrospect of the hardships she suffered here, to the view of her present felicity, which is my only comfort.

Have you read Lord Gardenstone's Sketches, or detached observations, I believe they are? It is very much the kind of reading that you like. I never met with any one that thought exactly as I do of Shakspeare, of David Hume, and Queen Mary, but he. In politics we should never agree. I am, dear madam, yours faithfully,

A. G.

* Mr. Macintosh.

Letter XXXVI.

TO HER DAUGHTER, MARY, AT PARKHOUSE, GLASGOW.

Laggan, October 19, 1796.

My dear Mary,

I had the pleasure of your letter, and I really began to grow impatient for it, being extremely anxious about poor little Archy Smith, of whom I am happy to hear such good accounts.

Do not be in the least discouraged to go on in a course like what you have begun, by the precision of my directions. People are so very apt to fall short of the proposed standard, that there is a kind of moral necessity for setting it higher than common practice attains to. Then the native indolence you have the felicity to inherit from your renowned ancestors urges me to use the spur to you, as frequently as I do the bridle to your sister Catherine, whose activity, eagerness, and acuteness of feeling require a constant rein; but, to do her justice, she is diligent, active, disinterested, and affectionate, in a very uncommon degree, and, in matters of common life, as self-denied as ever poor Moome was. Isabella has gone to spend a fortnight at Kincraig. Miss H. Macpherson sent a horse for her, but as she could not ride alone, we declined sending her. Isabella bore this with great meekness, but pined inwardly, so that Charlotte and Catherine insisted she should be indulged, but nobody could be spared to go down with her. In this sad crisis Isabella's good genius brought old Mr. S. here from

Inverness, and Charlotte found out that it would be
an excellent way to transport Isabella behind him on
the horse. She was mounted accordingly, and her
father told her, with great gravity, that he all along
suspected it would end in this at last, but he hoped
the Cannich would be kind to her. She began to
make rueful faces, and all the others laughed; in short,
there never was such a scene of mirth exhibited since
Christmas last; but the Cannich, heedless of the up-
roar, rode off in triumph with his prize. I
have no leisure to tell you of all the gaiety of the
Garagask balls, where all the belles and beaus of the
braes exhibited themselves. We all dined at Cluny,
with the Laird, the other day. He is the kindest
landlord I ever saw; he asks always for you, and
speaks of Isabella Ralia with a warmth of regard that
I really like him for.

I am obliged to Miss Coates for her partiality; and
the more as I did not expect it. I believe the impressions you have received of her are from some who are
prejudiced against her. She certainly possesses integrity, goodness of heart, and a most cheerful, even temper; and then she is very sincere, though perhaps not
very steady; but these, in tempers like hers, are quite
compatible. Lively, impetuous, and unaccustomed to
restraint, she forms strong and sudden likings to those
of whom she knows little. The consequence that invariably results from this temper is, being obliged to
change one's opinions, and relax in one's attachments.
A rage for novelty is the consequence of being in a
condition to have our wishes gratified as soon as they
are formed; and people courted for their wealth and

consequence, do not so often meet with faithful friends as you and I do. As for being satirical, I fear we should all be thought so if we said everything that comes in our heads, as she does, without regard to time or place. She wants softness, delicacy, self-command, and often complaisance; but heart, understanding, and probity she truly possesses, and such a wide range of memory, and happy facility in applying what she remembers, as makes her conversation very amusing when once one is reconciled to that boisterous vivacity which at first overpowers and silences a diffident person. She is very kind, too, and there is a cordiality in her kindness that shows she feels a pleasure in serving you, independent of what emotion it may excite, and she would serve you though you never knew of it. In short, few have gone through the fiery ordeal of high prosperity, unbounded freedom of will, and incessant flattery, that have preserved as much uprightness of intention and originality of character. Rich people are apt to misjudge us, thinking our sentiments must be mean and contracted, because our circumstances are so. We, on the other hand, are as apt to conclude that they are insolent and hard-hearted, merely because wealth puts it in people's power to show these dispositions with impunity. Laying aside the hostility that is so frequent between these opposite conditions, we may safely conclude that whoever, in confined circumstances, preserves a certain independence and elegance of sentiment, which enables them to converse on a footing with the prosperous, without envy or servility; and whoever, amidst the snares of affluence, retains natural manners, genuine feelings, and an innate respect for mind, however disadvantageously embodied, are kindred souls, and equally superior to the chances and accidents of fortune, by which vulgar minds are overpowered and enslaved.

Your brother, John, goes on very well; I hope we shall tame and cultivate him a good deal during the long winter evenings, which are to be in a great measure dedicated to the improvement of our young masters, who have danced away the summer, but must now think of something more important. I am extremely sorry to know that my poor father suffers so much. I beg you will let me know most particularly how he is when you receive this. I would fain hope that it is only the usual trial which the fall of the leaf gives to broken constitutions, and that he is by this time better. Let me know, too, how your friend Miss J. C. is, whose genius I admire, and whose goodness of heart I esteem highly. Yet I beg you to avoid the contagion of those principles which you own yourself she favours. Remember that one is not to be seduced by one's admiration of an elevated character to imitate its blemishes. Preserve your first notions and principles as a sacred deposit, and when you think of the system of religion, morality, and government you have been early taught to venerate, remember what the Apostle says on another occasion, —" If an angel from Heaven should preach any other Gospel, he is a deceiver." I am yours very tenderly,

ANNE GRANT.

Letter XXXVII.

TO MRS. FURZER, GLOUCESTERSHIRE.

Glasgow, April 27, 1797.

My dear Friend,

Your most acceptable letter was transmitted to me from Laggan, a fortnight ago, and gave me great comfort. I see your heart and soul are all alive, and am convinced you will be the very same Anne Ourry till the last hour of your existence. I likewise triumph in preserving my identity, and rising, like trodden camomile, from every depression, whether mental, corporeal, or pecuniary. But you outdo my out-doings; tranquillity and moderate cheerfulness cost me an effort; but your spirit and vivacity are peren-nial flowers, which bloom all day and every day. These gifts were bestowed on you liberally, but not superfluously, when one considers all the varied exigencies through which they have supported you. I think you have as much need of them in your pre-sent seclusion, as at any other period; though the sprightliness of your description sets some unpleasant things in so ludicrous a point of view, that one must needs be amused for the time. I sincerely lament what you must feel in seeing so deep a shade of im-perfection in a character you love and venerate. It is one of the severest trials we can encounter, to be deceived where we expect so much. Old age and solitude, or, what is worse than solitude, living always with most uncongenial people, may have produced an infirmity, which, after all, we should compassionate. There is one who will never deceive you, who I hope is by this time on his way to protect and comfort you, who will both excite and reward all the best affections of your heart. When we see how worthy persons of our sex are thrown away on the undeserving, we should consider a married woman as but too happy whose husband has plain sense, pure morals, and an upright heart of which his wife has the sole possession.

Now, after saying so much of you, it is but reasonable I should take my turn, and give some account of myself. Knowing I am a little addicted to complain, you will the more regret that I have been all winter distressed with a severe rheumatic toothache, much aggravated by my attendance on poor Charlotte during an illness, and my anxiety about Mr Grant's going to Ireland with his son, while his own health was so doubtful. In the spring I began to revive a little, and came here on the urgent invitation of my friends, who thought I was likely to derive some benefit from the journey. Here, then, I have been for two months, as happy as returning health, attentive friendship and kindness, and general esteem and civility can make me. My father has got a very pleasant house, surrounded by a garden and grass inclosure, near Dunchattan. I sometimes stay a week in town with my friend, Mrs. Smith of Jordanhill. Her husband has been very prosperous in business ; and, amidst their newly-acquired affluence, they possess a high degree of the public esteem, to which they are well entitled, both from their general beneficence and hospitality, and from the moderation and simplicity they preserve amidst this high distinction of every kind. After an interval of nine years, she had a fine boy lately. They are very happy, too, in their eldest son, who promises to be all they would pray for; but he is rather delicate in his constitution. The circle is never complete. I think Swift and Co., or some of those old friends of ours, remark, that they have seldom met with superior powers of understanding joined to amiable qualities in a woman, but that there was a balance of bad health to be set on the opposite side of the account. Amiable men are very scarce indeed; I do not know a dozen in my whole acquaintance; and, alas, I fear the same rule will apply to them! I do not mean a satire on the sex; I know good, worthy, and respectable men; but where soft manners, and a pure and delicate mind are added, I call the man amiable; and so does the world, for every one is delighted with an amiable man.

The alteration in Glasgow strikes me more forcibly than when I was in town last, because I have longer days to look about me. I see nothing but what reminds me of an old song, where a poor Highlander says,

" Scotlant pe turn'd an Englant now."

We have all manner of luxuries, pastry shops, and toy shops. I remember when there could not be a doll or a tart bought in town, but in a particular shop allotted for each. As for the luxuries of intellect, circulating libraries, &c., there is no end of them. There is a lecture, founded by the Will of a late professor,

that is to exalt and illuminate the citizens prodigi-
ously.*   The lecturer appears a very good, and, I am
told, is a very learned man ; though I despair of
learning much from him.   It might be a very harm-
less lounge for his female auditory, if the idea of being
greatly the wiser, for hearing a man talk an hour
about carbon and chemistry, would not lead to conceit
and affectation.   The having an additional place of
public resort, too, encourages that insatiable love of
change, that restlessness, which is, I think, the great
and growing evil of the age.   Shakspeare talks of
minds

> " That cream and mantle like a standing pool."

Modern minds will not remain quiet long enough to
allow the cream to rise.   I always thought a moderate
knowledge of geography and history a very desirable
acquirement for a woman ; because it qualifies her for
mingling in solid and rational conversation, and makes
her more a companion for her husband and brother,
and so forth.   The more pleasing and attainable
branches of belles lettres lie within her own province,
—that of the imagination and the heart.   What business women have with any science but that which
serves to improve and adorn conversation, I cannot
comprehend.   For my own part, I cannot conceive a
woman devoting her whole time and faculties to the
study of any particular art or science.   This must be
done by one who has an ambition to attain any degree
of excellence ; and why should any one plague herself

* Probably the Andersonian Institution.—ED.

and other people with dabbling and skimming the sur-
face of such subjects? If a woman were to talk pro-
foundly on philosophy, astronomy, or chemistry, for
instance, very few would understand her; if she talked
on such subjects in a conceited superficial manner,
no mortal would wish to hear her. That knowledge
which neither improves the heart nor meliorates the
temper, which makes us neither more useful nor more
pleasing, I cannot consider as a desirable acquisition.
I wish people would begin to work tapestry again.
I look on my Dresden apron with great delight, when
I consider how peaceably I sat to work at it, with
my thoughts at liberty for reflection, and, all the time,
forming the habits of quiet application and the love of
peace. I have no ambition to hear the modern belles
declare their "dark sayings on the harp," till such
time as I am convinced that they stay more at home,
have less vanity, and make better wives and daughters
than formerly.

I have teased you too long; you, who have no children to spoil, do not feel this subject as I do. I
dearly love young people; the gaiety, the candour, the
nature, the modesty one is so delighted with in young
creatures who have an unsophisticated character,—all
these are a great sacrifice to make to pert pretensions.
Adieu, my dear friend. Age *shall not* be dark and
unlovely to us, while we cherish our kindly affections.
The best way to do this is to have as little intercourse
with the world, and as much with each other, as possible. Retirement is certainly the only safe asylum
for delicate minds and delicate constitutions:

> " The world is frantic, fly the race profane,
> Nor you, nor I, shall its compassion move."

And we will not require it. God bless you, prays
your faithful friend,

A. G.

LETTER XXXVIII.

TO MRS. MACINTOSH.

Dear Madam, Laggan, July 8, 1797.

I hope this will find you in health and spirits;
for, I assure you, not even excepting Miss Pagan and
James Smith, I have left nothing behind me that I
am so anxious about. Little Charlotte and I had a
very pleasant day's journey to Perth. I found my
relations there very well, and cordially kind, and was
sorry I could spend but a day with them. I had
an agreeable day's journey from Dunkeld, or Blair
rather, with Charlotte, who proves an excellent travelling companion; always cheerful and full of observation, and easily silenced when I wish to indulge
my meditations. We took many long, considerate
walks, for I dreaded Paddy's being overloaded. Indeed, the last day, when I began to fear for both William and the horse, they appeared to me like Thomson's
traveller in the snow,

> " Stung with the thoughts of home: the thoughts of home
> Rush'd on their nerves, and call'd their vigour forth;"

so that we reached home by sunset. The Chaplain
had come a great way to meet me the day before, but

was disappointed, and would come no more. I found
all the young tribe waiting at the opposite side of the
river. Never shall I forget the extravagance of little
Charlotte's joy at seeing them. She cried in transport, " The children! the children!" fell into violent
bursts of laughter, and sprang up like a frantic creature, while we were crossing. The rest were as happy
to meet her. Mr. Grant and Charlotte the elder, I
believe, felt their share of joy too, though they were
not so outrageous in the display of it. Charlotte looks
thin, but most courageously combats the azure dæmons
by dint of activity and exertion. She has all things
in high order, and is become a great florist. My
daughter Moore is an engaging child,—quick, sensible, and very good-tempered; but such an odd,
staring, sun-burnt thing, you have not seen. It is
quite an original,—not the least like the rest; and
I think I like the creature with a different sort of
love. The Chaplain is all good and forgiving, and
does not reproach me for my stay so much as I feared, perhaps deserved.—There is nothing I look back
upon with such regret as not having seen Miss Munro
oftener while in town; and the more, because I flatter
myself the regret is mutual.—What an endearing
place home is, after all; the dwelling of true consequence and genuine comfort. M. and Bar, and the
Prophet in his mantle,* and all the satellites of the

---

* Mr. Evan Macpherson, here designated as " The Prophet," was
born and educated a gentleman, had been all his life very unfortu-
nate, but was, nevertheless, much revered for singular worth and
piety. He had, in early life, been sometime tutor to Sir John Macpherson, late Governor-General of India, who, in his old age, was
very kind to him, and wished him to spend his remaining days with

cottage, begin to move round their wonted orbits. See what it is to hear lectures ; even I am in a fair way to speak with tongues.

LETTER XXXIX.

TO MRS. MACINTOSH.

Laggan, July 15, 1797.

Dear Madam,

I have been now nearly six weeks in perfect ignorance about you all; I leave you to judge how my busy imagination has wrought. To think you grown careless, is inconsistent with the general steadiness of your character. What, then, shall I think? I am sure you are of my opinion, that nothing less than a want of integrity, or very intolerable caprice of temper, can cause a breach of friendship. I never lost a friend in my life that I know of. I have seen them depart to a better world, where I humbly hope

his (Sir John's) brother in the Isle of Skye. He was, however, so much attached to the parish of Laggan, where he had taught a school, and of which his brother had once been minister, that, when he thought his time drew near, he returned avowedly to die there. His great object was to be near us, having always declared our friendship to be his greatest earthly comfort. The wife of a substantial peasant, who reverenced the sanctity of his character, and esteemed his worth, did actually build a " chamber in the wall for the prophet, with a bed and a candle-stick." This circumstance, with a wide mantle he used to wrap around, and a peculiar kind of surly integrity, made us compare him to the Prophet Elijah. He was an excellent Gaelic scholar, and instructed me in that difficult language. He travelled through the Western Islands and Argyllshire with James Macpherson, the Translator of Ossian, in search of the Gaelic fragments forming the basis of that translator's works, and is mentioned in the late Report of the Highland Society upon Ossian's Poems. He died 16th December 1801, and sent me his dying blessing with great solemnity.—(1807.)

to meet them again with renewed and exalted affection; but I never lost one by change or unkindness. If I should meet with such a new species of affliction, you will be both the first and last to occasion it, for I will never, never open my heart more. Why multiply the ties that bind me to this vain world, or open fresh sources of affliction in the sufferings of others?

You would hear of poor Mrs. Macpherson's death, which happened very lately near us, at Dalchully. Hers was a truly useful life, divided betwixt the care of her soul and the care of her family. She had real principle, and great probity, though she was not gentle and conciliating. One reason why she was not so, was, that the rigour of her inflexible veracity and integrity could not bend to accommodate itself to other people's deviations; and she carried sincerity, if that were possible, to excess. I certainly ought to have grieved for her; for, though too much engrossed with more important objects to look for much gratification in social intercourse, she invariably showed marked attachment to me. But her case was so hopeless here, and so full of hope and assurance in what regards hereafter, that her death seemed a release, and apparent benefit to herself. Her boys will do very well; she has one girl, who is here now. We are all much pleased with the frankness and benevolence that appear in her disposition.

Let me know when we are to expect you here. It must be after the 6th of August; we shall then be solemnly engaged;* this could not be sooner, for it

* With the celebration of the Sacrament.

is only on the 2d that people return from the glens. One of the great concerns of life here is, settling the time and manner of these removals. Viewing the procession pass is always very gratifying to my pastoral imagination; I rise early for that purpose. The people look so glad and contented, for they rejoice at going up; but, by the time the cattle have eat all the grass, and the time arrives when they dare no longer fish and shoot, they find their old home a better place, and return with nearly as much alacrity as they went. I do love these vestiges of primitive life, that put me in mind of the plains of Mamre, and the flocks of Rachel. The season is fine, and everything thrives and looks well, from our flowers and our children, down to our pigs and potatoes. You must come in time to see the flax under its azure bells, and the potatoes in full purple bloom. These humble rustic beauties have charms for me beyond much finer objects. I will only add, " *Come and see.*" Adieu! simply, laconically.

A. G.

LETTER XL.

TO MRS. MACINTOSH.

Dear Madam, Laggan, July 20, 1797.

I am now in haste to thank you for a kind letter, which came just in time to abate fears and jealousies. Not that I think you can forget me; but you know unequal spirits and irritable nerves make dreaming people, like me, at times see things through a dark medium. It is not on my own merit I depend, but on your constancy of temper and knowledge of character, which must have taught you long since to relinquish the vain expectation of meeting spotless, perfect friends, to which no human creature is entitled, fallible as we all are. Yet, such expectations, unreasonably indulged, and justly disappointed, have made many a one go through life dark and chilly, without having their hearts opened, their countenances brightened, or their virtues invigorated, by the cheering cordial of friendship. This leads me to congratulate you on your present enjoyment of this nature. I feel true satisfaction in thinking how much you and Miss. Polson enjoy each other.

I give you joy of your heroic nephew's* arrival, and hope he will pay his duty to you on your return from your Highland excursion, which, I see, is likely to be deferred to the shortening days and weeping equinox. Consider the green delights of my Elysium, Fort-Augustus; the " Siberian solitude," as Johnson called it, of Stratherick; and the " sublime thunder" of Foyers. Not a word of the cottage, but that it contains your faithful friend. Farewell. If I see you again, it must be here. Yours, &c.

A. G.

---

* Captain (afterwards Admiral) Sir Graham Moore, of the Navy, who had just then distinguished himself under Sir John Borlase Warren, in taking some French vessels on their way to a projected invasion on Ireland, and carried them into the Clyde. Captain Graham Moore was brother to Sir John Moore, the hero of Corunna.

LETTER XLI.

TO MRS. FURZER, AT ADMIRAL OURRY'S, MARRIDGE,
OLDBURY, DEVON.

Laggan, December 10, 1797.

My dear Friend,

I heartily congratulate you on your return to Good-amere. What could induce you, so made to animate and adorn society, to bury yourself in a place like Colford? Your friend there is perfectly naturalized to the place, and lives among her old intimates, so that the benefit or comfort your society might afford her, is no counterbalance to your secluding yourself in a place so uncongenial.

I am now perfectly prepared to sympathize in all your cares and fears for the absent. We never intended John for the army as his permanent profession, but were flattered with the idea that the Fencible Regiments would be allowed half-pay at the conclusion of the war. He has been now a twelvemonth in Ireland, his education neglected, his morals in hazard, exposed to great expense from the frequent shifting of quarters, and separated from those who had the charge of him. How all this has preyed upon my spirits I cannot express. But now your old friend, General Moore,* goes to Ireland, second in command to General Abercromby, and I hope John will get a long leave of absence.

Mrs. Macintosh spent a month here last autumn,

---

* Afterwards Sir John Moore.

and to be sure we did talk about you! Her mate was in the North, visiting his friends in Sutherland, and spent a week here on his return. Charlotte the Greater, who loves and admires you, is now going South, I fear, to return no more. . . . . . .

An old acquaintance of mine, Miss Harriet Marchand, after she was turned of forty, has lately married Mr. Liston, our Ambassador to America,* and is now making disinterested friendly efforts, unsolicited by me, for the recovery of my father's American lands. I wish you saw what a pleasant creature my little daughter Moore is. A thousand warm kind loves attend you from this family. I am, in all truth and tenderness, yours unalterably,

A. G.

LETTER XLII.

Laggan, July 4, 1798.
My dearest Friend,

I am ashamed to own that I received your letters of March and June; but, believe me, though I have been so long answering the former, it gave me the liveliest pleasure, not only from the unreserved confidence you put in me, but from the strong characteristic originality of the contents. If you were to leave no other memorial behind, but that very letter, it would preserve the idea of what you are and have been. I

---

* The late Right Hon. Sir Robert Liston, afterwards British Minister at Constantinople.—(1845.)

think you were well entitled to say, on going to Goodamere, what Milton makes his Satanic Majesty say, on exploring his dark dominions :—

> " Receive thy new possessor, one who brings
> A mind not to be changed by place or time."

Now, after this *diabolical* comparison I must tell you of a softer and sweeter one. Do you know I have often compared you to a dove, which, though incomparable in constancy, varies its colours with every shifting ray; thus you, who are unchangeable in firm principles and attachments, have a constant play of fancy about you which makes your correspondence and conversation "for ever various and for ever new."

Speaking of imagination, I have been completely duped by my own; for I have been long pleasing myself with the thoughts of the great reformation which the advance of age, and prospect of death drawing near, was to make in two aged friends of yours, —how great a comfort they were to find in your society, how dependant they were upon you, and what a satisfaction it was to you to contribute so much to their happiness. But to my surprise I find they are as constant as yourself in a different way. I begin to believe there is some truth in your misanthropical maxim, that habits are quite incorrigible. Yet your practical benevolence has greater merit than mine; I do all the little good I can, hoping people will grow more deserving; you, quite hopeless, labour in the same way, from a pure motive of beneficence. I think that Bath is the fittest place in the world for your friends. Selfish people, that live idle, and study nothing but their little comforts and conveniences, are, I suppose, accumulated there into one insipid mass, neither animated by sensibility, cheered by hope, nor occupied by any generous or laudable pursuit. When I think of such a society I am ready to say, with Fingal, " Sufficient for me is the desert, with all its heather and deer."

If you were here this summer, you would think the desert far more tolerable than when you saw it last. We have made several little improvements, and this delightful season shows them all to advantage. We have had a delightful summer, such as we had at Fort-Augustus in the days of our youth, constant bright weather, and the little rain that falls is in the night. I have not seen so much sunshine, or felt so much heat, these twenty years. Then it is such a pleasure to look at the crop; the rich heavy soil of our meadows agrees with dry weather, and is now clothed with the finest verdure imaginable. I am glad to see everything look so well at this instant; for this is the day Colonel Macpherson of Cluny brings home his young wife, who has never seen the country before, and who, I hope, will be a great acquisition to us. She is the daughter of Mr. Cameron of Fassfern, a Highland laird in Lochaber, and niece to Mr. Cameron, the banker in London. I hope she will be a pleasant addition to our society, as she has resided much in the family of John Home, the poet, who is an amiable man, and sees the best company.

Mr. Grant has been much distressed with illness all winter and spring; my uneasiness on this account you may conjecture. John has got leave of absence from his regiment, and is now in Glasgow, that he may follow out his education—being only fourteen years or age—and acquire· some idea of business, for which, however, he has no great inclination, being obstinately attached to the military profession, which grieves me exceedingly, as he has prospects of being greatly patronized if he could bring his mind to business. The rest of the family are all well. I must now conclude abruptly. Sir John Macpherson forwards my letters, but I shall send this by post, for fear of delay, and you will very soon hear more from your own

A. G.

The Duchess of Gordon is a very busy farmeress at Kinrara, her beautiful retreat on the Spey, some miles below this. She rises at five in the morning, bustles incessantly, employs from twenty to thirty workmen every day, and entertains noble travellers from England, in a house very little better than our own; but she is setting up a wooden pavilion to see company in.

Letter XLIII.

TO MRS. FURZER.

Laggan, May 16, 1799.

My dear Friend,

I wrote to you fully last winter, and am sure you must have answered, if my letter arrived; so I conclude either it or the answer has been lost. I must now be brief and distinct in telling my sad story, lest

an event I hourly expect should arrest my pen, or, perhaps, finally close the scene. All spring I meant to write, but the perturbation of my mind, and the wearing anguish of suspense, put it out of my power. I cannot detail, but shall sketch, as well as I can. My dear, dear John, the most benevolent, sincere, and affectionate of human beings, who knew no stain of vice or meanness, but was all made of honour, truth, and generosity, was called away from a world that was not worthy of so much innocence and integrity, on the 3d of April last, two months after he had completed his fifteenth year. Judge how severe this must be under the weakness and apprehension of my present circumstances. Yet it has pleased God to support me, in a singular and unhoped for manner, under this overwhelming calamity. If my sorrow was great, so were my consolations; and I have been enabled to look with gratitude to my remaining mercies. I can think of the past with composure, nay, at times, with a mournful complacency. Mr. Grant sends love to you. He bears up like a Christian; but, from what he feels, and what he fears, is really an object of pity. Charlotte, senior, is here just now, come to attend me on the approaching occasion;* this is very inconvenient, and an exertion of more than filial piety. To compass it, she defers the happiness of an amiable and deserving man, to whom she is about to be united.†
She paid constant attention to her cousin during his

---

* The Author's youngest son was born at Laggan on 1st June 1799.

† Miss Charlotte Grant, the adopted daughter of the Author, was married a few months afterwards to John Smith, Esq. of Glasgow.

illness. He died in his grandfather's house, in Glasgow; he expected his fate for a month before, and his patience and resignation were singular and exemplary. That sense of piety, which sunk deep and early into his mind, continued unimpaired during his short journey through life, and supported him in the close of it.

Now, my dear, dear Nancy, friend of my heart, whom I think of daily amidst all my cares and sorrows, and always with a glow of affection undiminished, should this be the last letter you receive from me, cherish my memory, and look forward to the time when, through the merits of our dear Redeemer, we shall meet to part no more. May the God we imperfectly worship, the prime source and affection of pure affection, bless you through life, and support you in the close of it, prays your true tender friend to the last,

A. G.

LETTER XLIV.

TO MRS. BROWN, GLASGOW.

My dear Mrs. Brown,   Laggan, May 7, 1800.

Why am I so dead to memory? If you and your sister thought half as much of me as I do of you, you could not be so forgetful and silent. Yet I will not blame you. I hear from Catherine you are both much occupied in the hard task of attending your brother in an illness which appears dangerous. You may believe that he and his family have my sincerest sympathy. His goodness of heart, and constant kindness and good-will to me, made me always take a great interest in him. I am extremely concerned to find that the domestic comforts you all so eminently possessed, have of late been, in different ways, interrupted and embittered; but this is the lot of humanity. The cup of sorrow is in constant circulation; we must all drink, and most of us drink deeply. It is not material whether your turn or mine comes first; the thing is, to benefit by the draught; for it requires very little self-examination to convince us that we are unequal to prosperity, and unable to sustain it without either growing careless and selfish, or attaching ourselves too strongly to the things that perish, to the utter exclusion of those which are shortly to be our all. For my own part, the truth of the Psalmist's emphatic description of our nature, that "Man walketh in a vain show, and disquieteth himself in vain," was never so strongly impressed on my mind as at this very time. There is not a person I care for in this country that is not sunk in grief, from the loss of some near and dear connexion—lost, some of them, in the most aggravating manner, by dreadful accidents, duels from trifling causes, and the scourge of war, which has so long desolated the nations, though we are but beginning to feel its worst horrors. In Holland, there fell five or six officers whom I well knew, or was some way connected with. My reflections are to the last degree solemn and gloomy, and I still imagine myself surrounded by the hovering shades of the departed. It is lucky for me that the task of

nursing, besides unusual exertions in domestic matters, which I am obliged to make, so far engross me,
that I am not at full leisure to contemplate the dark
scenery which imagination continually presents. Indeed, there is no room for the play of fancy; real evil
surrounds me; sickness, aggravated by famine, calls
our attention daily, hourly, to new objects of distress.
I once thought to snatch a fortnight to see my children in Glasgow, and embrace you both; but it will
not be. The Pastor is appointed by the Duke to
overlook the distribution of grain which he charitably
allots to his tenants. He does not, on that account,
go to the General Assembly at Edinburgh, as he
once intended, and I cannot leave him.

LETTER XLV.

TO MRS. FURZER, PLYMPTON, DEVON.

My dear, kind Friend, *Laggan, May 9, 1800.*

I have long been indebted to you, which is not
usual: and if you consider my multiplied cares and
duties, you should not wonder at some wide chasms.
But when there is an interruption, you may impute it
to want of health, to the irresolute delay of a mind
worn with ardent solicitude, and constant exertion—
to anything but the selfish chill of increased years,
which I declare has never shed its torpid influence
over me. An enthusiast I was born, and an enthusiast
I will die. When I prefer my ease to the duties of
friendship, it is all over with me, and my faculties

must be on the decline; but while they remain entire, and my heart continues to beat, it will glow with those affections which have "warmed and charmed it" through the short journey of life. Time has done little to alter me; and the impetuous tide of vanity and luxury, which has overwhelmed and pervaded all habitable space, has produced no other effect on me than exciting my scorn and pity. I declare, had I my pilgrimage to begin anew through the wilderness, I would not give my share of the endearing charities of life, my bustles and struggles to procure ease and comfort to those I love, my faithful friendships, and

" My humble toils and destiny obscure,"

for all that wealth and fashion can bestow. I have seen just enough of it to show me how little is its real value; and could I get a little health, a little leisure, and a little sunshine, I know not whom I would exchange with; though I know very few would relish the state I am so reconciled to. But ease, liberty, and a kind of rough plenty, are become habitual to me; and I could scarcely find them in the same degree anywhere else. Yet the kind of ease I talk of is quite a distinct thing from leisure; that is an inheritance I am not born to.

I like very much the description you give of the manner in which you pass your time, and almost envy your reading leisure of evenings, and your fine climate, and flower-garden. We are just beginning to have a little elbow room after the temporary pinch occasioned by setting out our children; and now that we are easier and could do it, were I revisited with

such an attack as I had last spring, it might be found
expedient for me to go a little nearer the sun, though
the little birds of those gayer regions should wonder
at me, like an owl come into the sunshine. I wish
you were not so fearfully remote; Devonshire lies
almost beyond the reach of hope. Yet I have a strong
presentiment that I shall yet embrace you; I have
many inducements to carry me a part of the way, and
do not make desperate resolutions, like you, of never
stirring out of the place, though I have so many ties
to confine me. I have already told you so much of
what I think of wealth, that you are in no danger of
being pitied by me for not being rich, according to the
kind usage of the world. Nay, I insist, that in all
modest and rational computation, you are rich. You
contrive to be beneficent, munificent indeed in one
instance, after supplying all your wants; and then the
luxuries of a library and flower-garden are yours in a
superior degree, because both are, in a manner, of
your own creating, and you taste them so exquisitely.
At the same time that I admire your generous exertions for your little *protegé*,* I regret the self-denial
you must exercise to enable you to do what others, less
self-denying, must and would do, if you did not save
them the trouble. I think, as the world would give
us no credit for our Quixotism, even though we were
of consequence enough to be known as Quixotes, we
must even laud and praise each other. The approbation of a dear friend is certainly the very next thing

---

* Mrs. Furzer having been left a widow some time before, had
adopted a young boy, a relative of her late husband, Captain Furzer,
who is the protegé here alluded to.

to the sweet whispering voice of interior self-compla-
cency. A fine prospect is a very fine thing, but a
fine retrospect is

" The sober certainty of waking bliss."

I can easily conceive the blank you must feel from
being confined to the society of a companion who is
neither cultivated, nor capable of culture, however good-
natured or well-meaning. One regrets to see one's
companion excluded from sharing one's best pleasures.
Then you try to remedy matters, but find it sowing in
the sand. I found a good soil, and was richly rewarded
in Charlotte; but it cost me no little pains to unspoil
what early prejudices had done so much to spoil.

I have not leisure to describe to you the dreadful
fate of Captain Macpherson of Ballochroan, who, with
four others, set out before Christmas to hunt for deer
in a chase of the Duke of Gordon's, between this
country and Athol. There was a shooting-lodge or
cottage, of great strength and solidity, built in that
place to shelter the Duke on his summer excursions.
There the hunters repaired every night to sleep,
having provided fire and food to keep them comfortable for the three days they were to remain. But on
the third evening, December 2d, there came on a
stormy night; next morning, the father of one of the
young men of the Captain's party, went up to see
how they fared, but could not see even the house, the
roof, timber, and every stone of which had been carried more than two hundred yards distance. The
whole country was summoned out to discover and
bring home the mortal remains, and the Captain and

his associates were found dead, covered with snow, where the house had stood. The story is almost miraculous, and every one hereabout was filled with superstitious horror. We account for it from a whirl-wind or avalanche. You can have no idea what a gloom has overspread us; Mr. Grant was always partial to him. There are so many tender, as well as strange circumstances involved in this dismal tale, that the mind cannot shake off the impression.

My dear little good boy has cost me little in nurs-ing, he was so peaceable. Yet, in March, I found it necessary to banish him, as I began to give way fast. Anxiety for the dubious state of many poor people about us preyed upon my mind; even my unconquered spirit began to fail. Indeed, my heart trembled all winter for poor Charlotte,* who was in a very declining state; but Monday last I had the comfort to hear that on the 29th April she was safely delivered of a son. I am greatly relieved, and have heard since that she was in a fair way; I thank God I am hourly growing better since. She has been soliciting for one of the children all winter; I am going to send Anne for a few months. Mrs. Macintosh expected you would be much enriched by your uncle, the Admiral's, death; but I told her to cherish no such vain expec-tations. Mr. Grant sends his love, and wishes you to know what an excellent fisherman he is become. I am quite serious; we are never without a dish ex-traordinary of his procuring. Our lilacs and labur-nums bloomed last summer, and will now be in full

---

* Mrs. John Smith.

beauty. We had such showers of roses! and we are so pleased with our little flower nurseries, under the windows! and all this in the very teeth of climate; while you sail on your botanic voyage, with wind and tide in your favour. How much have I still to say! But I will leave it all unsaid, to beg that you may not wed yourself too much to your hermitage. Too much ease, convenience, and dominion, breed either apathy or peevishness, just as people are formed. Spend a little time with Miss Malliet in London; the revival of early and tender friendship renews the springs of life. You will relish your cot the more when you return to it. Adieu!

Letter XLVI.

TO MRS. MACINTOSH, GLASGOW.

Laggan, June 2, 1800.

Dear Madam,

How has your letter soothed and fed my sorrows, my hopeless, helpless sorrows!* For how can I remember without pain, and how can I forget *her*, whom long habit, ardent affection, and perpetual solicitude, had mixed with my very being, and entwined with every thought! Have I been a single hour awake, for twelve years past, without thinking of her? I did not meet with an occurrence at home, I did not see a flower in my walks, without considering what

---

* Referring to the death of Mrs. John Smith (formerly Miss Charlotte Grant), which took place at Glasgow, on 20th May 1800, three weeks after the birth of a son.

she would think of it. Everything is full of her; and it is so, and will be so. Still I see her graceful form; still I hear the language of truth and rectitude, expressed with artless elegance, and forcible simplicity. Dear, ever dear, lovely Charlotte, whose purity of heart was too congenial to superior natures to remain long here! I would not give up the sad satisfaction of constant retrospect, ideal conversation, and anticipated reunion, for all that apathy avoids, or vanity enjoys. Your feelings are so much mine, that to you, of all others, I will not attempt to describe them. What was she not to me, *daughter, sister, friend, counsellor,* —and, what of all binds closest, fellow-sufferer, and fellow-mourner! Have I been so many years shedding tears for her unequalled sufferings, and shall I now weep because she is released from them! The fleeting and unsatisfactory nature of all earthly things, will drive me for refuge and consolation to that Source from which all that was lovely and estimable first emanated, and to which it hastens to return; and then short will be our separation, and great my reward. Dearest, best child of my heart! how wonderfully has she been led into light, through the gloomiest and most intricate paths. With the highest spirit and the strongest feelings, she was made to drink the cup of adversity of its bitterest ingredients. Prosperity, we are told, is a harder trial; of that she barely tasted, and was summoned to share the abundant mercies of her Redeemer, in whose salvation I have reason to think she humbly trusted.

I envy you, however, the last poor comfort of knowing what she said, and felt, and looked, when the great change was approaching. I feel much, much for you; her affections were your dear-bought own. You were entitled to them, and could hope to enjoy them to the last: and true affection is no small matter to one who knows its value and its rarity. The Divine Goodness supported her to the last,—when she was enabled (at the very time when nature had sunk so low that she could not attend to her own infant, even in this extremity) to entreat you to bear no remembrance of the unkindness she had experienced from others. May we be enabled to imitate her noble example! Yours, dear Madam, very truly,

A. G.

Letter XLVII.

TO HER DAUGHTER, MARY, THEN IN GLASGOW.

Laggan, June 20, 1800.

My dear Mary,

I suppose Catherine has written to you fully, which will in some measure supply my deficiency, who am totally disqualified for everything, and have scarcely recollection enough to thank you for your letters, or to remark upon anything they contain. Yet it is no particular malady I complain of; merely want of rest, a kind of hurry and trepidation in my spirits, and great weakness. I wish I saw you; and you would set some value on that, if you knew how few things I wish for. Indeed, indifference to most things is my chief complaint, which you must allow to be very new to me, who enter with much ardour into other people's concerns.

Catherine and Miss Hall .are at length arrived. I think the former *semper eadem ;* (there is learning for you ;) the latter is a good, lively, little girl, quick and well principled, and ·needs much cultivation.   She sticks close by me, and seems much influenced by any-thing I say.   If I were not so borne down, and had a longer time of her, I could take a certain pleasure in rectifying her notions a little ; as it is, the attention I must needs pay her is of great service in diverting my mind from some things which wear it out cruelly.

Catherine's account of my poor Charlotte's latter days impressed me deeply. I could not think of her oftener than I did before, but it brought death so much before my eyes and my imagination, that I felt like a culprit under sentence. My dear, dear Mary, pray for me, that the bitter afflictions which it has pleased In-finite Wisdom to mingle in my cup, may be made pro-ductive of a salutary change ; may dissolve my attach-ment to a world in which my abode can be but short, and prepare me for the unchanging state to which we all hasten.   The snares of interest and vanity, which entangle the worldly-minded and selfish,—for what is vanity but a different mode of selfishness ?— had few attractions for me.   Intellectual enjoyments, the intercourse of virtuous minds, the interchange of affectionate hearts, this was my desire and enjoyment ; and few have cultivated it with more diligence and success. Yet even to the most refined of more earthly pleasures, it is not safe or warrantable to give up that heart and those affections which ought to be exalted and purified by the contemplation and love of Divine perfection.   To exercise our affections by tender and generous attachments, to enlarge our faculties by the acquisition of useful knowledge, is commendable. But it is stopping far short of that love and knowledge for which we are made, and which can alone avail us when every sublunary object evades our grasp, and nothing is left us but our hope and confidence in the merits of a Saviour, and the remembrance of what good we have done, not to please ourselves and procure praise, but to assimilate to that overflowing ocean of Beneficence which is ever pouring forth benefits upon its creatures, —to Him who giveth liberally, and upbraideth not. What can we give,—what have we to give in return for so many benefits, but our affections and desires, and a portion of that small part of time cut from the immense orb of eternity for our space of probation ?

With what keen remorse do I often think of the criminal waste I have made, and permitted others to make, of the day set apart for attending to those spiritual concerns which will soon be our all. Brought up in your grandfather's house, you have, in that respect, had the common advantage with me of seeing a very good example set ; and I entreat you to avoid, in time coming, what I now feel so painful, and to consider the Sabbath as a portion of time consecrated to the noblest purposes. A little relaxation in the evening I do not forbid : your confined mode of life may make that sometimes necessary ; but I hope you will, generally, spend it at home.

> " Lean not on earth, 'twill pierce thee to the heart,
> A broken reed at best, but oft a spear,
> On whose sharp point peace bleeds, and oft expires."

This is a truth which the dying testimony of the good

and wise, of every age, has corroborated, and to which my experience assents.

I defer writing to Mrs. Macintosh until Duncan goes to Glasgow, because I have papers to enclose in her letter. Pray offer my respectful compliments in the meantime. My duty to my parents, and love to dearest Isabella and Anne. I am, very affectionately, yours,

A. G.

Letter XLVIII.

TO MRS. MACINTOSH.

Laggan, November 14, 1800.

My dear Madam,

I had a very kind letter from you some weeks ago. I felt it, as I feel everything, in its full force and extent; I answered it from the overflowing of my heart, in the language of pure truth. I fear I shall never grow old in the true worldly sense, but die in a hurry, some day, with all my sensibilities in full expansion. Yet a week's added age brought so much caution and reflection with it, as made me burn this effusion. I will take very good care not to risk being supposed a flatterer. I am sensible the glow of my affections, and the rapidity of my ideas, might lead me to say too much on a subject where I am deeply interested, but thus far I am safe. I never praise any one for virtues the person is not generally allowed to possess; though I might not think it necessary to publish to the world the particulars in which my friends were deficient or

blameable. But I am in a fair way to do well, when
I have already begun to digress and egotize.

I congratulate you on the gleam of comfort which
lights up the declining day of your valuable friend,
Mrs. Dunlop,* whom I regard with a kind of affectionate reverence, not entirely owing to her genius, or
her virtue either, but that she has some singular notions, in which I have the honour to share,—that she
regards objects with indifference that I think unworthy
of attention, and admires where I admire. Poor Edward Mayne! † What an honourable death was his,
and how worthy of his unspotted life. At first sight,
there is something very aggravating in seeing a valuable member of society snatched away in the very act
of risking his own life to save another; which often
happens, as in this instance, from a pure motive of humanity, without any tie of previous affection. Yet, in
the course of my little reading and observation, this
case has occurred so often, that I am convinced they
are summoned in the moment of glorious exertion,
that they may be taken away from the evil to come,
and escape the temptations that might degrade or sully
virtue so exalted. I knew a little of poor Edward's
father once, and pity him exceedingly. So I do Mrs.

---

* Mrs. Dunlop of Dunlop, the friend and patroness of Burns.
† Edward Mayne, son to Mayne of Powis in Stirlingshire. This
excellent young man being on board the Queen, Indiaman, (which
was burnt in the year 1799, in some port which I do not remember,)
as he, with others, were going into the boat, he recollected a passen-
ger who was lying in one of the births below, and was unable, from
lameness, to make his escape. This generous youth immediately
returned, lifted the gentleman on his shoulder, and was carrying
him upon deck, when the ship blew up, and they were both killed.—
(1807.)

Trumbull,* whom I like better than any one I know
so little, because she is so totally disinterested; she
will suffer more than others, but she will enjoy more.
It is a short, shifting scene at best; those who live
merely for themselves will quit it as soon as those who
live for others; but they will have fewer pleasing re-
trospects, and leave less regret behind them.

It relieves me to hear you give testimony to the undiminished gratitude and attachment of our departed
friend; and I have no doubt of your keeping sacred a
promise so solemnly asked and given, especially as the
objects of it are not undeserving on their own account.
What you say of her concluding sentiments is exactly
what I should expect. Had it been otherwise, I should
have no faith or trust in anything human. I should,
indeed, have been for ever haunted by the phantoms
of inconsistency and insincerity; though I should have
had that best consolation, of leaving no duty unful-
filled, with regard to that much-loved object of my
long solicitude. Adieu, dear madam. Write soon
again to your very faithful

A. G.

Letter XLIX.

TO MRS. MACINTOSH.

Dear Madam,   Laggan, November 23, 1800.

I hoped to have sent your goose to-day, but cannot;

---

* Afterwards the Honourable Mrs. Henry Erskine of Ammondell.

he and the two blue cheeses, however, will, I trust,
soon find their way; and with them you will receive
an answer to part of your last letter. I have not yet
seen Ralia, to hear how well you look, and how merry
you are. My mirth and beauty, which he celebrates,
are not much increased this fortnight, but, thank God,
I am much better these two days. What is better,
the whirlpool in my brain has in some measure sub-
sided; nay, I find the relapse to calm sorrow, a relief
from constant perturbation, " *Tha solas an tuireadh le
sith, Ach claoidhidh fad thuirse soil doruin.*"* As I
cannot cure the evil habit of quotation, you see I have
changed ground, and taken shelter in another language; but Mr. Macintosh will translate it for you. I
make no doubt of what you say of our dear departed
friend still hanging about your heart, and am sure she
will continue to do so " while memory holds her seat."
If this is your case, amidst affluence, prosperity, and
various society, judge what must be mine, in the utter
seclusion to which I now devote myself,—in a place
where seven years' residence had naturalized and do-
mesticated Charlotte so much, that her image makes
a part of every scene around me. Though the agitated
state of my mind has for some time interrupted that
kind of mystic intercourse which fancy delights to
hold with the souls of the departed, I gratify myself
by paying a kind of delicate homage to her memory,
in showing kindness to those she loved, and doing

---

* This quotation from Ossian has been elegantly, and not unfaith-
fully, translated by James Macpherson. It runs literally thus:—
" There is enjoyment in mourning with peace; yet long mourning
wastes the children of calamity."

things that I think would please her. The most
soothing retrospect I ever can have, is in recollecting
the many conversations we have had together upon
that awful futurity, which she has entered on only a
little before us; being, perhaps, prematurely ripened
by a succession of sorrows such as few experience.
My thoughts hover perpetually over the grave; yet I
trust in that Infinite goodness which has hitherto supported me, that the gloomy prospect will be enlivened
with some rays of hope and consolation. Speaking of
those whom she regarded, her old friend, Mr Ewen
Macpherson, who is a sincere mourner, is returned
from Skye, merely that he may die in this country;
and, no doubt, that his last days may be spent near
that once happy cottage, which was a central refuge
for affliction, before it was darkened by successive
sorrows.*

I hope the persons you mention at the close of your
letter will at all events respect themselves, and preserve their own esteem. It signifies little, when the
short chapter closes, in what class one has stood; the
great matter is, to have been near the head of that
class. I would rather be the first of peasants than
the last of kings; besides, the darker we find our
prospects here, the more diligently we explore the
light that leads to heaven. May that light shine on
you, and comfort you when all other comforts fail! So
prays your true friend,

A. G.

* This is the same gentleman previously referred to, by his familiar designation of " The Prophet." See Letter of July 8th, 1797.

Letter L.

TO MRS. MACINTOSH, GLASGOW.

Laggan, January 15, 1801.

Dear Madam,

I think I have it now in my power to fulfil the promise I made of sending you a translation from the Gaelic. You judge rightly that I am vain of knowing so much of that original and most emphatic language. I shall soon send you a literal translation, which I have by me, of part of an ancient fragment—a genuine one, remember, and hitherto untouched. The present subject, however, is modern. The mourner whom the bard personates is, indeed, " soft, modest, melancholy, fair;" and the deep and real distress which the song commemorates, is yet recent. Mrs. Reid, a lady in the neighbourhood of Athol, went to the summer shealings,* in the mountains, with three remarkably fine children, a boy and two girls; the boy, who was eldest, was distinguished by a remarkably good ear for music, and, though but eight years old, played on the violin very sweetly. The children caught a pestilential fever, which some poor neighbour had brought up into the glen, and, being very remote from all assistance and the convenience and attendance that sickness requires, the death of all the children was the consequence, at a very early period of the disease.

* Summer pasturages, with temporary accommodation for the dairy-maids and others in charge of the cattle.

The bard who soothed the sorrows of the parents by this composition, appears to me to possess native genius. Let him speak for himself:—

" Ah! still must I languish,
  Thus pining in anguish,
  For my joy and my pleasure,
  My heart's dearest treasure,
    The fair sunbeams that brighten'd my soul!
  The loud storm blew boldly,
  The bleak blast came coldly,
  My sweet buds all blighted:
  Forlorn, and benighted,
    Ah! nothing can ease or console!

" Where was beauty, fresh blowing,
  Where was stature, fast growing;
  Where was truth and affection,
  Where was thought and reflection,
    That so early appear'd in full bloom?
  At midnight, when musing,
  All comfort refusing,
  I hear, through my groaning,
  Your voices low moaning,
    Oh, speak to me once from the tomb!

" The sighs of my mourning
  Arise with the morning;
  And when evening's soft showers,
  Weep fresh o'er the flowers,
    My tears fall as silent, unseen.
  Who hears me lamenting,
  But, sadly consenting,
  Must pity my grieving,
  Since Heaven, thus bereaving,
    Has wither'd my fair plants so green!

" The viol so sprightly
  Who touches so lightly?
  O, peace to its sounding,
  My troubl'd heart wounding,
    For my son shall awake it no more!
  Nor my daughters, gay smiling,
  My cares once beguiling,
  From their cold bed returning,
  Shall banish my mourning,
    Or hear me their absence deplore!

" O, children beloved,
  Where are you removed?
  Have you left us so early,
  Who cherish'd you dearly,
    For the dark silent chambers of death!
  The fair sun, returning,
  Shall light the new morning;
  Fresh grass on the mountains,
  Fresh flow'rs by the fountains,
    Shall wake with the spring's gentle breath:

" But no morning, new breaking,
  My children shall waken;
  'Tis hopeless to number
  The days of their slumber,
    The long sleep that awakens no more!
  Shall the cold earth's dark bosom
  Still hide each fair blossom?
  Have angel's not borne them
  Where bright rays adorn them,
    Where on wings of new rapture they soar?

" On my fancy thus beaming,
  My eyes, ever streaming,
  My breast, ever heaving,
  Their image relieving,
    Shall soothe into pensive repose:
  In beauty transcendent,
  In brightness resplendent,
    I shall meet them where life has no close!"

I have preserved, as far as possible, the simplicity of
the original; but its tenderness, the solemn sadness
that runs through it, its pathetic beauties, I am sensible I have not reached. I have left out many verses.
Poetry, in the ancient style, knows nothing of concen-
trating thoughts; it was the object of undivided and
unwearied attention to minds susceptible of all its
beauties, unchilled by interest, unhardened by vanity.
Children of nature did not turn wearied and satiated
from the expression of genuine feeling, to listen to every
rattle by which novelty allures frivolous minds. Now
you have a modern poem, which, if I have not spoiled

it in the translation, will give you some idea of the language of nature and true sorrow. The stanzas are in a form unusual and uncouth; but I could not think of deviating from the original measure, which is adapted to a wild plaintive tune quite in unison with the sadness of the subject. If you set a due value on my effort to oblige you, I shall send you the " Tale of other Times" very soon; and am, in the meantime, with all due respect for your laudable curiosity, yours, very truly,

A. G.

LETTER LI.

TO MRS. BROWN.

My dear Mrs. Brown,   Laggan, January 26, 1801.

I took your last letter very kindly indeed, though my long delay in answering appears rather against me. This *young* family of mine, which seems destined to be ever young and ever growing, engrosses me more than ever, as I grow more than ever indifferent about other matters of this world. Not that I love my children better than formerly, but I love other things less. And though I have not, as yet, made any extraordinary progress in that easy and pleasant science of self-love, I still love myself so well as to fly the approaches of despondency, whom I consider as cousin-german to despair; and the best mere earthly refuge I know, is constant, earnest employment. Yet I could contrive to find time to write, if I could find spirits; but all the melancholy events of the last year, with their more melancholy consequences, did so overwhelm me when I endeavoured to write to any one whom I knew to be conscious of my feelings, that I shrunk from what used to be my consolation. My heart has been so softened, so melted by distress, that I feel more than ever the kindness of my few remaining friends; I cling to them in idea with a stronger grasp. The value you express for my correspondence, and the sense you retain of our long endeared intimacy, is a cordial to my sick heart. I am cheered by the reflection how much Providence has suited the kind and degree of comfort, allotted to me, to my taste and inclination; indulging my love of freedom and tranquillity, and giving me a warm interest in so many worthy hearts, and making those with which mine was most intimately blended, all I could wish. Without this, the world would have been a desert to me, and all its most envied enjoyments splendid trifles. You will rejoice to hear, after all the sorrows and sad privations I have suffered, that I have an increasing stock of comfort in my children. . . . . . . Such have been my comforts under this illness. How many, many languish in vain, amidst splendour and affluence, for these high peculiar blessings, that can only be given or received by minds of a certain description.

How are Mr. Brown's monarchical spirits supported under the triumphs of the great Consul? We are here all in sackcloth and ashes. I did not give myself credit for so much public spirit as this occasion has called forth; my blood really chilled with horror and anguish. Alas, for the poor Swiss! I fancy the wits of all your politicians are sharpened by hunger. We are better off than most of our neighbours; our crop, I hope, will feed us till the new one comes. I wrote to your sister about a commission of rice for the Duke's tenants, which I thought your brother might procure. We long to hear from you. Mr. Grant joins cordially in every good wish to you and yours, with your affectionate friend,

A. G.

LETTER LII.

TO MRS. MACINTOSH, GLASGOW.*

Dear Madam,　　　　　　　Laggan, December 17, 1801.

If sympathy could alleviate the greatest of possible calamities, mine might be softened by the sincere and tender compassion of my friends, which is beyond what I could have hoped. Yours I believe to be not only sincere, but very painful. Willingly would I lessen your pain by showing you how Divine mercy has enabled me to soothe my own. The storm of adversity has indeed been let loose upon me, and shattered my fabric of happiness; so frequent, so heavy were the shocks, that it is no wonder I lay stunned among the ruins. But I have not abandoned myself to sinful despair; I am gathering up the fragments to build a little hovel, where I may live the appointed time on hope and recollection, and then die in peace. I will

---

* Written after the death of the Rev. James Grant, the husband of the Author, which took place on the 2d December, 1801.—ED.

not describe my sorrows; I will not tell you that when half my heart was torn away, the other half ached at the separation. All this you must know, for you too have a heart. But you have been too prosperous, to know how minds, not inelegant, are endeared to each other by retirement, and sharing sorrows and difficulties. But I meant to tell you my resolutions. Pecuniary evils I neither feel nor fear. God is all-sufficient, and my trust in him is unlimited.

* * * * * * *

Dear madam, what right have I to repine, when the time must needs be so short till the period that reunites us? In the meantime, I will hover round his remains as long as I possibly can?—I cannot at this time write longer, or I would tell you how indulgent the Duke of Gordon has been, in permitting me to continue somewhat longer on the farm, at the old rate. Our affairs were in much better condition than could be expected, considering my husband's liberal spirit and numerous burdens. No friend need take the trouble of a long journey on my account; my cousin, Captain R., and Mr. Anderson, our neighbour Clergyman, have volunteered their assistance, which will be quite sufficient. God bless you both!

Your concern about the pension expected for the widows of chaplains, is very kind indeed. Mr. Grant's agent will inquire about it: if others get it, I shall; I have no peculiar claim. I am, dear madam, yours sincerely,

A. G.

LETTER LIII.

TO MISS DUNBAR OF BOATH.*

Laggan, January 1, 1802.

Dear Madam,

So young, and such a novice in sorrow, you have not yet learnt the weakness, the extreme languor, into which the mind sinks when the first violent bursts are over; incapable of raising itself to the true source of consolation, and ready to lean on every reed. In this state sympathy is most availing, and in this hopeless and dispirited state your letter found me. Why then apologise for what excites my warmest gratitude? Your dear worthy mother and you I have long known and esteemed, through the medium of your humble friend. This proof of your goodness to so great a stranger, convinces me that you are all I have been taught to imagine you.

You wish to know how I bear the sudden shock of this calamity. I bore it wonderfully, considering how very much I had to lose. Still, at times, the Divine goodness supports me in a manner I scarcely dared to hope. Happily for me, anxiety for a numerous orphan family, and the wounding smiles of an infant, too dear

---

* This and some following Letters were written in answer to one Miss Dunbar had, at her mother's desire, addressed to the Author, condoling with her on the loss she had recently sustained.—(1807.) Miss Dunbar was the only daughter of Alexander Dunbar, Esq. of Boath, in the county of Nairn, and sister to the late Captain Sir James Dunbar, Bart., R.N. She was a lady of cultivated taste and lively manners, and continued to correspond with the Author until her death, which took place at Forres in the year 1835.—ED.

to be neglected, and too young to know what he has lost, divide my sorrows, and do not suffer my mind to be wholly engrossed by this dreadful privation, this chasm that I shudder to look into. A daughter, of all daughters the most dutiful and affectionate, in whom her father still lives (so truly does she inherit his virtues, and all the amiable peculiarities of his character); this daughter is wasting away with secret sorrow, while, " in smiles she hides her grief to soften mine." I was too much a veteran in affliction, and too sensible of the arduous task devolved upon me, to sit down in unavailing sorrow, overwhelmed by an event which ought to call forth double exertion. None, indeed, was ever at greater pains to console another, than I was to muster up every motive for action, every argument for patient suffering. No one could say to me, " the loss is common, common be the pain ;" few, very few indeed, had so much happiness to lose. To depict a character so very uncommon, so little obvious to common observers, who loved and revered without comprehending him, would be difficult for a steadier hand than mine. With a kind of mild disdain, and philosophic tranquillity, he kept aloof from a world, for which the delicacy of his feelings, the purity of his integrity, and the intuitive discernment with which he saw into character, in a manner disqualified him; that is, from enjoying it. For who can enjoy the world without deceiving or being deceived? But recollections crowd on me, and I wander. I say, to be all the world to this superior mind, to constitute his happiness for twenty years now vanished like a vision ; to have lived with unabated affection together even thus long, when a constitution, delicate as his mind, made it unlikely that even thus long we should support each other through the paths of life, affords cause for much gratitude. What are difficulties, when shared with one whose delighted approbation gives one spirits to surmount them? Then to hear from every mouth his modest unobtrusive merit receive its due tribute of applause; to see him still in his dear children, now doubly dear; and to know that such a mind cannot perish, cannot suffer; nay, through the infinite merits of that Redeemer, in whom he trusted, enjoys what we cannot conceive! Dear Miss Dunbar, believe me, I would not give my tremulous hopes, and pleasing sad retrospections, for any other person's happiness. Forgive this; it is like the overflowing of the heart to an intimate; but your pity opens every source of anguish and of tenderness. Assure your kind mother of my grateful esteem; and, believe me, with sincere regard, much yours,

A. G.

Letter LIV.

TO MRS. FURZER, BERNERS STREET, LONDON.

Laggan, January 12, 1802.

My dear Friend,

I have perused your affectionate letter again and again; but how shall I answer it? Day after day, week after week, I have deferred, in hopes of a serene hour. To you I could pour out my heart, and from you expect the sympathy this cold world has not to bestow. But two things I see clearly: that mine is a growing sorrow, like other streams, widening as it proceeds; and that I am utterly incapable of arranging my thoughts at present: one overpowering recollection absorbs everything. . . . .

Now that I have gone through this bitter narrative,* you will be sensible how sudden, yet how aggravated, the stroke has been. Very delicate he was all summer, and much enfeebled, in consequence of his illness last spring. However, it was a delightful summer; we had got matters arranged to our satisfaction, and shook off some embarrassments that had arisen from the expense of enclosing, improving, &c. Our farm was well regulated, and productive in consequence. Isabella came home, and her improvement, in every sense, afforded us great pleasure. In short, from different favourable turns with regard to our children and our affairs, we were relieved from many anxieties which had preyed on his delicate and sensible spirit. We were indeed all cheerfulness, harmony, and peace, enjoying the highest domestic comfort, and the most pleasing prospect of a calm evening of life. He was delightfully pleasant; I never saw him enjoy himself and his family more. A boy, the most promising one, the greatest tie I have now to life, was sent us for a comfort when my dear John was taken away, and was the charm and amusement of this last fatal year. I never saw his fondness carried to such a pitch, though he treated all of them with the most endearing

---

* This narrative is here omitted.

tenderness. My dearest Nancy, were I to choose so long a period to live over again, at any time of my life, I think it would be the very half year, the close of which swallowed up my hopes of earthly happiness. . . . . I will not torture myself with particulars. I had not ten minutes' warning; it was a thunder-stroke. Yet if sudden, it was comparatively easy; the doctor was not alarmed till the last half hour. I cannot either leave off or go on. . . . . I thank God, no one can have better children. My friends, too, seem disposed to do all that can possibly alleviate what is incurable. The Duke of Gordon humanely indulges me in keeping the farm in the old way, till the period when it shall be found expedient for me to leave it. Our affairs are in better order than you could expect, when you consider a man so charitable and generous with so large a family. My intention is to hover round his remains here as long as I can; and when I remove, it shall be to a town. You will hear something of me hereafter, that will surprise you, yet not more than it has done myself. I use every means to calm my mind, but the hiatus is dreadful. Write to me soon; in this state one leans hard on friendship. Adieu.

A. G.

LETTER LV.

TO MISS DUNBAR OF BOATH.

Laggan, April 24, 1802.

Dear Madam,

I wrote a hasty scrawl to accompany the poetical fugitives you wished for, which I sent to Bar,* to be forwarded; but Bar, " whose meaner stars have shut her up in wishes," has every inclination, but no power, to transmit the important packet. So I must brandish the quill once more, though scarce able to lift it; for I have been, for ten days past, sick, spiritless, forlorn, and dejected. I am no whiner, and love my friends too well to inflict my sufferings upon them, when I suffer moderately. Indeed, when I do not positively suffer, I do positively enjoy; for which reason, it is more peculiarly my duty to suffer patiently, and enjoy gratefully. Now, you will reasonably expect a definition of what I call enjoyment. It is, when the sensibilities of my heart are excited, and find objects worthy of them; it is, when I can meditate in peace, and return to my first love, the fair face of nature, with serene complacency; at times heightened into an enthusiasm equally tender and solemn; it is when I can indulge recollections that exalt my mind while they soften it; it is when my sorrows are asleep, lulled by the

---

* " Bar" was a familiar abbreviation, in the Author's family, of the name of Miss Anne Dunbar, who taught, with much success, a school at Laggan, attended by the children of the Author, to whom she was endeared by many deserving qualities. She was well known to Miss Dunbar of Boath, and her name frequently occurs in Mrs. Grant's letters to that lady. Miss Anne Dunbar still survives; she lives at Elgin, in Morayshire, esteemed by many friends.—(1845.)

cheering smiles of playful infancy, or the easy artless conversation of the young, the innocent, and the affectionate. I say nothing of the humanizing muse, her ladyship having, at times, a great propensity to point the stings of pain, and being, at best, but a capricious comforter.

Now, you must needs be tired of egotism; but who such egotists as the sick and sorrowful? and what so improving to the young, the gay, and prosperous, as to know how suffering may be endured, to know the ingredients of that wholesome, though unpalatable cup, of which we must all drink by turns! I owe you, after your patient endurance of this homily, some lighter theme. I must tell you the origin of the song of " Cro Challin," which Mary, improperly, called a translation. You must know that, in the progress of Highland society, there was a kind of intermediate state, to which a good deal of pleasing, fanciful poetry owes it origin. But then it is so local, so peculiar, so untranslatable, it is absolute sal volatile. The heroic age, as you well know, was entirely divided betwixt war and the chase. Love, in such an age, appears not in a voluptuous or seducing form; man, always born to suffer and to mourn, then suffered more severely, and mourned more deeply. Love was a solemn, serious passion, interwoven with the ruling one of heroic achievement. A man loved his mistress much the better that he had obtained her by some warlike exploit, and mourned her loss the more, as it was generally attended with that of his far greater idol, honour. He often won her by war, and supported her by hunting. This inferior war gave scope to those pursuits that elevated the minds of the Highlanders into that sublime melancholy with which their love, their poetry, and their music were so strongly tinctured. When their extravagant and restless knight-errantry had almost occasioned the extinction of the Fingalian race of heroes, a new tribe appeared, more industrious, and less enterprising. In short, the pastoral age commenced; and the first tenders of cattle were regarded by heroic bards and lovelorn maids (who were of course musical and poetical) as a degenerate race, who had not spirit or ability to encounter the hazards and fatigues of a life of hunting. These are the sons of little men, so contemptuously spoken of, and indeed considered as the idle and cowardly part of the community. However, the tide of property and consequence changing, that prejudice changed with it; the muse deserted to the pastoral vale, and maidens began to boast the peaceful plenty of their lovers' folds, and describe their herds and flocks with rapture. Others, again, praised the valour of their hunters, the wild variety of their pursuits, and the sylvan scenery they traced in search of their game. The authoress of the sweet wild strain, " Cro Challin," provoked to emulation, extols her Colin's herds and flocks, and ascribes singular properties to them. They require no fold, no herd, no restraint; she dwells with delight on their beauty and swiftness :—

" O where are thy flocks, that so lightly rebound,
And fly o'er the heath without touching the ground ?
So beauteous, so varied, so dappled their hue,
So agile, so graceful, so charming to view.
In all the wide forest, sure nought can appear
Like the flocks of my Colin, my hunter, my dear," &c.

All ends in the discovery that her lover was a hunter;
and the animals, whose beauty and vivacity she had
been admiring, were deer, roes, and fawns. This I
some time ago transfused (for translate I could not,)
into English for Mr. Thomson.*

I have been tedious, and feel myself the better for
being so, but am tired. To-morrow night I will spur
myself up to be tedious again, and answer all your
queries with regard to Burns. Good night. Sleep be
upon thine eyes, peace in thy breast !

A. G.

Letter LVI.

TO MISS DUNBAR.

Laggan, April 25, 1802.

Now I have to satisfy you as to my favourite poem
of Burns. Doubtless the "Daisy" is the most finished,
and excels in simple elegance ; " The De'il himsel" in
humour—exquisite, peculiar humour. I confess, if
decorous people could be reconciled to blackguardism,
John Hornbook is the very Emperor of blackguards.
Only think of that despotic power over the fancy,
which can unite, what the creative Shakspeare himself never united, the terrible and ludicrous. Yet,
where Death is personified meeting the bard, I am

---

* George Thomson, Esq. of Edinburgh, the friend of Burns and
of the Author, whose letters to the Ayrshire Bard appear in the
correspondence published by Dr. Currie.—" Cro Challin," as translated by the Author, is included in the fourth volume of Mr. Thomson's Collection of Scottish Music.—(1807.)

sure you would laugh, if you were not afraid. The same power reappears in " Tam o' Shanter," which I allow to possess superior excellence, though not the very sort of excellence most to my taste. But if you talk of my very own taste, I find myself quite at home in " The Epistle to Davy," and " The Cottar's Saturday Night." The latter, indeed, draws aid from the true source of the sublime and beautiful in composition, the sacred Scriptures. The Epistles have a strength of thought, with a playful ease of expression, a mixture of sound sense and sportive gaiety, which is really delightful. The " Auld Farmer to his Mare Maggy," is a very great favourite of mine ; and " The Lament" has more nerve in it than all the love laments, I ever saw, put together. Then the songs—what a wilderness of sweets is there, and how puzzling is choice among such contending beauties! I, who delight in Scotch landscape and simple pathos, overlook songs richer in poetry, to shelter under the bard's plaid.

> " O wert thou in the cauld blast,
>   On yonder lea, on yonder lea,
> My plaidy to the angry airt,
>   I'd shelter thee, I'd shelter thee."

Or to

> " Wander wi' Jean in yon glen of green bracken,
>   Where the burnie steals under the lang yellow broom."

If, indeed, I could resist the soft attraction of

> " O wha is she that lo'es me,
>   And has my heart in keeping?
> O sweet is she that lo'es me,
>   Like dews in summer weeping,
>   In tears the rose-buds steeping," &c.

If you ever know, as well as I do, what it is to have your heart wrung with agony,

> " On the past too fondly pondering,
> O'er the hopeless future wandering,"

you will feel the force of Isabella's complaint :—

> " Raving winds around her blowing," &c.

Hear the true language of despair :—

> " Life, thou soul of every blessing,
> Load to misery most distressing,
> O how gladly I'd resign thee,
> And to dark oblivion join thee !"

In extreme bitterness of soul we all should say this, if
we knew how.   One more Elysian flower from this
rich wreath, and I have done :—

> " ' And wear thou this,' she solemn said,
> And placed the holly on my head—
> Its polish'd leaves, and berries red,
>   Did rustling play,
> And, like a passing thought, she fled
>   In light away."

Let the doors of the temple of fancy be for ever barred
on those who can read this without turning, involun-
tarily, to gaze on vacancy, and startling at the rustling
leaves, when Coila flies " in light away !"

Letter LVII.

TO MISS DUNBAR, BOATH.

Laggan, May 4, 1802.

I now hasten to your queries.   I cannot tell you
how much I admire and despise Peter ; * he is every
way original, and most original in this respect, that I

---

* Peter Pindar, the assumed name of John Wolcott, a witty, but
low, and mischievous writer of verses.—(1807.)

know not that ever any other object at once excited
my contempt and admiration. His humour is most
peculiar, most unaffected, most irresistible. Yet, for
what end Providence intrusted a weapon so dangerous in the hands of one who avows his disregard of
everything sacred and venerable, is very difficult for
us to conjecture. I am the more fully convinced of
the bad tendency of his writings, from the amusement
I derive from them, forearmed as I am by a disgust
at his want of principle and decency. "Bozzy and
Piozzi," however, is above praise and beyond censure:
there the satire is so just, so pointed, so characteristic,
that one can laugh without self-reproach. The Lou-
siad, however, I regard with a mixture of contempt
and disgust. Burlesque spun out so long is loathsome:
it is a farce of five acts. Besides, to make royal weak-
nesses, should they even exist, a subject for ridicule, I
think immoral as well as impolitic. This scandalous
license would be intolerable, though we were not, as
now, ruled by a virtuous and exemplary Prince. It
is necessary for the good of society that we venerate
our rulers, unless they oppress us by tyranny, or show
a corrupting example. Whoever applies a magnifying
glass to every speck of human infirmity, shakes the
main pillars that support government—the love and
respect people have for their rulers—and this is laugh-
ing at too great an expense.

I greatly admire the songs of Burns you mention;
"Jessy" is exquisite. But my selection was from
songs not so generally popular, but which have, to my
taste, transcendent merit. From songs to singing the
transition is easy, which leads to another of your

queries. All my young people love music, but only those inherit their father's fine taste and passable voice, who are so happy as to resemble him otherwise. These are Catherine and Moore. Duncan, too, has a very fine voice and ear. Musical talents we could not afford to cultivate,—paying the shoemaker's account for such a host is a serious affair. Mary has, in most things, a very good taste; you may depend more on it than on mine, ever blinded, as I am, by partiality. She thinks you have made the most of your subject; but it is not a happy one; nothing very lively or very tender arising naturally from it, giving no room either for pathos or gaiety. Your lines on your brother's return, which she met with in one of Bar's written books, delighted her—so elegant, easy, and tender; you would be vain if you knew what so calm a critic thought of them. You dazzle and overpower one with Miss Frazer's* character; I think I, too, would indulge her favourite propensity, if I had scope for it. Improving the face of nature I had almost called a divine amusement. She, who has made the desert to blossom as the rose, is the benefactress of the unborn as well as of her contemporaries. I was ready to cry out, on reading your description of her, " Lady, you are the cruellest she alive, if you will lead those graces to the grave, and leave the world no copy." Perhaps the lady might answer from the same author, " I will not be over-mastered by a valiant piece of clay," &c.

I have left no room for acknowledging your generous and highly successful exertions on my account, but I am run away with by Miss Frazer. I do feel a

* Miss Frazer, of Castle Frazer, Aberdeenshire.—(1807.)

little exalted at knowing there are such women in the world. Remember me in all kindness to your unequalled mother. I am always yours,

A. G.

LETTER LVIII.

TO ROBERT ARBUTHNOT, ESQ., EDINBURGH.*

Laggan, June 21, 1802.

My dear Sir,

Your letters were wont to be a great cordial to my spirits.; but the last gave me a tremour of anxiety, from which I have not yet recovered; for though I am sanguine in the extreme, and apt to hope against hope, when once I do fear, terror is with me a most acute sensation. Why did you not subscribe your letter? It was that which alarmed me most; yet you directed it, and I flatter myself will, ere long, direct another which will set my mind at ease on that head.

Shall I tell you how much I feel Mary's departure? I have been so little accustomed to stand alone, that I must needs have somebody to lean on, and she was

---

* Robert Arbuthnot, Esq., late Secretary to the Trustees' Office at Edinburgh ; an elegant scholar and amiable man. He was nearly related to Dr. Arbuthnot, the well-known associate of Pope and Swift, whom he resembled in steadiness of principle, cheerful equanimity, and entire resignation to the Divine will. He lived in intimacy with the most distinguished characters of his day for talents and for worth. The venerable Mrs. Montagu, Professor Beattie, author of the Minstrel, and the late excellent and much lamented Sir William Forbes of Pitsligo, were among his most particular friends.—(1807.) Mr. Arbuthnot was father of the late Sir William Arbuthnot, Bart., so created on the occasion of George the Fourth's visit to Edinburgh in 1822, of which city Sir William was then Lord Provost.—(1845.)

absolutely my prop. I have, by the greatest accident, heard of the Waterhouse family (Mrs. Protheroe's), from a young relation who has been lately in their part of Yorkshire. They rise upon me in everything that I hear of or from them. I am very much of David's mind when he talks of the excellent of the earth, in whom his delight was placed. My greatest comfort in my pilgrimage through many struggles and difficulties was, that I had always some intercourse and connexion with superior and unsullied minds; and is not this what one may call " the dim faint dawn of pure celestial day ?" This is a subject which I cannot touch without being rapt, as one may say. I think of my living friends with tenderness; but of those departed with enthusiasm that raises me above myself.

I feel bitter remorse lest I should have said anything that you might misapprehend about Mr. A. My strong way of expressing things might make me overcharge my own meaning. He has a solemnity, a certain pompous manner, that Mary always said you would dislike, and that, truly, I dislike myself. I wished to prepare you, in case you saw him, that you might, as we do, separate the inward from the outward man. You have really made me proud and happy by your kindness to my poor John's* outward man, though his ignorance of all polite languages makes his inward man inaccessible to your inquiries; he has as much of the genuine old Highlander as any one I know.

I have read your Translations with much pleasure,

---

* An old servant from the Highlands, whom Mrs. Grant had recommended to Mr. Arbuthnot.

not only for their elegant simplicity of language, but because I find the subject very congenial to my feelings, which, like your own, have undergone very little alteration from time; which I attribute to my having been so singularly happy in my friendships and connexions. I hope you will not *resent* the unauthorized liberty I have taken in inscribing the Gaelic translations to you. The prefixed Thoughts on the authenticity of Ossian, I have thrown together, without giving them any regular title, for I do not think it is a disquisition; but I appoint you and Mr. Thomson sponsors, and allow you the choice of the name.

In the hurry I have been kept with Mary's visitors taking leave of her, and the winding up of my volume, to which my nervous shattered *conformation* was very unequal, I have thought of the past and future for sometime as one dreams. One very pleasing vision, however, floated in my fancy, suggested by some past conversations with a *protegé* of yours. I thought I saw you on your way to Peterhead, tiring of the old beaten path, and resolving to vary it by going the way of Laggan, where the grandeur of the solitary majestic Grampians would be so contrasted with the humble tranquillity and social comforts of your friend's little cottage, swarming with population,—let Mary say the rest, and tell you how much I am Mrs. Arbuthnot's, Miss Arbuthnot's, and yours most gratefully,

A. G.

LETTER LIX.

Laggan, June 26, 1802.

My dear, kind *Helen,*

There, now, is the requested freedom, which, as you justly observe, ought to exist between those whose affinity of soul is felt, and claimed by each other. Besides, my matronly character and years entitle me to treat you if not maternally, a little *auntishly.* I need not, indeed, take much matronal consequence to myself, for, with my grown-up daughters I live like an elder sister. But now to my delay. Your last letter, inspired by the very soul of warm, young, active friendship, would have charmed me in the perusal, though I were not, myself, the obliged and grateful object of that friendship. But, before I answer it, I must tell you, that I have just parted with two friends whom I may never meet again, and who have been both very useful in supporting my spirits during this period of calamity. The preparations for their departure have not only engrossed, but overpowered me. One is the Book of Books,* the revisal of which had almost turned the brain of brains before it was completed. The other is the daughter of daughters, even my Highland Mary, who is now on her way to Eng-

---

* This alludes to a Volume of Poems, written by the Author of these Letters, and published in 1803, which was playfully called the Book of Books by Miss Dunbar.

land, and has left me under much depression. But, resolved not to yield to it, many a hard battle have I fought with despondency, and often, as now, have I been playful, for fear of being doleful. If I had not a firm reliance on Providence inwardly, and an active mind, that impels and enlivens my struggles outwardly, how could I still exist, after the hard pulls my heart-strings have had? The motives of this journey I shall explain hereafter, for I never could narrate when my head ached. We spent " one day of parting love," as Burns says, at Dalwhinnie, from which her young cousins, Isabella, and I, returned to-day. I took refuge in my haunt in the deep dell, where the Bronnach dashes impetuously over its rocky channel; there I wrote a few lines with a pencil, which I will retrace and inclose for your perusal. But the meaning of this effusion connects so closely with the scenery, that, without a commentary by that cool critic, Bar, you will not half taste it. Let *her* paint the landscape which she has so often seen and felt; let her tell you how the Bronnach is born in the recesses of the Corry-buie,* very near Charlotte's beautiful fountain. From this kindred stream it diverges, and turns its course towards our cottage, before it descends from the eminence under which we are sheltered. Never, sure, in a quarter of a mile's course, did a mountain-brook assume such various aspects, and speak such different languages. Turbulent and hoarse, it first descends, over rocks and great stones, through the

---

* Corry-buie is a name applied to a large verdant hollow, something like the crater of a volcano, near the summit of a mountain. It means, literally, yellow or flowery bosom.

deep chasm which its wintry tumults have formed in
the steep descent; when it reaches the house, close to
which it passes, the channel is stony, but not abrupt;
its murmurs are still loud, but regular and not unpleasing; a little further on, it runs over smooth
pebbles. Its borders are verdant, and its sound equal
and almost musical. Presently after, it enters a
meadow rich and flowery beyond all compare, fertil-
ized by the overflowing of Spey, beautiful with luxuriant herbage, and diversified by the windings of this
wandering stream, which becomes here a perfect
meander, circling round so often, that it seems inclined
to revisit its source. Its brink affords shelter, amidst
the tufted flowers, to an incredible number of larks;
and its channel in this rich mould is so deep, that the
sound is softer and sweeter than any other stream.
When I walked alone, to indulge sorrow, I always
went up the banks of this stream. How many tranquil evenings have I traced its wanderings through the
meadows, with those who, alas, will never more share
my peaceful enjoyments! But now to the purpose:

LINES ADDRESSED TO THE BRONNACH,

*A small Stream that descends from the Mountains behind the
Manse of Laggan.*

Rude stream, that com'st dashing the wild rocks among,
And drown'st in thy tumults the pastoral song,
How oft thy hoarse clamours have softened my care,
When pining with anguish, or sunk in despair!

When nature lay hushed in oblivious repose,
When nothing was waking but I and my woes;
When the stars all beheld me with bright eyes of fire,
And bade me resign, and their Author admire.

Then, where by my cottage thy turbulent course,
Like sorrow subsiding, diminish'd its force,
When the heart, overburden'd, could seek for relief,
Thy murmurs how placid, how soothing to grief!

When morn in fresh beauty enlightened the skies,
When the sun was preparing in splendour to rise,
Among the smooth pebbles, in melody clear,
Smooth gliding, thy waters more lucid appear.

But when in the meadows, at ev'ning's soft hours,
On thy borders I wander, 'midst verdure and flowers,
Where, hid in thy channel, in whispers so sweet,
Thou art heard in a cadence for sympathy meet;

My musings, tho' pensive, are free from despair,
While soothing I feel the soft balm of the air;
When from thy low banks, they ascend to the sky,
My soul seems to follow the larks where they fly.

When the sun from the west, with a soft parting ray,
Irradiates thy stream, where it mingles with Spey,
While to seek the wide ocean thy pure waters roll,
How soft, yet how tranquil, the calm of my soul!

The stream that with thee in the mountains arose,
In whose dark recesses your sources disclose,
Whose parting thy murmurs lament all the way,
Tho' forc'd from beside thee so early to stray,

Now again shall rejoin thee, and flow in one tide,
Nor part till to ocean together you glide:
How blest, who arrive at that sea without shore,
Where currents rejoin, to be sundered no more!

LETTER LX.

TO MRS. SMITH, JORDANHILL, GLASGOW.

Laggan, June 27, 1802.

My dear Friend,

For my life I cannot recollect which of us wrote last, but I think it is, I am sure it ought to be myself. The hurry I have been kept in with concluding the Book you know of, which has been so corrected, enlarged, and be-noted, that you would not know it again, has really done me some hurt, though, on the whole, more good. Intense thought is a disease with me, for as thoughtless as you imagine me; but the misfortune is, I give too few of these profound meditations to the important, urgent, present moment. I dwell on the past, I muse and recollect, till the fire burneth, and then I fly for relief to the future, and expatiate in the waste regions of space and possibility. The intellectual labour this same book required was at once a stimulus and an opiate,—it fixed my attention, spurred on my exertions, and, at the same time, constrained me within " the flaming bounds of space and time ;" and abridged the power of restless, painful memory. However, I know the state both of my frame and my feelings too well to indulge in indolent reflection. From morning to midnight I am constantly employed, and always in motion, when not engaged in this or some such way. I reap benefit from this exertion, being more cheerful than you could expect from a heart torn to pieces as mine has been

for sometime past. But then I am fallen off to a
mere skeleton, which, I suppose, must be the consequence of sleeping so little as I do. I tell you all
these particulars, because I fear Mary will not see you
on her way to England, as she is to stay but a night
or two in Glasgow. I miss both the bustle of the
Book and Mary, who, without doubt, is one of the
pleasantest housemates I ever met with; her temper
is so equal and cheerful; she is so domestic, so active,
so versatile; her character is so perfectly natural, and
she has some traces of her father's correct judgment
and dignified sincerity. Alas, what comfort have I
equal to tracing all I can find of their amiable father
in my children. What would I not do or suffer for
his children!

I have been under the necessity of taking what is
called a flying crop off the farm, because it was in
such a high state of culture and preparation, that it
would be considered absurd to do otherwise; but all
things will turn to the greater advantage at the term
when they are sold off.—Pray acknowledge warmly
for me Dr. Reid's exertions. Speak of me as I am to
Mr. Smith; that is, as his and your obliged, affectionate, unalterable friend,

A. G.

LETTER LXI.

TO MISS MAXWELL PAGAN.

My dear Maxwell,   Laggan, August 4, 1802.

I will by no means delay answering your kind letter, though it costs me a greater effort than you are
aware of; for I have really got a surfeit of writing of
late. First, that tiresome Collection* which I had to
arrange for the press; and now with answering letters
which I had been obliged to defer till that task was
concluded. Of these letters what shall I say? I wish
you did but see them. Of more than forty, moderately speaking, which I received on a late melancholy
occasion, not one speaks the cant of condolence. Some
of them are from people I never saw, though I know
them well through the medium of mutual friends;
others from *lang syne* acquaintance, by whom I thought
myself entirely forgotten. Some of these epistles are
singularly elegant, some piously affecting, some simply
pathetic; but it is very singular, that, among so many
there should not be one studied or affected expression,
or one hackneyed phrase. They all breathe, in various
tones, the genuine language of feeling and compassion
for the living, of esteem and veneration for the departed. All this tender regret for modest worth, hid,
during the short pilgrimage of life, in obscurity; all
this amiable sympathy for orphans, some of them too

* The volume of Poems before alluded to.

young to know the extent of their misfortune, and for their unhappy mother sinking in an unheard-of corner, under the depression of narrow circumstances, accumulated cares, and an enfeebled constitution—form a powerful body of evidence against the prevailing notion, that every creature acts from some selfish or sordid motive, and that vanity or interest are the sole actuating principles. Behold, here are so many who have not bowed the knee to Baal,—who are not entirely swayed by that world which is at perpetual enmity with its Maker. What motives, but the purest and the best, could any one have for taking so warm an interest in those who could promote no one's advantage, and gratify no one's vanity?

We have had letters from Mary since her arrival in England, and even since she went to Devonshire. Her journey, which was full of novelty and amusement, and which, as far as possible, she has shared with us by her description, was rendered more safe and agreeable by the company of a particular friend of mine, Mr. Anderson, a neighbouring clergyman, who, being obliged to make an excursion for his health, accompanied her to London, and on to Sidmouth, a watering-place where she found her new friends, together with some others of the family. The elegance of their manners, and the cordiality of her reception, exceeded even her expectations, which had been highly raised by their previous correspondence.* Here I must waive the true and entertaining narrative of her travels, to recite something more extraordinary than

* The late Edward Protheroe, Esq., M. P. for Bristol, and his family, are here alluded to.—(1845.)

anything that occurred to her observation in that world of wonders, London itself, during her short stay in it.

*   *   *   *   *   *

I have not left room to tell you of the goodness of Divine Providence, as it appears manifested to the children of a worthy man, in the kind and considerate attention of many to their affairs. Know me always, yours truly,

A. G.

LETTER LXII.

TO HER DAUGHTER, MARY, AT EDWARD PROTHEROE'S, ESQ.,
PARK ROW, BRISTOL.

Laggan, August 17, 1802

My dearest Mary,

Do not think me fanciful. Late last night your letter came ; the night before, like many others, was mostly a dreary vigil, occupied by those recollections which, sad as they are, must be ever dear and desirable to me. I slumbered two hours in the morning, and awaked in an agony, bathed in the tears I had shed on your account, during the dreadful visionary horrors from which I had just escaped. I dreaded, from my dreams, that all was not right with you; and though exceedingly sorry, I was not surprised, at all, at your dejection, or at the forlorn, helpless sense of vacuity and insignificance which has invaded, and for the time subdued your mind. Perhaps I should be, in one sense, sorry it were otherwise till habit had reconciled, and affection naturalized you where you are. Your dress, your table, your lodging and attendance, are better where you now live; but your associates have not more sentiment, discernment, or information, nor can they as yet have as much affection. If you who have lived always in a kind of intellectual luxury, surrounded with people who, compared to the world at large, were all heart and soul, with cultivated understandings and warm affections, of which you were the darling object; if you, who never knew a vacuity in your heart or in your time, could at once make an abundance of exterior comfort supply to you the place of all this, I would renounce you from my affections as a selfish being, unworthy to be a member of such a family as ours, who possessed among ourselves so many of the prerequisites for rational and refined happiness. But this torpor of the soul, this chilling sense of solitude in the midst of society, will gradually wear off. I shall write largely every week,—my letters shall be so long, so Scotch, so marmalade,—such a mixture of bitter and sweet, of harsh precepts and amusing information! In the meantime, consider how much we still possess in the midst of our sorrows and privations; and what need we have of something to drive us to the great and unfailing Source of consolation, in whom are the well-springs of life, and whose mercy endureth for ever. Think, dear Mary, on your enlarged power of doing good; say to yourself, when your spirit dies within you,

> " Alas, what crowds, by ceaseless labour worn,
> What millions sigh to be as blest as I!"

Since you have lost my letter (no small loss I assure you, for it was full of anecdote, and very long),

I must again tell you that I have the kindest possible letter, all heart, all herself, from dearest Mrs. Furzer, whom I love better than anybody out of my own family. She earnestly requests you to visit her, and I as earnestly advise you to do it. She says the passage by sea from Bristol to Plymouth is made at a very moderate expense. Go by all means when you return from Bath. Next summer, please God, we shall meet again.

Frequent and earnest devotion is the first resource I advise you to; the next you will think childish, silly, and ill-bred, yet you will find it very efficacious —it is a little egotism once removed. Speak often to Mrs. Protheroe—who will bear it first patiently, and then pleasantly—of your absent friends, of our cottage and its inmates, of your dear father and his dear children, of Highland customs. By degrees this, though foreign at first, will interest her; and that again will make her more interesting to you. There is a native eloquence that gives life to our language when we speak of those we love. You will become amusing to her, and then be interested in *her* localities. I wonder very much that gratitude does not make your heart warm. Love, and make yourself beloved, and all the azure demons will return to the place from whence they came.

The garden here is in full glory: convolvolus, poppies, roses, and nasturtium thriving beyond example with warm soft rains, which have renewed the face of nature, and covered the earth with an abundant prospect; the flowers abovementioned blowing daily in rich redundance. The porch is enchanting past all conception; numbers of pansies spring in your borders, and pinks, the wonder of all beholders for number and variety; and I, Adam and Eve in one, propping, weeding, and handling the hoe and spade with equal dexterity. Then for fruit, there is such a quantity, that we are giving jam and jelly to all the neighbours. The abundance of black currants is incredible.

I have Mary Macpherson with me, just come from Cluny, where she paid a visit for ten days. She grew upon me much: she is an admirable creature, rude from the hands of nature. Mr. Arbuthnot was charmed with the *Book*. I have received numberless compliments on it. Rejoice, for his son tells me he is much the better of his Aberdeenshire jaunt, recovered from his late illness, and in great spirits. The Grants are all in glee, having foiled the Frasers with much ado at the election. Charles Grant, the new member, is my old friend Mrs. Sprott's brother. The country swarms with shooters, among whom are some of the heroes of Egypt. I had a levée on Monday, at which appeared the Marquis of Huntly, Colonel D. Gordon of Aberdour, and Sir John Gordon of Park. I will tell at more leisure what they said, and how they looked. I expect my father hourly. God bless my dear child, prays

ANNE GRANT.

LETTER LXIII.

TO GEORGE THOMSON, ESQ., TRUSTEES' OFFICE, EDINBURGH.

Laggan, September 3, 1802.

Dear Sir,

The great desideratum with me, in thought, word, and deed, is method. I wish I knew where a " commodity of good methods were to be bought." I would be as willing to purchase them as Charteris would have been to buy a fair character, which he rated so high from a similar motive, knowing its value from its want. Some disarranged folks pretend to be above method; but I humbly own it to be above me. I am determined that this letter, as a proof of my honest endeavour to reform, shall proceed methodically, and never once " reverse its march," as Laing most affectedly says, when any plain Christian or honest soldier would say " retreated."

I shall cut and alter all you bid me about the poem of the " Highlanders;" and am daily more and more sensible, that without a pilot, such as I have been so happy as to find in you, it would be madness in me to venture from shore. Unaccustomed to disguise, and hitherto having no motive for it, I shall appear to the world such as I really am, formed by the accidents of education and situation,—a solitary anomalous being, not thinking in the common track, or classing with any sect or party. Such once was he, whose steady judgment directed, and whose intuitive penetration enlightened me! What class of beings will now own or protect me? I shall be like the bat, whom mice and birds alike shunned and disclaimed. The Jacobites will not endure me, because I honour the memory of the Revolutionists. Whigs will detest me because I have a great liking for the Stuarts and their adherents and dread all these factions who would make a cypher of their sovereign, and crown King Hydra, whom I always thought a worse monster than fables have yet feigned, or fear conceived. Philosophers will regard me as a superstitious bigot, because all the powers and faculties of my soul repose with full confidence and joyful hope on

> " Father, Son, and Holy Ghost,
> The God whom heaven's triumphant host,
> And suffering saints on earth adore."

I quote the doxology to show that my faith is purely orthodox, and because I regard the sacred writings with admiring reverence, as the pure fountain and original prototype of all that is truly sublime and beautiful in composition, as well as of useful knowledge and sound morality. Devotees, again, will utterly renounce me. Piety, even when very sincere, has been lately driven by " the world and its dread laugh" to take shelter in tabernacles and conventicles, where spiritual pride is continually narrowing the limits of salvation, and within whose limits I could never confine myself.

It is among the lovers of truth and nature alone that I am to look for my partizans. Who that admires Mrs. Robinson or Miss Seward will ever tolerate me? I have read no modern authors, except in extracts that I have chanced upon here and there. But the only female writers of poetry that I can recollect at present, who have kept their garments unspotted, are Carter, Barbauld, and Williams. All the rest have sat too long at their toilette, and are so bedizened,— they nod such spangled plumes, and trail such pompous trains,—that, like every other artificial and superficial thing, they are only calculated for the fashion of the day—to please and dazzle for a moment: But of the two former, particularly, one might say,

> " The teeth of Time may gnaw Tantallon;
> But *they*'re for ever."

Miss Williams has since disfigured her style with the slang of party: But how elegant were her first productions! I am told the song,

> " Where Avon mingles with the Clyde,"

is hers. I should have been charmed though I had seen that only. Burns's Poems always excepted, I have seen no lyrical production of latter days that has power over my feelings.

Pray do not omit to tell me how far your feminine poetic taste agrees with mine; and how you like Darwin's Botanical Garden, of which I got a sight lately. They are really Hesperian gardens, glittering all over—the fruit gold, the leaves silver, and the stems brass.

It is odd how many people, without comparing opinions, should coincide in the same sentiment; but Mrs. Macintosh, Miss Dunbar, and Mrs. Furzer have all said to me just what you say about publishing Letters. The latter says, in her lively way, that she has herself of my letters what would make an interesting volume. Whatever I do, it will be always my fixed opinion that it is wrong and indelicate to publish correspondence in the author's lifetime; and even were I persuaded to do such a thing, my opinion would remain unaltered. Pope did it, indeed; but then he was head of a sect that looked up to him as infallible, —was a deep thinker, and wrote on literary subjects. I do not speak of his genius; for I do not think that greatly appears in his familiar letters: they are valuable for something that comes more generally home to the heart than genius itself. The only series of mine worth preserving were addressed to Charlotte. Written with all the ease of confidential intimacy, they were at the sametime meant to enlighten a strong and pure mind,—a mind whose early culture had been utterly neglected, and its very first principles warped by haughty illiberal prejudices, which it was my labour for years to obliterate. In those letters was all that my reflection and observation, and the reflection and observation of one who saw far quicker and far deeper, could suggest for the direction of a young person in circumstances delicate and difficult beyond example. *There* was the minute and faithful history of twelve years, during which very severe sufferings were blended with very superior enjoyments. Even now that I am drinking the bitter dregs of this salutary mixture, I gratefully acknowledge that its best ingredients are such as I hope to meet exalted and refined hereafter, and its worst, perhaps the easiest and safest mode of trial here.

This collection of letters, however, my girls, with extreme reluctance, committed to the flames, at the dying request of the person to whom they were addressed. She knew there was nothing in them that ought to have offended any human being; yet callous minds and restless curiosity might have found endless matter of speculation and conjecture, among figurative expressions, remote allusions, and fanciful flights quite out of the common way; so she summarily desired them to burn all the papers in her repositories. They did this, with great regret; and there remains nothing else, either connected or instructive. Though they did remain, we should still suspend the production of farther localities till we see the reception the public gives to those already submitted to its mercy.

Laing, whom I have read with great attention, and who has more plausibility and deeper research than any writer I have read on the subject, has not in the least shaken my Ossianic faith. If I were a man, which I always wish to be when I feel very angry and very helpless, I would soon apply Ithuriel's spear to his fair semblance. Indeed, his etymologies, in which the whole strength of his detections lie, fall to the ground with a touch, like a house of cards, as I shall hereafter prove to your conviction. I am going to abstract myself from all the weighty concerns of potatoes, flax, and children, to transcribe the Dissertation on Ossian's Poems, by which I shall live and die. Adieu, kindly,

A. G.

Letter LXIV.

Laggan, 10th September, 1802.

TO MY NEIGHBOUR STREAM.

Rude stream, that com'st dashing the wild rocks among,
And drown'st with thy clamours the pastoral song,
How oft thy hoarse tumults have softened my care,
When pining with anguish, or sunk in despair!

[*Here followed the remaining verses of the Lines to the Bronnach, printed in a previous Letter, page 186 of this Volume, and which are therefore omitted her*e.]

There, now, is simplicity its own self;—the first verse written long ago—the rest traced with a pencil on the burn side the week after you went away, when I was dying with despondency and headache. Dear burn;* how shall I ever leave it? I love its very ruggedness. Pray tell me honestly, not what merit this has, but how you like it;—nobody else has seen it but Isabella and Miss Dunbar. I thought to write fully to you; but since Isabella and your other friends here have been so voluminous, and my letter will not be intelligence, but merely advice, for which people generally wait very patiently, I will defer writing in folio till your grandfather leaves us, whom I expect to-night, which expectation agitates my mind too much to allow me recollection for writing as I intend. I wish with all my heart, as the greatest rarity that

* Burn, *Scotticé*, for brook; the one here alluded to after descending from the mountains, flowed past the Manse at Laggan.

could go from this aerial region, that I could send you the second sight, which I begin strongly to suspect myself of having from the many lively pictures I draw of you and the house of Protheroe, whom I esteem for their own sake, and like for yours. If you were but a gifted sorceress, you might see me at the dining-room window, before which poppies, pinks, and sweet-william flourish beyond all belief. You would see Donald More driving up hay, and John Peter and Moore both at present looking very well—she very soft, and he very spirited, waiting the return of the cart, and Isabella arranging flowers for the windows. The shepherd and the goatherd should appear in the background of the piece—the former grinning complacence, the latter pensively smiling,—and, to give an elegant finish to the whole, Betty, with the gentleness of a Madonna, telling them in soft accents that the *brose* is not only ready, but cold. A distant view of the dairy-maids descending like mountain nymphs from the Corry-buie, where the cattle have been these ten days, and bearing a libation of milk to my shrine, would complete the family group. Now when will you be so picturesque and so particular?

While I am drawing and describing, I will sketch the Marquis of Huntly and his group as they appeared on Monday. The Marquis, then, has lost the boyish look he retained so long, but appears more manly and decided. He has his mother's fine eyes, and, on the whole, is a genteel, spirited figure, with a countenance animated and penetrating; and so it ought, for he observes like our gillieroy,—nothing escapes him. Colonel D., who commands the heroes of the Black

Watch, and is therefore not a little interesting, has a face—I never saw such a face but once, and that was on the stage in the character of Bardolph—so fiery, so carbuncled ; they must have been Invincibles, indeed, that could have encountered such a portentous meteor. I was glad to find I was not the only person this face had astonished. The Marquis says, that the Prince of Wales asked the Colonel what his face cost him ?— The veteran coolly replied, he could not tell till it was finished. G——— of A. has nothing extraordinary about him, but that at twenty-five he is married, and has already five daughters. Sir John Gordon of Park, without being strikingly handsome, is one of the finest youths I have seen. Such an ingenious countenance, with so much nature and modesty in it, and frank withal.

I, too, have got Burns, and he has absolutely given a twitch to my heart-strings that I shall not get the better of for a while. I could write a folio on all my corresponding pangs, and will at more leisure give you my sentiments at length, with regard to that most extraordinary man ;

> " A beam ethereal, sullied, and absorpt ;
> Though sullied and dishonoured, still divine."

While reading over the glowing reflexion from his ardent mind, which his letters convey,

> " By turns I felt the answering mind,
> Disturbed, delighted, raised, refined."

Adieu to this copious theme. Farewell, dear Mary. Write soon to your affectionate mother,

A. G.

LETTER LXV.

TO GEORGE THOMSON, ESQ., EDINBURGH.

Dear Sir,   Laggan, September 15, 1802.

Your last letter found me in the very altitudes of rural occupation. What use have I not made of these fine days! I have been in the court every morning, seeing the sun rise; and at the river side every evening an hour after its setting. Potatoes rich in purple bloom, large as melons, and numerous as dew-drops, how shall I leave you! Lint, whose azure bells I meant this day to scatter;—mildly fragrant hay, on whose half-finished stack the labourers dance to tunes, how shall I forsake you! But, above all, sweet, smiling children, who move round me like obedient satellites, and exercise all your little ingenuity to attract me, how shall I frown repulsive, issue forth the cruel mandate that forbids playing before the window, and leave you only the sad alternative of imprisonment in the nursery, or banishment beyond the burn! Here, alas, must I sit immured, and instead of your animating gambols, see only opposed the poppies in the flower-pots, nodding their heavy heads with sympathetic dulness; or the convolvolus looking still bluer than myself, and emulous of my curiously involved periods; while carnations, whose endeavours at display seem checked by the ungenial clime and declining season, warn me against a public exhibition under similar disadvantages. Now you must have patience with this prelusive flourish, and consider it merely as a trial of the instrument which is just about to play a lesson of your own setting.

I confess that Ossian in the hands of his translators sometimes swells into tumidity; but then Ossian was mortal, and Homer is allowed sometimes to nod. I like the style and character of " Morduth," as a warlike poem, better than most of his warlike poems. Tell me how I have executed the version. There is a certain style of poetry adapted to a certain style of landscape, as well as to a particular turn of mind. The inhabitant of a level and cultivated country, who dwells amidst a smiling landscape, where all is regular and tranquil, supposing the principles of taste to exist in his mind, will find them modified by the scenes around him. His soul will be soothed and softened into the love of order and elegance. When brought to admire the rugged grandeur of solitary mountainous wilds, abrupt precipices, dashing torrents, expansive lakes, and echoing caverns, he will try to be pleased, and partly succeed. But the repulsive ruggedness, the cheerless gloom, the bleak aspect of desolation, will affect his regulated spirit and cultivated feelings, in a far different manner from what they would a native, possessing originally the very same principles of taste. To him the deep-toned blast that sweeps resistless down the mountains, sounds a welcome prelude to the storm that exalts while it agitates his mind. The dun solitude of the heathy waste, the steep acclivity of the pathless rock, and the darksome recesses of the narrow wooded glen, have to him peculiar attractions. He views them as scenes distinguished by the exploits,

and hallowed by the songs of his ancestors, the favourite haunts of the hunter, the hero, and the bard.   It
is needless to add, that each finds a strain of music
and poetry congenial to those feelings excited by his
situation, and endeared by his habits.

At different periods of my life, and under various
circumstances, I have been very differently affected
by the same objects.   I believe I might very early, in
some degree, affect the wonderful and wild; for I
liked thunder exceedingly, and one of the strongest
wishes I remember, when standing on the banks of
Lake Ontario, viewing the passage of innumerable wild
fowl to the upper lakes, was to mount on the wings of
a swan, to explore the depth of the luxuriant forests on
their banks.   When I came a few years after to Scotland, Ossian obtained a complete ascendancy over my
imagination to a much greater degree than ever he
has done since.   Thus determined to like the Highlands, a most unexpected occurrence carried me, in my
nineteenth year, to reside there, and that in Abertarffe,
the most beautiful place in it; yet it is not easy to say
how much I was repelled and disappointed.   In vain
I tried to raise my mind to the tone of sublimity.   The
rocky divisions that rose with so much majesty in
description seemed like enormous prison walls con-
fining caitiffs in the narrow glens; those, too, seemed
the dreary abodes of solitude and silence.   These feelings, however, I did not even whisper to the rushes,
but in the meanwhile was busied in all the little arts
of self-deception.   I made myself believe that I admired a bold projection of rock; but, on reflection,
discovered it was the fantastic tufts of flowers growing

out of the crevices that had attracted me. I tried to
think that a dark morass looked cheerful when the
summer sun shone on it, but I soon found that the
silken tufts of cannach waving in the gale, and the
groups of *rhoit* which perfumed it were the charms
that engaged my fancy. Thus I went on with more
industry than success trying to create a taste suitable
to my dwelling, like Satan, when he said, " Hail,
horrors, hail," &c.; but I could not with him add,
" one who brings a mind not to be changed by place
or time," as the sequel will show.

Four years after (in 1777), I went from the Highlands on a visit to my friends in the south, and
thought myself in duty bound to talk rapturously of
Alpine scenery, the only affectation with which I can
charge myself. Yet my heart did so warm to Stirlingshire, and my mind expanded in those Elysian fields,
where everything wore the aspect of tranquil cheerfulness. I discovered that, however my fancy might be
delighted with particular spots, the general aspect of
things within the girdle of the Grampians was not
congenial to me ; and then the wild mountaineers,
whose language I did not understand, and to whose
character, of consequence, I was a stranger! But, like
the potent Prince to whom I just now compared myself, I had nothing for it but to return to the place
from whence I came, where it was my fate to be
planted and naturalized. There my activity of mind
and love of knowledge were confined to very narrow limits indeed; but, like water whose channel is
impeded, they took a different course. Whatever
appeared to me a subject of laudable curiosity, I had

seized and appropriated. New objects, perfectly compatible with my new duties, appeared, and I pursued these with proportionate eagerness. The language, the customs, the peculiar tone of sentiment and manners of the people, the maxims, traditions, music, and poetry of the country I made my own with all possible expedition. I learnt them in the fields, the garden, and the nursery, in such a manner as rather to promote than interrupt my necessary avocations. And then I spoke of plants, from the fir on the top of Craigellachie to the house-leek on the cottage wall. What a scene did this open to me! What an interest did it create in a country walled in from the world; where the language, customs, and traditions have remained for so many ages unimproved and undepraved—the native region of heroic, musical, and poetical enthusiasm;

> "There was need to purge my visual orb,
> For I had much to see."

I felt like a gifted seer, from whose eyes the unseen powers had suddenly removed the veil of separation, while solemn visions of renowned heroes, departed bards, and the fair of other times pass in airy groups before him.

I am sure you are saying by this time that if I had much to see, you have had rather too much to hear. But stay a little. In 1793, I again went southwards, and began to look for the beautiful country I had formerly traversed with so much pleasure. It was gone; I saw nothing round me but tame flat nature, and formal frigid art. The people were such a set of new sprung, insulated beings, so uninteresting; and for the mobility,—bless them, they were so ungraceful

and ungracious, so devoid of all courtesy, and all sentiment; the worst of them were like bears, and the
very best like sheep at most. O how I did lift up my
joyful voice when, on my return to the Highlands,
I drew near the mountains of Perthshire; and at the
Pass of Killiecrankie I worshipped the genius of the
mountains with devotion the most ardent. This morning I mounted the height above the house,—beheld
the sun irradiate so many beautiful wreaths of mist,
slowly ascending the aerial mountains;—nay, more, I
had the whole parish in my view at once, and saw the
blue smokes of eighteen hamlets at once, slowly rising
through the calm, dewy air, every one of which hamlets had some circumstance about it that interested
me, or somebody in it that I knew or cared for. How
populous, how vital is the *strath!* And with what a
mixture of emotions did I behold it! And all this I
must leave, and something that I value more than all
this.

There is no saying where this current may carry
me; but, before I go quite out of sight, I shall methodically deduce the inference from all this. I have
never had so clear a view of the origin and progress
of taste, or of its distinct modifications in any other
mind, as its gradations and changes in my own have
afforded. The result of those changes is what I may
call a catholic taste. Notwithstanding my raillery
on my native Lowlands, these transitions have only
enlarged my capacity of being delighted, as I may
very truly style it. I can now repose among the softer
scenes of nature, taste the more gentle and elegant
beauties of art, and, with equal relish, " mount in the

rapid chariot of the soul" to the regions of sublimity, or sink as suddenly among the paper kites of levity, and pass through all poetical gradations, from the Paradise Lost of Milton to the fireside bagatelles of Swift, without missing pleasure or instruction.

Now, do not be angry with me for tiring you, and, in return, I will not be angry with you for being tired. Through what endless interruptions I must write! It was very judicious in the ancients to make Minerva a maiden lady; had she had as numerous and as noisy a family as mine, they would soon have teased her out of her wisdom. Over seven children and seven servants must I extend the sceptre of authority. I cannot describe the sudden palpitation that seized me when I heard you were all at Dunkeld; and Mrs. Brown, too, to come so near without coming nearer. To see me anywhere else than here, would be but seeing my ghost, and that a wandering discontented ghost. Send me a brief account of your travelling occurrences and opinions. You will see that my spirits are much better; but you little know what need I had of this lucid interval. I would not live over the last month for the Indies. Tell her whom I admire and pity most, that I enter into her present feelings, in a manner in which few others can. The departure of him whom she must ever lament, would make life insupportable, if he did indeed depart. But he must remain mingled with every idea; he is the companion of her solitude—the subject of her meditations—the vision of her slumbers. Long may you remain in happy ignorance. Adieu!

A. G.

Letter LXVI.

TO MISS DUNBAR, BOATH.

Laggan, October 5, 1802.

My dear Helen,

Your return from Aberdeenshire was matter of consolation to me on various accounts; my two great props, the " Book of Books," and Mary, being taken away at once, I fell into a relapse of despondency; the image, which must ever live in my heart, and dwell in my meditations, entirely engrossed me, to the exclusion or diminution of every other concern! I never sleep much; but, during this " double gloom of nature and of soul," I knew only the painful transition from deep dejection to severe anxiety; and, when exhausted by the labour of the mind, I sunk into a state that more resembled a heavy torpor than refreshing slumber. I waked with a sudden start before the dawn to horror inexpressible. Yet I never took more pains to soothe a sick infant, than I did to reason down the throbbings of unconquerable anguish. All the singular instances of the Divine goodness, which have shone upon me since I was left alone in the world, I have made to pass in review before me, and reproached myself for sinking while thus supported. Were you ever struck with an affecting instance of the true sublime in the Old Testament?* It is where Moses, encouraged, as it should seem, by being

* Exodus xxxiii. 18, 19.

P 2

admitted into so near communion with the Deity,
entreats that he would shine forth upon him in full
resplendence : " Lord, show me thy glory." " I will
make all my goodness to pass before thee." What an
answer! How condescending its beneficence—how
rich its meaning! How cold must be the heart that
does not make the suitable comment on this emphati-
cal definition of true glory.

Confess now that I am not in the habit either of
lamenting or preaching to you. " The heart knoweth
its own sorrows, and a stranger intermeddleth not
therewith." I do not mean to cloud the gayest
thoughts of gayest age, where there is so much reason to believe it an innocent and warrantable gaiety ;
and I know too much of the source from whence you
draw your instruction, to believe it in my power to
make any valuable addition to it. But, sometimes
the overcharged heart will seek in sympathy an alle-
viation, where there is no hope of cure. Your late
indisposition and depression will make all this intelli-
gible to you. I can assure you my concern and apprehension about Anne was one of my morbid terrors ;
and, through the gloomy medium in which I beheld
all objects of fear, you yourself—*you* were another of
my disturbers. Judge, then, whether I was glad when
I got your letter, and whether I was grateful when I
saw with what alacrity you went in search of Anne ;
and how determined you were to think the best of her.
I do not know whether I remarked to you before,
that I never knew a creature who enjoys, in a higher
degree than this daughter of mine, that " eternal
sunshine of the spotless mind," which Pope gives to

his vestals. She goes on rejoicing in her course all day, and every day; and this without animal spirits, —mere cheerfulness of heart. I am happy to hear your Aberdeenshire *jauntey*, as Burns calls it, has been so serviceable to you. You have been quite in high life in Aberdeenshire, where I should not like to have been with you; for early did I say,

" Vain pomp and glory of this world, I hate you."

But perhaps you will call this sour grapes. Not quite, neither; I love elegance in sentiment, in language, in manners, though I do not care for the externals and insignia of it, nor can I bear it at all when disjoined from simplicity. Artifice, spleen, vanity, and false refinement, are the demons by which the upper regions of life are haunted. Must I confess that grossness, vulgarity, and indelicacy puddle about like pigs and ducks in the lower world. We made a little world to ourselves here, where ease, simplicity, and a kind of negative elegance, gave an undefinable charm to our cottage. This made people of genuine feeling and uncultured taste like it, without being able to tell why. Sweet cottage! must I leave it? I will tell you, sometime or other, how our poppies and convolvolusses nod into the low windows, and how richly the woodbine clothes the porch, where we have so often sat together, contemplating a mild showery evening, that would let us go no farther. But what does this avail? I do not mean all this to detract from the merits of Miss Frazer's elegance, which, I doubt not, is regulated by her taste, as well as dignified by her virtues. Is Lord Lyttleton son or grandson to the virtuous and poetical nobleman of that title? The verses he left at Castle Frazer are sweetly turned.

I give you joy of having " the dark rider of the wave " for an inmate; he will make a frigate of the house, in which the BRAMIN will be midshipman, you first lieutenant, and your mother master and commander;* he will be an animating acquisition. I think, brothers are the only possessions I ever envied any one. For more than twenty years, the sense of this desideratum was effaced; but now I feel it more than ever. How rich are you in these enviable relations;—a mother that is sister and friend, as well as guide and monitress; and peace and leisure; and music and literature; and taste and health; and sense to set the just value on all these blessings; and sympathy to keep your feelings from hardening in prosperity. Look round now, and see if there is any other so happy. I leave you to the grateful contemplation of all these blessings. Adieu, Felicia! . . . .

I am sorry I mentioned Mr——'s eulogium of you; a consciousness of that kind is destructive of ease of intimacy, and it is agreeable to be on an easy footing with a rational man who expects nothing. Once more adieu,

A. G.

* Alluding to Miss Dunbar's brother, Captain D. of the Royal Navy, then on a visit to his home at Boath.

Letter LXVII.

TO MISS DUNBAR, BOATH.

Laggan, October 15, 1802.

Once more, my dear Helen, give me your pity and your prayers, and then farewell for a while; your dear mother, whom I love and revere unseen, will give me hers. I am just setting out for England; I will anticipate no evils, but ask the Divine aid to frame my mind to something between hope and resignation, while I leave this group of orphans, loving and beloved as they are, to attend the sick-bed of one, whom absence and calamity have made best and dearest in my eyes for the present.* I cannot now narrate; but her recovery from a slow nervous fever is so dubious and unlikely, that Mrs. Protheroe, obliged to leave home by an urgent call of similar distress, wishes, before she sets out, to have one of Mary's relations from Scotland to attend her. I am the fittest to undertake this task; my anxiety would be doubled if either of her sisters went alone in stage-coaches at this season. Isabella is too timid and too delicate, and Catherine has an arduous charge of various concerns, and feels too strongly to act properly among strangers in such a trying emergency. I got your letter last

---

* The Author's eldest daughter, Mary, who had been for some months resident in the family of Mr. E. Protheroe, M.P. for Bristol, was seized with an alarming illness at this time, which induced her mother to go to England to attend her.

night; it would give me pleasure if anything could; but my chief comfort just now is to recollect promises of Divine consolation and support from Him who will not afflict above measure.

> " With the Patriarch's trust,
> Thy call I follow to a land unknown."

This passage of Young runs in my head like the prevalent idea in a delirium. I should bewilder you as well as myself by leading you into the howling wilderness through which my mind wanders. Only this, let not poor Anne* know of the impending cloud, or my departure. I am glad you and dear Mr. Mackay like her so well. Hers is the milder merit of the heart; but such a spotless heart, and a temper so unclouded. In the depth of despondency I sometimes lay hold of a ludicrous idea to play with; such is that of your house being turned to a frigate. Do not mistake me; I know your brother is no *mer-man*. Nautical skill, as a man of science, and the resolute manliness of his profession, are, in his case, I am told, blended with easy manners and an improved mind.

No longer whimsical or sportive, behold me a suppliant for a life dearer than my own, and shivering with fearful expectation. Adieu. May every blessing attend you.

A. G.

* Then attending school at Nairn, near Boath.

Letter LXVIII.

TO MISS DUNBAR, BOATH.

Glasgow, Nov. 7, 1802.

My dear kind Helen,

Worn, as I am, by the pressure of many sorrows; divided, as I am, between necessary occupation and many visits of sympathy which I receive; can I go to England, and remain for a time in dread suspense so far from you, without bidding you farewell—without expressing my gratitude for all your kindness to Anne, so amply detailed, and so warmly commented on, by that paragon of grateful damsels? I hope this will find you in some degree recovered from the indisposition she lamented so much. Perhaps the time may arrive, after all these clouds are overblown, when I may, from the occurrences of my journey, and short stay in Edinburgh, furnish out an amusing detail; but now "chaos is come again," at least in my brain.

Since writing the above, I have witnessed a very impressive scene; it was the departure of a young lady* who resided in my father's house for sometime past. Her father had been Chaplain to a settlement abroad, and left her in easier circumstances than generally happens to the children of Levi. She only meant to stay a few weeks at my father's, on her way to the north, where her friends live. There she was arrested by sickness, her lungs being in a decayed state before;

* Miss Kennedy.

and there she has been since June last, lingering a
life that might well be called a protracted death;
Catherine, in the meantime, doing all in the power
of compassionate attention to alleviate her sufferings.
At Edinburgh I heard that Mary was so much better
that I needed not proceed. I gave up my intention,
yet thought, as I was so near, I would see my parents,
and arrange my Stirlingshire establishment.* I wrote
to Mary, that if she felt a wish for my coming, here
I was, and there I would go. Now, while I sat in
security, and, moreover, heard from Mrs. Protheroe
that she was walking out, I began to breathe a little;
when another letter informed me that her frequent
relapses, and the danger of her lungs, made it necessary for her to remove to the Hot Wells, near Bristol,
unless she soon grew better. The agony it cost me to
relinquish my intention of returning to the dear family
I have left, is unspeakable; but it must be. I should
have gone yesterday, but could not forsake this poor
dying girl. Last night she expired, and O how forlorn and friendless! No creature to bestow a tear on
her departure but ourselves. Why do I enlarge thus,
or who can understand the state of my mind? Yet
let me, in this wounding exigency, do justice to the
unwearied kindness, the tender sympathy I receive.
Who ever needed, who ever met with so much? All
this is incoherence, but we must lay our account to
suffer as well as enjoy with our friends; it is a proud
pre-eminence, and worth buying at a high price, to
be a friend. I entreat your worthy mother's prayers;

* The Author had made arrangements for removing, in the en-
suing year, from Laggan to the neighbourhood of Stirling.

I know how you will mourn over the dear children I leave behind. Adieu, my dear Helen. I will write to you when I am more at ease. Peace be with you!

A. G.

LETTER LXIX.

TO MRS. FURZER, PLYMPTON, DEVONSHIRE.

Bristol, Hot-well House,
December 14, 1802.

My dear Friend,

I can hardly reproach myself for a delay which elicited from you such a proof of warm, unchanged affection. How gratifying are these lively marks of kindness, when the heart, stripped of its wonted shelter, languishes in a strange land, chilled and forlorn. I have now the comfort to acquaint you, that the benefit Mary receives from these waters is beyond my hopes, so that her recovery seems nearly completed. This is wonderful, for there was so great an inflammation on her chest, that the doctor says, were it not that she has a most excellent constitution, he should have entertained little hopes of her. I was treated with all possible kindness where I was, and owe more than I can express for sympathy and attention. Yet it is a great relief, in my present state of life, to be here at liberty. Without the uneasy sensation of disturbing the quiet, and poisoning the comfort of those who are deservedly happy, I would wish my comforts to be shared as much as possible with my friends; but my sorrows and anxieties I would keep as much as possible to myself.

This, sure enough, is a beautiful, dismal place; but though the mind were not, like mine, overloaded, I wonder how people can taste pleasure where death haunts you in so many forms, that you seem to have entered his vestibule. The number of the young and prosperous that appear drooping like faded flowers about these "sacred springs!" And then to see the vapid, futile phantoms, in the form of nervous, splenetic, and hectic women of fashion, settling their card parties, and talking over their winnings, at the very pump, and in the very presence of the poor wretches for whom the grave is visibly opening! I cannot tell you how I am shocked at these incursions, that vanity is hourly making into the precincts of mortality. The crowds who elicit gaiety from each other, have the opposite effect on me. Accustomed to walk complacently round the narrow circle of those whom I knew and loved, I am not cheered or amused by the crowd here. It only impresses more forcibly on my mind how many are here that regard me with indifference or contempt, and how great the change. I am so cheered when our kind friends from Bristol come to ask for us! but that cannot be often. I have, however, the very best accounts of the little flock at home, and hear my deputy-matron, Isabella, does wonders. When a burden is laid on such young shoulders, there are generally great complaints; but my young heroine conquers difficulties with all imaginable ease; indeed, she commands tried and faithful forces; for, as everything I have, you know, must needs be extraordinary, no one has such faithful and attached servants. Of this I have had many proofs ; and in the depths of my calamity, it was a consolation to me to see, that the kindness of a most indulgent master had produced so much gratitude. I love to find these soft features of human nature where one least expects them. Yet why not expect them ? if these people are uncultured on the one hand, they are unspoiled on the other.

My health begins to yield to the pressure of intense anxiety. I cannot, must not stay an hour after my patient is able to move ; but, before she takes a long journey to a northern climate, I will endeavour to carry her, for a single week, to see your retreat. Your gay painting of summer scenery must not tempt me ; matters of the utmost moment depend on my reaching home by April. . . . . You shall have proof sheets of my poetical volume to exercise your criticism ; they have been transmitted to me, and give me the idea of a scaffold I am about to mount. But we shall discuss abundance of topics, literary and domestic, when we reach your Arcadia. Send me a bill of health in the meantime, and accept of your pupil's affectionate regards, and the tender affection of

A. G.

Letter LXX.

TO GEORGE THOMSON, ESQ., EDINBURGH.

Bristol Hot Wells, December 20, 1802.

Dear Sir,

If you do print the Dissertation on Ossian, pray

soften everything that might irritate or give needless pain. Yet I do not know,—truth supports itself in the long run. The noble plant rises, while the choking weeds decay. I would not willingly give pain to any human being, unless there was some good purpose to be answered by it. I know the enemies of the good *new* old cause will think I have said too much in James Macpherson's favour; and his few personal friends will wonder at my confidence, living poor, as I do, to diminish in the smallest degree the consequence of a man who died rich. They little comprehend how small value I set on this extraneous part of his character, or how very little of the grace of humility I derive from the defect in mine, which, in their view, should awe me into silence. At present I cannot afford to be humble; but if ever my wings are wet by a fertilizing shower, you will find my nest in the furrow.

Every man, if not the artificer of his own fortune, is, at any rate, much the artificer of his fame. Had James shown as much candour and justice to himself as I have done to his character, this last would not have lain under the reflections which are now become so general, and believed as just. I am not afraid of poor and stingless resentment; and will do all the justice to his memory that truth allows, in spite of the ignorant prejudice which will, I doubt not. regard this offering to the shade of departed genius with thankless malignity. I have said my say, and closed my evidence; further I shall never by any provocation be led. My feet are much too tender to tread the thorny paths of controversy. I feel elastic and thankful as the period draws near when we shall

all shelter in that blessed asylum, Woodend. This, to be sure, is a very beautiful though very dear place. Mary, for whom the waters have really done wonders, walks about in a fine mall and crescent, just below our window, with some very agreeable Irish acquaintances. Feeling myself to be unpleasant, I keep very free of *pleasant* people, merely such. I sit here, like an owl in a turret, contemplating the scene I have no desire to mix in. Sometimes I go for a short time down to the pump-room, but oftener to the woody rocks that rise above our dwelling, to see Mr. Protheroe's ships sail by; or to catch, with complacence, the cold blast from Caledonia, and think I see it waving the amber locks of my dear boy, or bending the trees, planted by his still dearer father round our once happy dwelling.

Do not you be concerned about people's imputing exaggeration to me, with regard to the Utopian scenes and Arcadian virtues of my Alpine regions. What would you have? You know I have always represented the country as wild and barren to the last degree, and the inhabitants living in a state of great poverty and hardship. When I describe particular glens and sylvan scenes as possessed of wild and singular beauties,—when I impute to the natives tenderness of sentiment, ardour of genius, and gentleness of manners beyond their equals in other countries,— every one that knows anything of them must know that these have always characterized them. I am not afraid of being laughed at: ridicule is not in this, nor in many other cases, the test of truth. In a word, I expect, but do not dread ridicule on this head.

Adieu. I wish sometimes that the Book were in the well; and when I am in better humour I feel disposed to put the well in the book, in return for the benefits I have derived from it. Suppose I should begin—

> O fount benign! in which I fain would drown
> My sad reflections, and this new half-crown.

Or,

> Why, greedy stream, dost thou, with whirlpool's power,
> My purse, and peace, and poetry devour?

This you will call. low and prosaic. No such thing. Do not you see the figure by which the well swallows my poetry, which stands for the profits of my book, and the alliteration in the last verse? Pray, now, " let desert mount," and put this into the volume.

I feel a little like poor Parson Evans, who sung because he was full of melancholy. But of this no more. I spend all my sorrow where I spend much of my time,—among the tombs. And surely nowhere are tombs so eloquent as here, when so much intellectual light has been extinguished, and so many of the fairest human flowers withered in their prime. Death is everywhere a glutton, but here an epicure. Once more, adieu.

A. G.

Letter LXXI.

TO MISS DUNBAR, BOATH.

My dear Helen,   Bristol Hot Wells, January 20, 1803.

I am sure that distance, and sorrow, and care have

not extinguished that ardour of benevolence, which
was formerly rather excited and heightened by the
causes that generally freeze the friendships of the
world. I feel myself already in danger of moralizing
and speculating. If once I wander into digression,
farewell to order, connexion, and information; and to
you, of all others, I am most apt to digress. Now for
a succinct, dry narrative. Very dry indeed it will
prove; for, from the harassed state of my mind, looking back only to grief, and forward to terror, I heard
things without listening to them, and saw them without looking at them. First, now, behold me in the
streets of Glasgow, preparing to enter the mail-coach,
which was occupied by two gentlemen, one well dressed, well bred, and rather youthful-looking, whose countenance bespoke good humour and intelligence; and
much veracity of countenance he had, as shall appear
in the sequel. The other,—how shall I describe him?
for he was all chagrin at the time, and looking his
very worst; but, through his neglected, heavy figure,
and harsh, sun-burnt countenance, some gleams of the
gentleman broke dimly forth; yet I really shrunk
from him, and thought of Sterne's Smelfungus. He
was sick, and he was splenetic; and he did nothing
but growl and murmur, and tell his grievances, all the
way to Hamilton. But, though he was surly, he was
not vulgar; his language was that of a manly and enlightened mind, through which gleams of feeling and
gentleness broke forth unconsciously. In short, by
the time we reached Moffat, I thought him like the
ghost of Matthew Bramble. Mr. Macintosh, our fellow-
traveller, softened him and amused me. Mr. M. was

intelligent, gay, facetious, and accommodating; he had been, a few days before, at Dr. M.'s, whom he seemed to know intimately. He is a native of Inverness-shire, and had already been in both the West and East Indies: Laggan was familiar to him, but I could not make him out. At Moffat Mr. M. went off, proceeding to London, but I took the west road, in company with my new friend, who, by this time, saw my distressing anxiety, and appeared to take considerable interest in me; I saved a hundred miles by this course. I had a letter to a lady in Carlisle, where I should have stayed a night. Unable, in the ferment of my mind, to sleep, and unwilling to lose my fellow-traveller, whom I began to look up to with a kind of respect, I proceeded without sleeping; for, in a carriage, I never can. That day we could neither get a mail-coach, nor a partner in a post-chaise, so we took places in a right miscellaneous voiture, emphatically called the long coach, and very long indeed we thought the time we were in it: I never felt such degradation, or witnessed such depravity and grossness. My new friend was indignant, and disgusted beyond measure, and protested against any such association for the future; so, after vainly searching the good town of Lancaster for an associate, we took a post-chaise to Liverpool, being now perfectly known to each other through mutual acquaintances. His name is Allardyce; he is sovereign, I presume, of some little *grenadilloe* in the West Indies, and is married to a lady whose connexions I know, and with whom he appears to be very happy. He delighted in speaking of his children, to which, you may believe, Desdemona did seriously incline, for I like those domestic traits, and he seems a fond parent indeed. We had many wise discussions on education, and much nursery discourse, &c. Besides, I, who love to know a little of every-thing, know more now of West India matters than ever I thought to have done. This " fair discourse " brought us to Liverpool. There I found no rest for the sole of my foot, for my anxiety about Mary " had murdered sleep."

You wonder I give you no account of the places I went through ; I really cannot, we passed so rapidly. Only this, I did not like the face of either Cumber-land or Lancashire. They were flat, bleak, unvaried ; having neither the romantic variety of dear Scotland, nor the mild features and rich culture which I expect-ed, and afterwards met with in England. Indeed the season, and my mind were so gloomy, that I should scarcely have done justice to Elysian prospects, and, I dare say, I did great injustice to Liverpool, which, I am sure, is a fine town, could I but think so ; but my eyes, half closed, could not admit its symmetry, or contemplate its regularity. I was disappointed in their farm-houses too ; for it is in that scene of life, and not among fine people, or wealthy citizens, that I look for discriminating lines of character, to be traced in their habits and form of life. But, O, these are gross and unrural !—brick farm-houses, built on the very edge of the road, as if to stare at the excluded traveller ; offices at the very end, without a rural court, or any form denoting taste or social order. They have, in-deed, little gardens in front, but they are such confined, formal, suburban-like things, that they banish the idea of rustic simplicity, nay, even of rural ease. Every place, too, is covered with tiles, which are my antipathy. My own dear cottage, with its mossy thatch, its woodbine porch, its green court surrounded by shrubs, and its outer court of offices, the image of comfort and regularity, came sadly sweet to my recollection, like joys departed never to return. I heard, in idea, the roar of my mountain-streams, and the blasts from the hills of my fathers, while England faded from my view. I meant to tell you what I saw, and I find myself vainly trying to describe what I felt. Well, but I meant to say, the formal windmills, and sluggish clay-coloured waters made me recollect, with painful pleasure, the pure streams that poured, like melted crystal, from our Alpine hills; and the romantic recesses and sweet waterfalls, where our Highland peasants grind their scanty crop. What pleased me most, was the distinguished beauty of the Lancastrian women, not void of the more attractive charms of grace and softness; for they have, for the most part, good figures; and, with them, fine dark eyes are often united with a soft complexion; clear pale, which, you must have observed, do not often meet elsewhere. I was absolutely dazzled, I do not know how, when I saw so much beauty set off with so much elegance; for every one is well dressed; and this descends to the lower classes.

I am sure you are very tired, and will not object to my going a while to dream of the fair Lancastrians, before I proceed. I never had so much writing leisure since I was a girl, and I fly to it, as a refuge from " the pains and penalties of idleness;" and those eating cares that follow where we fly, banish sleep, and

embitter reflection. Good night. I shall resume the
account of my journey to-morrow.

A. G.

Letter LXXII.

TO MISS DUNBAR, BOATH.

Hot-well House, Bristol,
January 21, 1803.

My dear Helen,

Now, I come to reclaim your attention to my sorrowful pilgrimage. I do not much like the English
towns; the streets are narrow, and, except those of
Liverpool, they have all an unsocial look, that I
cannot tell how to describe. I should not include
Lancaster; it is more cheerful, built of stone, and
derives an air of dignity from its Castle, which, somehow, brings back very forcibly to the imagination the
red roses and holy Henry, and

" Anjou's heroine, and the paler rose,
The rival of her crown, and author of her woes."

I have not terms of art to describe the Castle; but it
is in a style of architecture which pleases me very
much, and I have just negative skill enough to be
sure it is neither Grecian nor Gothic. From Liverpool I set out about eight in the evening, most reso-
lutely, but avoided the long coach. In the short
coach, however, I found one gentleman, the top being
loaded with drunken sailors; my companion was a
Scot, and the son of a clergyman. In the morning
we breakfasted at the very pretty town of Litchfield,

which appeared to me haunted by the ghosts of Johnson and Darwin, whom I could not get out of my head while I staid there. I saw a fine old cathedral, beautiful gardens, and, for the first time, clear streams, which Narcissus himself could not view with greater pleasure. Through what an enchanting scene did I pass afterwards; it was a part of Staffordshire, where I found precisely the compact image of plenty, content, and simplicity, that I wished to see in the farm-houses. Charming varieties of rising grounds, luxuriant vales, solemn shades, and winding streams. Then such noble seats; such rich overhanging woods, dressed in every mellow tint, from dusky red to the palest yellow; such a soothing air of tranquillity and comfort; and, above all, such visible possibilities of human happiness. I had no idea that mere landscape could have such an effect on a mind so worn with grief and anxiety. But the matchless beauty of this landscape was animated by cheerful countenances of peasants going to their early labour, and brightened by the first rays of a mild autumnal sun. O, how I enjoyed the drowsiness of my fellow-travellers, which left me at leisure to be delighted.

At this rate, my paper will be filled before I reach Bristol. Suffice it, then, that I arrived before dinner at the shocking, disagreeable, town of Birmingham, where I languished in restless impatience all the afternoon, and imagined I saw everybody and thing about me looking cold, selfish, and venal. In the morning I set out by three o'clock, in another long coach, in which, luckily, were only two ladies, mother and daughter. During some conversation about our arrangements in the coach, I happened to use a Scottish phrase (*better do.*) " O how that phrase delights me," said the youngest; "it reminds me of dear Scotland." This was touching an accordant string, and very great we grew immediately; for it appeared these ladies, who reside in a village near Bath, had been on a pilgrimage of love to visit their relations, who are some of the most respectable people in the west of Scotland, and were now on their return. The old lady was a native of Scotland, and the young one fond of it to enthusiasm.* This day, too, we passed through a fine country; saw the bloody field of Bosworth, and passed by Tewksbury, where the Usurper's corpse was carried. It is a fine old town, with houses in it, the most curious, antique fabrics imaginable: I dare say king-making Warwick, and old Nevill, were in some of them. They were in a style of architecture different from anything I had ever seen or imagined. The church is a stately edifice; the whole end of which is formed into a most noble window, that has a striking effect. We passed through Gloucester, large and populous, full of antique towers and spires, and surrounded by a very rich and beautiful country. The latter is picturesque, with frequent farm-houses, in the true old English style, and shady with orchards. There the country people were not bedizened, nor modernized, but had just the rusticity that I like in their buildings and appearance. In the evening we

---

* Mrs. Simson of Keynsham, near Bath, and her daughter, Miss S., afterwards Mrs. Conway of Chantry-Netherbury, Beaminster, Dorsetshire, are the ladies referred to. They became afterwards esteemed friends of the Author.—*See* Letter of 12th March, 1803.

reached the full majestic Severn, which is really a
noble-looking river. Then were my eyes regaled with
a distant view of the Welsh mountains, and my ears
with the sound of Bristol bells; these latter were to
me like a knell, and my terrors increased every moment as I drew nearer. My new friends were all
kindness and sympathy, and procured a chaise to carry
me to Park Row at eleven, where I entered the door
trembling, and was glad to find, by the stir through
the house, that there was nothing funereal about it.
I found my patient on a sofa, with her kind friends
about her. Worthy people, what do I not owe them !
There is no doing justice to their merit and kindness.
In two days she had an alarming relapse, occasioned
by inflammation in the breast, for which the doctor
ordered her to resort to the Wells, as soon as she
could be moved with safety. It was a month, however, before this was thought proper.

We are now settled in very pleasant and convenient
lodgings at the Hot-well House, which I would describe to you, if you were not already surfeited with
description. Now, thank God, I think I can, from
our experience, recommend the Hot Wells to every
one threatened with a similar affection : and I am
convinced the reason they are not generally effectual is,
that people defer too long coming to them. We have
lived a month here in more profound retirement than
ever we did in Laggan, not knowing any one in this
quarter, except the Protheroes, in their various branches,
who are, indeed, invariably kind. Yet, amidst all this
melancholy leisure, my mind has been so engrossed by
intense anxiety for the absent, and reflections on the

past, and melancholy anticipations of the future, that, except mere bills of health and necessary business, I have written to no creature but yourself. Now I hope you will have the grace to set a due value on this proud pre-eminence.

One very stormy night lately, I could not close my eyes, nor yet read; so I had recourse to my pencil for relief to my overburdened mind, and here is the result of this vigil of sorrow, at least as much of it as I can transmit in a letter.

Yes, to my soul, those northern winds are dear,
That howling blast is music to my ear.
Blast, whose swift wing has swept our Alpine snows,
The rocks of Morven, and the hill of roes,
Say, hast thou wak'd my wild harp's mournful strings,
Bear'st thou the voice of sorrow on thy wings?
Or hast thou rush'd along the sacred shade,
Where those my heart must ever weep, are laid?
From my dear native land begun thy flight—
Bring tidings to my soul, O blast of night!
When shall I view again my narrow vale,
And hear a voice in every whispering gale?
See spring's first violets deck the hallow'd ground,
And trace my children's fairy footsteps round?
Then, in a tender trance of anguish'd joy,
To my fond bosom shall I clasp my boy,
View the soft radiance of his full blue eyes,
Warm the fresh roses on his cheek with sighs,
And, while his curls of waving amber flow
With varying lustre o'er his neck of snow,
The dawn of manly beauty let me trace,
The smile benignant of his father's face;
While hope, auspicious, points her wand of gold,
Where future days the latent bud unfold,
And bid hereditary virtues bloom,
To deck with kindred sweets a father's tomb!

Such are my meditations, and such my hopes.

Now to tell you what I mean to do. I cannot remove Mary till the milder months arrive. Next week I go to Bristol, to dear, good Mrs. Protheroe; the fol-

lowing one down to Devonshire, to take my last farewell of my dearest friend, Mrs. Furzer, whom it is
scarcely possible I shall ever see again. Perhaps this
is not coldly and precisely prudent; but I have no
notion of friendship that merely exhales in breath, or
flourishes on paper. Cromwell's saints got at last above
ordinances; and I have long since got above indul-
gences. Ease, and what the world calls pleasure, I
despise; I have no sacrifices to make to luxury or
vanity; but a gratification so dear to my heart, so
necessary to my peace of mind, I cannot, will not deny
myself. I know there are those that will wonder at
me, to say no more, for this single indulgence, self-de-
voted as I have ever been to the advantage and satisfaction of others. Yet it were hard to grudge this
cordial drop in the cup of bitterness appointed for
me. . . . . I heard once of you through Bar,
who, I hope, is, like a good friendly hen, spreading
her wings over my chickens in my absence. I get
heroic epistles from my young housekeeper too, whose
spirit seems to have risen to the occasion. I never
feared her doing anything wrong; yet, when I think
of her diffidence and inexperience, I am agreeably
surprised to find her so constantly and decidedly right.
Remember me in a manner at once affectionate and
respectful to your mother; and tell your brother how
much I was flattered by his kindness to Anne. I am
very warmly and truly yours,

A. G.

Letter LXXIII.

TO MRS. FURZER, PLYMPTON, DEVONSHIRE.

Bristol Hot Wells,
February 13, 1803.

My dear Friend,

I have deferred writing to you till I should take my resolution about my future measures, that I might have something decisive to inform you of. Now, my dearest, kindest friend, do not be in the least disturbed or fluttered at a sudden and, alas, short visit which I am about to make you. There is a gentleman at Bath, an old friend of ours, lately arrived from Grenada, and confined in that city since his return by bad health ; he has urged us to return to Scotland with him, which will be a measure accommodating to both parties. I am alarmed with an account of my father's being seriously ill, and ought, on that account, to set out immediately ; but Mary, though quit of inflammatory symptoms and looking very well, still grows feverish when agitated by much exertion, and so long a journey will as yet be rather too much for her. In the beginning of the week, however, we propose setting out on a visit to you of a week at most, when you must·be as firm as an oak, and not by any means melt or agitate me ; for the consequence will be, as it always is on such occasions, a nervous headache of no short continuance. We do not meet as people to part for the last time. It is to little purpose that we have gone through the furnace of affliction, if we have not learned to look to a better hope, and the belief that we shall know our friends in a happier state. But this and many other things shall be the topics of future discussion. May the Almighty bless our meeting, and grant that it may prove a source of comfort and improvement to us both, prays your most faithful and affectionate friend,

ANNE GRANT.

Wednesday or Thursday, I hope to clasp you once more in my arms. A. G.

LETTER LXXIV.

TO MRS. FURZER, PLYMPTON, DEVONSHIRE.

Keynsham, near Bath,
March 12, 1803.

My dear Friend,

As I suppose Mary has given you an account of our journey since parting with you at Plympton, it is needless for me to go over that ground. I have not been .very well since I came up, and it recruits me and calms my spirits to pass these three days with this truly amiable family.* They are people possessing a degree of refinement and delicacy, a good breeding, and sentiment not often found in higher stations, with the purest morals and warmest piety. We have been more obliged to them than I can express. I shall leave them with regret.

---

* The family of Mr. and Mrs. Simson, before alluded to as the Author's fellow-travellers to Bristol.

Though trembling at the task which I have undertaken, I feel like a soul released from purgatory. What a dreadful winter I have gone through! Yet how thankful I am, and ever shall be, that I have once more embraced you; that I have renewed, and, I hope, strengthened, that affection which will last while any earthly tie remains. How we do lament your dwelling among those who are unfitted to appreciate or comprehend you! But you have many little comforts; and that superior comfort of looking back to a well-spent life, and forward to the peace which passeth understanding.

Now, my dearest friend, in what words shall I acknowledge your active, cordial, considerate kindness! How it has supported my spirit, I cannot express. Pray tell Mrs. Cholwich I shall always remember her, not with gratitude only, but pleasure. I am charmed to think so much goodness has opened to itself such a source of innocent and laudable enjoyment, to soothe the evening of life. Adieu!

A. G.

LETTER LXXV.

TO MISS DUNBAR, BOATH.

Laggan, April 11, 1803.

My ever dear Helen,

You surely have not received my letter from Bath, that was sent thence by Mr. Guthrie, and which inclosed one for our mutual friend, Mr. Mackay; for if you are the same unaltered and unalterable Helen, you would not let me blear my dim eyes, and wear out my grey goose quill with pompous narration, and veritable description, without once saying, "thanks, gentle Anne." But you never would make this acknowledgment. I must, in compliance with the entreaties of your great and grateful admirer, Anne, thank you for numberless favours conferred on her, while near you at Nairn, which are her nightly dream, and daily conversation.—Thus far I had written when your letter appeared, and my doubts vanished.

I am happy that, in the irksome gloom of my late exile, I had it in my power, by a faithful though brief transcript of what occurred to me during my too rapid journey, to afford you any degree of amusement. I am now literally "weary worn with care," and a hundred objects press at once upon my attention; but when I can breathe at leisure, I shall tell you a few more tidings. Yet how painful it is to me to retrace the steps of that sad pilgrimage, where too much leisure for my present state of mind, made all that ever I lamented recur so forcibly to my sick imagination, bereft as I was of my comforter and support. Let me quote myself:

I had sigh'd o'er the bud, I had wept o'er the blossom,
   And beauty full blown I have liv'd to deplore;
But the voice that was wont, to speak peace to my bosom
   Shall whisper compassion's soft language no more.

No more shall the bosom, when heaving with anguish,
   In the kind breast of sympathy seek for relief;
While helpless I wander, or hopeless I languish,
   Ah! cold is the heart that would share all my grief.

Except Mr. Protheroe's family, whom I can never think of, or mention without esteem or gratitude, our correspondence with the living inhabitants of Bristol

was very small indeed; but I could give some tidings
from the dead, among whom I spent much time.—

> "The great, the gay, the noble, and the sage,
> And boastful youth, and narrative old age,"

are to be found there, from all parts of the kingdom.
The most distinguished people come there to die; and
the whole Cathedral at Bristol, and church at Clif-
ton, are hung with marble tablets, with ingenious and
affecting inscriptions: two only I will particularize.
Mason to his Maria:

> "Take, holy earth, all that my soul held dear," &c.

The other, a large tablet of exquisite white marble, in
the form of a shield, with figures in low relief, admir-
ably designed and finished. Surely you have seen
Sterne's Letters to Eliza; if not, do, without delay,
read them; it is her monument I am describing. The
inscription is simply this:

> "Sacred to the memory of ELIZABETH DRAPER,
> Wife to GENERAL DRAPER,
> Who died at Bristol in the 28th year of her age.
> She was eminent for Genius and Benevolence."

There is an urn, with a drapery hanging in such loose,
easy folds over it, that you are tempted to lift it up.
On one side is a female figure of matchless grace and
elegance, " her looks commercing with the skies;"
she leans pensively on the urn with one hand, and
holds a flaming torch in the other. This represents
Genius. On the other side is a figure of a less dignified air, but, "soft, modest, melancholy, female, fair,"
who seems to look compassionately into a nest of
young birds, which she holds in one hand and feeds

with the other. This is Benevolence. Beyond these, on one side, a broken column denotes the fragility of the most perfect human forms, which moulder and decay like the noblest productions of human art and ingenuity ; on the other, a palm, the emblem of immortality, appears like the undying spirit. But I must not indulge this descriptive mood, to which my journey northward would give full scope, had I leisure. Yet fain would I describe Devonshire, the English Arcadia; its pure streams, its pastoral hills, its rich vales, and softly genial climate ; that, indeed, is the region of picturesque beauty. There I went to meet the spring, for there " she first unfolds her mantle of green." There, with a dear friend, Mary and I spent part of an April-like March, in the enjoyment of a felicity that I did not hope to taste during my earthly pilgrimage. Fain would I give you a faint idea of the undiminished excellence, the unwithering spirits, and unchilled affections of her

> " Who heard with pain my parting sighs,
>   And long pursued me with her eyes;"

In short, of my own self-same Anne Ourry, now Mrs. Furzer. But a theme that wakes all the powers of imagination and memory, and makes the heart and eyes overflow at once, deserves, and shall have a letter to itself.—The *book of books* has been delayed to my great vexation ; for I believe, had it come in time, it might have obtained some notice in England, where Burns's mighty, overpowering genius has swept down the mounds of prejudice in its impetuous progress ; nay, it has absolutely made way for a partiality for Scotch productions. This merit may, no doubt, be

divided with Campbell, who is, indeed, forte-piano in
a very superior degree. My impression, however,
thanks to the active zeal of my friends, is the largest
ever printed in Scotland; but the same printer has
the Court of Session Reports (formidable rivals indeed), to print all winter. They were busy with my
beloved old Bard when I came away, and had only
the subscribers' names (to me, and many others, the
most interesting part) to finish. I know, by the
mental pangs I have suffered for some days past,
that the book is born, and you may expect to hear
it some day squalling at your door. But, alas, those
rough nurses, the critics, whose hands do not spare,
nor their eyes pity! Bitterness may be borne,

> " But what high heart could ever yet sustain
> The public blast of insolence and scorn?"

And who believes or cares for that want of leisure, and
numberless other wants which you know of, among
which I wish, for the sake of my repose, want of feeling could be included in the present instance? The
Edinburgh Review is (woe is me!) a work of ability,
from which there lies no appeal. Those young cen-
sors, however, seem to have studied Shakspeare well;
and to be emulous of the character of Cesario, of
whom Olivia says,

> " O what a deal of scorn looks beautiful,
> In the contempt and anger of his lip!"

They seem to expect the public will regard their *beautiful scorn* with the same partiality. For my part, I
am rather inclined, like Orsino, to dread what they
may prove, " When time has sowed a grizzle on their
case ;" as they are already so apt to be scornful.

I met two very agreeable women at Mr. Thomson's, one of whom is a sister of Mr. Mackay's futura ; I like her much. Of your friend's choice, I can only say that I heard Mary speak highly of her, who knows her very well. Shut out, as she must be, in some measure, from the vain and busy world, by the peculiar nature of her duties, what a delicate and superior happiness must hers be, to whom is allotted the charge, so like that of a guardian angel, to preside, invisible to him, over the comforts and enjoyments of one of the worthiest and most amiable of mankind, still more beloved as he is more dependent !

Why have I not left room to tell you, how sweetly rural and sequestered I found my future dwelling at Woodend,* or of the transport that filled the dear family, both native and adopted, when I arrived at home ? The dear creatures are all improved. Isabella has done wonders, and my poor servants, too, worthy creatures, it would be ungrateful not to record their fidelity. One misfortune I have to lament ; my little boy speaks nothing but English : I am so provoked at his losing the native tongue, though it appears to be the only loss which my family sustained in my absence. I regret your collateral losses ; yet it is some consolation that your beloved sailor will be permitted to worship his household gods a while longer. Farewell. I have a thousand urgent demands on my attention. Though I cannot write, rest assured of the attachment of yours ever,

A. G.

* A sequestered but beautiful retreat near Stirling, to which the Author removed some months afterwards.

LETTER LXXVI.

TO MISS DUNBAR, BOATH.

Laggan, May 10, 1803.

My dear Helen,

Very sick and very busy as I am, I am so charmed with your goodness, in being so mindful of me under such a pressure, that I lose no time in thanking you, and in congratulating you on the recovery of a mother, a friend, and an exemplary model of every social and domestic virtue.—Do me the justice to believe, though urgently advised to take the measure you mention when I was in England, pressed for money in a land of strangers, that I not only rejected the proposal, but the rejection cost me so little effort, that I never once thought of telling you I had refused it. I should consider it as a stain to the memory of the most delicate and disinterested of human beings, if I, walking so long in the pure light of his spotless mind, should be induced to do anything that could bear the construction of disingenuity, to benefit his family. By the Divine blessing, there is little danger of their wanting what is necessary, and it is my duty to endeavour to limit their wishes within narrow bounds. I hope this will find you in some degree recovered, though it will take time to restore your usual strength; I do not add spirit, for that seems unimpaired. I know you now perfectly, in the simplicity and very similitude of Anne's description, for you are her daily theme.—Your patience in illness raises you not a little with me. I can-

R 2

not bear the tribe of croakers; they are indeed, "like
the black raven hovering o'er my peace," no less a
bird of omen than of prey; for they really prey on my
comfort.   I do not believe these *dismalites* feel half
what I do; if they did, they would be glad to seize a
respite when they could.   I believe you to be very
deserving; yet if those clouds did not intervene, you
would have more than your share of those showers of
manna allotted to support us in our travels through
the wilderness.   I do think you gather more than an
omer, when I take brothers, and music, and literature,
into the account.   I have my share, too, though I am
doomed to eat it, like the paschal lamb, with bitter
herbs.   I hope there will be no war, and that your
brother will take root and flourish in his native soil.
What a feast must rural and domestic life be to an
uncorrupted mind, after tossing about in a profession
where the mode of life is so unnatural.

I will give my opinion, such as it will be after a
hasty perusal, of the poem you had the goodness to
send me; but you, in return, must give me yours of
Dr. Cowper's Malachi.   I did not tell you how very
ill I have been of the Cowper-mania.   I do not now
mean the Doctor, but the delightful author of the Task.
Read his letters and his life by Hayley, as I did, and
you will find them

> " Of power to take the captive soul,
> And lap it in Elysium."

Your young cousin's Poem to Science is a wonderful
proof of premature abilities.   It shows genius under the
direction of wisdom, and does equal honour to his judgment and his poetical faculties.   No wonder that those

on whom the culture of so fair a flower has devolved, should carefully attend to its unfolding; but if it were mine, I would not have it reared in England. Who will care for Scotland, after being bred in so fine a country? I would have a son of the Muses be a patriot and a true-blue Scot. John Bull is not so much alive either to the tender or ludicrous, as we are. And why? he has too much ease, and too many conveniences, which he cultivates to a degree injurious to social life and social love, and which will produce the same effect on us whenever we attain them. It is partly to this apathy that irreligion, the source so fruitful of every evil, is owing. We struggle by the light that kindles darkness into day, through hunger, poverty, and hardship; our blest enthusiasm lights up the dreariest prospects with rays that stream from heaven. Earth-born views are so bounded, that the soul soon sickens with the reiteration of unvaried comforts, and languishes amidst all its enjoyments. There are, doubtless, very many pious people in England among the more enlightened middle classes, but our " virtuous populace " is our peculiar and invaluable blessing. I am now speaking of devotion merely as an earthly comfort.

Our final day here is the 11th June.—Did I tell you of the Marquis of Huntly's visit? Was it not very considerate and good? Farewell; I am tired out of measure, and will not bestow another word on you or him, well as I like you both. Good night.

A. G.

LETTER LXXVII.

Laggan, May 13, 1803.

Dear Madam,

I received a letter, two days ago, from our dear friend, Mrs. Furzer, in which she mentions your having the goodness to execute a commission which she gave you on my behalf. I was proud to find you so solicitous about having the books. By the time you receive this, I hope they will have arrived; for I ordered them to be sent to you sometime ago. I gladly seize this occasion of expressing the sense I entertain of the zealous interest you and good Mrs. Malliet have taken in my affairs; and how useful your kind exertions proved in the unlooked-for emergency which occasioned my journey to Bristol. We were much flattered to hear you were disappointed at our not returning by London; I never made such a sacrifice of inclination to prudence in my life, as I did in coming home by the west road. I am not clear I could have done it, had I been sure of getting credit for my principal motive, which, in truth and verity, would have been to see you; but I was sure of meeting with many Eliabs who would say to me, " Why camest thou hither, and with whom hast thou left those few lambs in the wilderness? Surely I know the pride and naughtiness of thy heart; to see the *city* art thou come?" Did you know the struggle it cost me, you would give me credit for self-command

and self-denial—qualities very necessary for a person
whose duty it is to act and think solely for others. I
little thought, during my remaining pilgrimage through
this world, to taste so much of the pure and tender
satisfaction which connects with our early warm affections, as I enjoyed during the few happy days I spent
with Mrs. Furzer at Plympton. Have you ever met
with anybody like our friend? I think neither you
nor I need lament the want of a sister, while we divide
between us a heart so pure, so liberal, and so faithful.
To know the world so well as she does, and yet retain
all her integrity, untainted by its corruption, unbiassed
by its prejudices! In this particular she stands unrivalled and alone. Vehement she is; but if she were
not, she would not love us so well as she does. She
is, indeed, "made of the firm truth of honour." I
cannot enough admire the resources her active and
affectionate mind creates to itself. Her garden, which
she has half animated; her birds, who seem to have
caught a spark of her own vivid intellect; and her
young botanical pupil, whom she has refined and civilized almost against the bias of nature, are only less
wonders than herself. Yet, though she will always
create something to love and take solace in, it is griev-
ous to see the benevolence of that kind, and the energy
of that ardent mind, evaporate among those good little
gossiping women at Plympton, who understand her
just as well as I do algebra. Her strength of character puzzles and overawes them; they are afraid of
being scorched by that lambent flame, by which we
should be cheered and delighted. What pity it is that
a person so made for all the duties and enjoyments of

friendship, should live in a state that may well be called a solitude of the heart!

It is time that I should tell you that Mary is, thank God, recovering, or rather recovered; that I found my children well, and my young deputy-matron at home acquitting herself beyond my warmest hopes, and that I am soon to remove to a beautiful sylvan retreat on the banks of the Forth, such as even you, accustomed as you are to the luxuriant scenes of your happy native land, might be pleased with.

Your *spiritual* relation here, Anne Louisa,* is just recovered from the influenza, and grows like asparagus. Pray, when you write, let me know what *other people* think of my poetical volume. On your judgment I lay no weight, for I should be very sorry you were impartial. With grateful and respectful compliments to Mrs. Malliet, I am, dear madam, your obliged obedient servant,

A. G.

Letter LXXVIII.

TO MISS DUNBAR OF BOATH.

My dear Helen,   Laggan, May 17, 1803.

You must have felt some of the pains and penalties of authorship, to have any idea of the cordial satisfaction I derived from reading Mrs. Rose's† elegant

---

* God-daughter to Miss Malliet.

† Mrs. Rose of Kilravock, whose taste and talents are universally known and respected in her own country.—(1807.)

criticisms on my poetical volume. I insist upon it,
that it betrays hardihood, insolence, and indeed some
hypocrisy, to affect indifference about public opinion,
when one has once left the safe and peaceful shades
of privacy. Very reluctant, indeed, I was to plunge
into that stream; but now that I am in, I most un-
doubtedly would wish to keep above water as long as
possible, and consider such approbation as Mrs. Rose's
as an excellent cork-jacket to assist my floating. The
Della Cruscas, and many others who fed the public
with gilt gingerbread, to the great delight of all
masters and misses who loved glitter and tinkle, took
very suddenly with their admirers, and sunk as suddenly into deserved oblivion. Plain common sense,
with few and simple ornaments, will be relished by
the lovers of nature, only, at its first appearance. But
the power of those judges, in some respects, resembles
that of a certain great aërial potentate—it is invisible,
indefinite, and unacknowledged; yet daily increases
and extends over all manner of people, and tongues,
and nations, and many act under its influence who
imagine themselves free. agents. I will run this
parallel no farther, but merely observe that, in the
long run, good sense generally recognises and obeys,
as arbiters of taste, those who are best qualified to fix
the boundaries of opinion. Praise from the praise-
worthy is, of all gratifications, the highest and most
delicate; and poor authors militant, " who must far-
dels bear," &c., have much need of some such cordial.
But, after all, the local character of my subjects, the
narrow circle I walk round, must for ever preclude
me from exciting general interest.

By the pains you take to soothe my feelings with regard to the wrath of those who ought to thank me for my well-meant efforts, I should fear I had expressed too strongly my opinions on that subject;* but you ought never to indulge a thought that I could be displeased at the generous concern you express lest it should be hurtful to my interest or reputation. In that matter, I have gone to the barrier of truth, and beyond it I will not go for mortal; and for jesuitical concealments, I know no art but silence. If delicacy or prudence forbid being explicit on any topic, I can let it alone; but if I touch a subject† from which a thousand public discussions have long since drawn the veil of concealment, I will tell the truth, the whole truth, and nothing but the truth. I should like, at any rate, to be tried by my peers—that is, by people who know as much about the subject as I do. Far from being displeased with you, I consider this as an additional proof of that active, zealous, and unwearied friendship, which does honour to your own character, as well as to me, and which I often think of with admiration equal to my gratitude. No one has had warmer and more faithful friends; but you are the only invisible female friend who has made distinguished exertions on my behalf; for Miss Malliet I place to Mrs. Furzer's account.

I have lately made a great acquisition in an invisible male friend; but, alas, I can hope for little more than

---

* These opinions were expressed in an Essay on the Authenticity of the Poems of Ossian, printed in the Volume of poems published by the Author of these Letters.

† The translation of Ossian.

his parting blessing, for he is full of days and honour, and drawing near the verge of time, yet takes such a lively interest, and writes so like a gentleman, a Christian, and a man of taste and intelligence. *More I must not say.* But I feel a kind of triumphant satisfaction, in finding that age has no power to damp those virtuous feelings which ennoble our nature, when they flow from the proper source.* My dear, worthy Mr. Arbuthnot, another instance of generous enthusiasm illuminating life to its closing period, is fast decaying, and has not been out of his room for many months. The very last letter he wrote, was to me, and if ever I see you, you shall see it, and be convinced I do not overvalue the writer. I hope you received favourable accounts of all your brothers, particularly your beloved nautical hero, who, I imagine, has a very ample share in the division of affection. He is quite in, or rather on his element now. Speaking of the sea, have you seen Campbell's glorious effort on the Tyrtean lyre?

> " Her march is on the mountain wave,
>   Her home is on the sea."

I wish you would tell me, whether you admire Campbell's " words that glow, and thoughts that burn," as much as I do ; and whether you are tempted to have a little Teraphim image of Cowper in your chamber for

---

* There can be no reason now (1845), for withholding the name of the late excellent John Richardson, Esq. of Pitfour, as the person here alluded to. He introduced himself to Mrs. Grant after reading her Poems, published in 1803, and continued her warm friend and frequent correspondent until his death in 1821. Several of Mrs. Grant's letters to Mr. Richardson, are printed in her lately published " Memoirs and Correspondence."—ED.

your private devotions; and whether you are very
proud that so many women, distinguished for elegance
and intellect, as well as virtue and piety, gave up the
pleasures of this vain world for a time, to extract the
thorns from his heart, and pour in the wine and oil of
consolation. I am always glad when I can warrant-
ably boast of my own sex. We are better than men,
upon the whole. Indeed, the few amiable men I have
known had many *femalities* in their tastes and opinions;
but, then, I must allow the most respectable women
have some masculine traits too. Nature does nothing
wrong. It is those women who affect and assume the
masculine character, that are insufferable. Tell Bar,
for it will charm her, that two of the most respectable
women, and firmest, truest friends existing, are about
to form an union with each other, by domesticating
and living as much together as circumstances will
admit, as I shall hereafter explain. She will know I
mean Mrs. Furzer and Miss Malliet. Have you seen
my rhyming description of our house? Perhaps I
may conclude it, some quiet, gloomy evening, with an
account of the oaks of Woodend, &c. O that you
came to Edinburgh! Then would you surely visit
" my cabin that stands by the wild wood," and cast a
look of kindness on its inmates. Anne, who now,
thank God, enjoys perfect health, is always begging
me to send her love to you. She will never have done
speaking of Boath, which she considers as the abode of
taste, elegance, and felicity. I wrote to our friend,
Mr. Mackay, congratulating him with heartfelt pleasure on his new connexion, and entreating that his
beloved would *own receipt*. But no—so you see it is

not you alone that are washed from recollection by the
tide of happiness that has flowed in upon our correspondent. But fear not ; we shall yet emerge ; we are
too *good* to be forgotten ; and his chosen is too generous to engross him. Pray write, and be sure you tell
me everything, about everybody. I am resolved to
like all your people, because you like all mine so well.
Isabella Macpherson of Ballochroan, for instance, who
is elegance, vivacity, and truth personified. Remember
me to your excellent mother ; I am not more pleased
with her regard than yours, but I am prouder of it.
Adieu, my dear Helen ; write soon, and think kindly
and often of your affectionate friend,

A. G.

Letter LXXIX.

TO MRS. FURZER, PLYMPTON, DEVON.

Laggan, June 15, 1803.

My dear Friend,

. . . . Have you read Hayley's life of that
dear, amiable saint, Cowper ? I have no patience
with Hayley for expatiating so minutely in praise of
Cowper ; whose life and works praise him beyond all
that he can say. It is just as if one should assure you
that the sun was a bright luminary, and then gravely
add, that the ocean was both wide and deep. Cowper
wants no stilts to raise him in the esteem of any person possessing either feeling or understanding. He is
exactly everything that I delight in ; the bright gleams
by which his mental gloom is occasionally lighted up,

throw a kind of mild splendour round his natural and original character. But I will neither anticipate your judgment, nor do what I have so much blamed others for. Examine him by his own light; and pray observe, in this illustrious instance, how necessary every man of genius, who is at the sametime a man of virtue, finds the charm of female society. The graces, the sprightliness, the softness, and the innocence, let me add, of female conversation, the tenderness of female sympathy, and the fidelity and warmth of female friendship, are cordials to a mind too delicately toned for the rough tumults of the corrupt world. What a constellation of female worth shed its sweet influence round this inspired sufferer! It is worth consideration, how many of the great and gay, who have made a noise and bustle on the stage of life, have sunk into quick and deep oblivion; while we follow with eager interest every step this obscure, unobtrusive mortal makes among his flowers or shrubberies, and are more interested in his very hares and robins, because he loved and tended them, than in all that ever dazzled and amused us among the children of art and vanity. . . . . Tell me how your Book Society relish the nosegay of heather, birch, and cannach, which I have sent them. —Are you deep in Scriptural studies? Does not your heart burn within you, when you throw the world at a distance, and drink deep at the true fountains of Inspiration? . . . . . . It is a fatal fashion that prevails of late, of calling every one a Methodist who goes a little out of the beaten track of mechanical forms.—I dare say this illiberal cant drives many into sects, merely as a sanctuary from ridicule; for it does not require so much courage to share ridicule with a numerous body, as to face it alone.

> " O bless'd retirement, friend to life's decline,
> Retreats from care which *ever* must be thine."

What sacrifice can be too great to make for peace and liberty? And yet I am not quite satisfied with your retreat. This should not be said. Farewell tenderly,

A. G.

LETTER LXXX.

Woodend, near Stirling.
July 8, 1803.

My dear Friend,

It is a sure proof that I was very little capable of writing that your kind letter is thus long unanswered. I cannot easily make you understand what a cordial it was to me, when I was so " weary worn wi' care," that nothing less that the soothings of friendship, and the dim, distant views of peace beyond this world, could allay the fever of my mind. But before I say one word of the ordeal through which I have passed, I will answer your letter.

I am glad, that others doing what they ought, relieves you in some measure from the dilemma you were in about your *protegé*.* To send him fluttering away, thus early and unformed, from the nest where he has been so tenderly cherished, must have been a

---

* An adopted son of Mrs. Furzer, before alluded to.

severe alternative, after all the pains you have taken.
When one does a generous action merely from the
pure delight it gives the heart, it is very mortifying to
be obliged to stop short before the plan of beneficence
is completed. I am greatly pleased matters continue
on the old footing. It would be a dismal blank to
your warm, active mind, to have no object near you to
exercise its affections. Now, at the distance at which
you keep him, he excites interest, without teasing and
wearing you out; and then your holidays are so joyful
to him.

Now, how shall I briefly, and at the sametime
clearly show you the track I have trodden since I
left you. . . . . . . Alas! for my beloved cottage!
But I will not distress you with the retrospect. You
will be pleased to hear that nothing could exceed the
general kindness and considerate and friendly attention of my neighbours that were. As it is, I see much
beauty and many comforts about my new abode.
When the mists that overcloud my mind are a little
dispelled, I hope to taste what I now merely look on
with cold critical approbation. You, who live so
much in the fair creation of your fancy, need not be
told what a pang it awakens to part with a home,
where everything, as it were, owes its existence to
you; where one has suffered and enjoyed what self-
lovers can form no idea of, and which is endeared by
being, in a manner, rendered sacred to the memory of
those we love.—The letters with the accounts of my
poor father's death, came before I left Laggan, but
were concealed from me till the bitterness of parting
with my late home was over. What an asylum, what

a comfort has that dwelling been to many others besides the family that inhabited it! There, indeed, social life, and social love seemed the warmer for being compressed within narrow bounds. There I lived, and moved, and had a being in some degree useful and interesting to others. Hereafter I shall indeed exist; but my highest hope must be to spend

" Quiet, tho' sad, the remnant of my days,"

far, far from my old haunts, my old habits, and my old associates. I will not balance the account, for you will do that for me, and reproach my croaking to boot. I am all penitence and submission, so pray be moderate in your reproof of yours tenderly,

A. G.

Letter LXXXI.

TO MRS. FURZER, PLYMPTON, DEVONSHIRE.

Woodend, July 12, 1803.

My dear Friend,

The cheerful tenor of your last letter was a great cordial to my spirits. I rejoice exceedingly at the prospect of your removal to Richmond; not that I expect, or would have you expect, that everything and everybody will be quite to your wish where you are going. In vain would we encircle the globe by successive removals, in search of an accumulation of comforts ;—those comforts, which the frugal, though bountiful hand of Providence has scattered in various proportions, to alleviate the sorrows and sufferings of a state only meant as the pathway to felicity. Yet of those ingredients of happiness, on which an elegant and sensible mind is most dependent, I am confident many await you; and, amidst all the wealth of Flora, which your industrious ingenuity had lavished around you, and all the softness of a genial climate, I always thought of you with an anxious and desponding tenderness, well knowing your heart was not at home, *could* not be at home, among people who so little comprehended you. Your warmth of heart and energy of character were quite beyond them, and you would have continued a stranger after fifty years' residence. I would carefully banish from my mind the absurd and silly fastidiousness of working myself up to relish no conversation but that of wits and savans; it would be a regimen of pickles and marmalades, without bread or water. Common sense, and common integrity, with some degree of heart, I insist on in my companions. Knaves and fools I will positively have nothing to do with. Some one mind that thinks and feels as I do myself, is indispensable. It is like my morning tea, the only luxury I care for, which habit has made necessary, morally necessary, because this favourite indulgence, this mental banquet meliorates my temper and expands my heart. I do not pity any person merely for being deprived of pleasure, however innocent, or however elegant. The time of trial is hourly shortening, and the hopes of futurity proportionally strengthening, to those who look forward to another state of existence. But, I think, where one finds the kindly affections continually chilled and repelled, and the disposition to spleen and censure as often excited, it may truly be called a state of temptation.

The more I think of your change, the more I am pleased with it. Miss Malliet's constant attention to you at such a distance, has demonstrated the strength of her attachment, and established her claim to yours. Johnson says that Pope and Martha Blount were necessary to each other, because the events of their past lives were pictured on each other's minds. It is one of many attractions you have towards each other, that the same may very truly be said of you. Of your mutual friendship I shall only say,—may it be perpetual! Adieu, affectionately,

A. G.

Letter LXXXII.

TO MISS SIMSON,* KEYNSHAM, NEAR BATH.

Woodend, near Stirling,
July 15, 1803.

My dear Miss Simson,

A constant succession of labour, care, and sorrow since I saw you has not been able to efface from my memory the traces of the kindness I received from your most estimable family. Keynsham was to me, in my sad wanderings, like the olive tree to the poor fugitive dove, and I carried away the cordial recollection of genuine kindness, like a leaf plucked off, as a promise of peace and security in my future changes of abode.

* Afterwards married to ——— Conway, Esq. of Chantry-Netherbury, Dorset.—*See* Letter, January 21, 1803.

s 2

You would hear from Mary of my father's death, and how reluctantly I have torn myself from my long-loved cottage at Laggan. The peaceful shades of Woodend, of all places the most sylvan and seques-tered, now promise us an asylum, after all our cares and sorrows, such as the weary soul in adversity so often vainly figures to itself.

I make no apology for sending my poetical volume. To love of Scotland and of the author, I am proud to say, another powerful inducement may be added to insure your partiality. It is the love of truth—truth of sentiment, truth of character. So all my friends tell me, and may, at some future time, tell you; and in this, truth like charity, must cover many faults. I have seen your letter to Mary, and congratulate you on the return of Mr. Bright. Such a paternal friend, so loosened and distinct from the world, with a mind so purified by devotion, warmed by benevolence, and refined by taste, is a treasure of which you are truly deserving, because you know how to estimate its value. Believe me I, too, know how to estimate yours; and often, amidst my saddest musings, I have in fancy listened to you and your brother singing the vesper hymn, in melodious chorus, with your sweet instrument. But I must check feelings to which I have no leisure to give vent.

I feel extreme concern at your mother's too frequent illnesses. I hope they prove a furnace of trial from which her piety and fortitude will acquire a higher lustre. Give my reverential love to her, and to that primitive saint, your father; and tell your brother to continue always the amiable and artless character nature meant him to be, without being dazzled with, or emulating any one's fashionable or witty pretensions; so shall he prove worthy of his parents and sister, and as happy as so much benevolence and understanding ought to be. I am, dear Miss Simson, very truly yours,

ANNE GRANT.

LETTER LXXXIII.

TO MRS. SMITH OF JORDANHILL.

Woodend, near Stirling,
July 17, 1803.

My dear Friend,

You wonder I have been so long answering your kind letter; I too wonder, and must account for my silence in a manner no less wonderful. Do you know my mind has, at length, lost all its elasticity. That happy faculty, that inestimable cork-jacket, by the aid of which, however deep I might plunge, I still rose buoyant on the waves of calamity, is gone. Here I am, safe ashore, and yet I gasp in amaze, like a creature removed from its native element. Time and habit may amend this; but at present I am, like Orpheus, at the hazard of my peace, looking back to the gloomy region I have left behind, and from a somewhat similar motive;

" For so to interpose a little ease,
Do my frail thoughts dally with surmise."

All this is very fine and very fanciful, you will say; but the plain truth, I believe, is, that my mind was so exhausted by a long succession of painful exertions, that quiet, now I have attained it, is like the faint stupor of a person cast ashore from a wreck. Yet I cannot call it leisure, either; for, arranging and adjusting everything belonging to so large a family, in an entire new establishment, kept me very busy; and when I was not busy, I was stupid. My mother grows more composed, walks out in the air, and her sleep and appetite return. Little Grant Smith, the dear son of my lamented Charlotte, is another of my tender cares; I thought him puny, and brought him here for a little country air, and that he might know and love me. But he will not stay long enough, nor come back soon enough to form or renew affection. His father will never be at ease till he gets him home; nor would it suit me to keep him.

Of this place, suffice it to say, that the house is excellent, capacious, airy, and well laid out. It is sheltered, at a small distance behind, by craggy rocks, and surrounded on three sides by pleasant woods, through which there are many openings, walks, and sloping glades; and for birds it is a perfect aviary; I could not have conceived so many to be contained in one wood of this extent; they find covert in various beautiful shrubs, which, with woodbine and hazel, greatly abound. These woods, too, are diversified by every kind of tree that bears our climate. The front of the house commands an extensive and varied prospect over a level and fertile country, bounded by mountains lofty and wild, whose fine marked contour is always noble, and at sunset beautiful. This same house stands in a circular enclosure or lawn: it is surrounded by a wild hedge, after the Devonshire manner, mixed with fruit-trees, and allowed to run into a little becoming disorder, which nearly emulates "the negligence of nature, wide and wild." In short, the place is neither trimmed nor rolled, and I like it the better. Yet it has no air of savage wildness, but, on the contrary, looks very tranquil and domestic, the garden excepted, which is in a most slovenly undress. But it is so wood-surrounded, musical and sequestered, that I like it much. It lies on a slope, and a little brook runs through the bottom of it ; opposite, a wood rises, "shade above shade," on an ascent. I meet with much civility from some fine people who live near us. I am, on the whole, thankful; yet not satisfied : there is a cold void in my heart. I am accustomed to love and be beloved by those around me, and I miss the cordial glance of sympathy and kindness. It is no one's fault ; but it is my misfortune :

> The voice that was wont to speak peace to my bosom,
> Shall whisper compassion's soft language no more!

I do not solely allude to the breach that is irreparable. There are a set of good, kind of people, perhaps unsusceptible of the delicacies of friendship, whom long habit, and the interchange of kind offices, has endeared to one ; who sincerely lament our misfortunes, and cordially enjoy our comforts ; whom we regard with that kind of instinctive affection, which a susceptible mind will bestow on the trees that have sheltered, or the brooks that have murmured to us for any length of time. These ties, which, though not tender, I find very tough, are all broken by a change of residence ; and here are no materials to spin them anew. The common people here are so gross, so sordid, they neither love nor esteem their superiors. And how should they, when these last regard them with such scornful indifference? The middle rank, that most valuable and happiest link in the chain of society, which superadds the polish of the upper, in some degree, to the strength of the lower, and was wont to connect and strengthen both; that class of society where, I might say with the Psalmist, "all my delights are placed," has here, I think, ceased to exist. I have my children, and they are worthy of my love, but necessarily more each other's companions than mine. I feel this desideratum, more for their sake than my own. I ought to be pleased, and shall, I hope, be tranquil; but not yet. Do not tire of this querulous length of letter, for it has done me much good to tell you all this, and to think how sorry you will be.

You are too happy and too lazy to visit me here; and yet you have done many idler things, and I should be so thankful to see you. With love to all your dear fireside, believe that I shall always be much yours,

ANNE GRANT.

APPENDIX.

APPENDIX.

ESSAY

ON THE

AUTHENTICITY OF THE POEMS OF OSSIAN.

BY

MRS. GRANT OF LAGGAN.

[The following Essay, which was appended to the Volume of
Poems published by Mrs. Grant in 1803, having been frequently
referred to in the concluding Letters of the foregoing Series, and
containing some interesting facts respecting Mr. Macpherson's journey to the Hebrides in search of materials for his Translation of
Ossian's Poems, is here inserted by the Editor for the benefit of such
readers as may desire to peruse the Essay, and have not an opportunity of referring to the volume in which it was originally published.—ED.]

The time is fast approaching when it will be impossible to throw new light on the question respecting
the authenticity of those celebrated productions of the
Celtic Muse. The most conclusive evidence which the
nature of the subject will admit of is fast fading away.
It consists of traditions co-relative to the Poems, a
kind of poetical phraseology derived from them, and
a resembling strain of sentiment in other compositions
of great, though not equal antiquity, which no one
could ever have had any motive to falsify or alter.
There is another clear, though now decaying evidence.
Old people can very well remember, before Mr. Mac-

pherson ever thought of translating those remains,
when many comparisons and allusions, to be found in
them, were as correct as scriptural quotations in the
last age among the peasants of the west of Scotland.
" She is as beautiful as Agandecca, the daughter of
the Snow,"—" She is musical as Malvina,"—" He is as
forlorn as Ossian after the departure of the Fingalians,"
—" Such a one is as alert and nimble as Cuchullin,"
were phrases in common use. Whatever embellishments, or whatever anachronisms the injudicious vanity of a translator may have grafted on these Poems,
no person who lived in the country of their reputed
author ever doubted their existence or antiquity. There
every stream and mountain, every tale, song, or adage
retained some traces of the generous hero or the
mournful bard. But there was little chance of getting
at the truth of this question, while the contention lay
betwixt learned people, on the one hand, and national
vanity on the other. The former were accustomed to
consider letters, not as the vehicle, but the essence of
knowledge ; accounting all unlearned people utterly
savage and barbarous, and unable to conceive how any
one could entertain noble or generous sentiments without deriving them from classical models. The latter was
unwilling to confess how little the Gaelic language had
been used in writing, and to what a narrow district
of the kingdom it had been, even in remote ages, confined,—which was the real cause why no connected
series of these Poems had been written down, and
why they had been so long hid in obscurity. To the
same motive may be attributed the silent acquiescence
of the Highlanders in the alterations and embellish-

ments added to these Poems by a Translator more ambitious of adapting them to modern taste than of adhering strictly to the sense of the originals; more studious of his own fame than of the addition to be made to the science of human nature, by developing, truly and closely, the manners of the heroic age; by which I understand that intervening betwixt rude barbarity and the regular establishment of law, property and agriculture.

It is obvious that the greatest literary attainments do not enable a man to judge whether a work written in a language he does not understand, differing in its form and construction from every other with which he is acquainted, be faithfully translated or not. It was highly absurd in the opponents of Ossian to cry out for written evidence, that is, original manuscripts of a work composed long before the signs of words were heard of in the country where they were composed. It is no shame for a man of learning and taste to be ignorant of the rude unwritten language of a savage people; certainly not. But he ought to be ashamed to decide upon facts without obtaining the necessary previous information. We have no right to strip the laurels off the tombs even of savages, until we clearly ascertain that they ought not to have been planted there. Let Fingal continue to be a hero and Ossian a poet, were it but by the old rule of prescription, till those who challenge their right acquire their language, and are thus enabled to decide upon the question.

But it has been asked why were the Poems not committed to writing when the knowledge of letters

was introduced, being so much admired by the people,
and cherished as sacred vestiges of their heroic age,
and venerated memorials of their ancestors? Here
the ignorant defenders of Ossian erred; their national
vanity would not allow them to confess that, except
the monks of Iona, who held the heathen poems of
Ossian in abhorrence, and laboured to eradicate the
prevailing passion for works of fancy, there were very
few who did write Gaelic, and the writings of these
few were confined merely to theology and to family
archives, unless in some rare instances where a young
chief, before he became entirely engrossed by war and
hunting, might have written down some favourite
passage, composed or recited by a bard, or some old
chief preserved on parchment a genealogy delivered
by a Sennachie.

Though the imagination may be delighted with
fiction when the pictures drawn by the flowery pencil
of fancy, resembled something that we know or believe
to exist, yet the love of truth is happily so fixed in
the human mind that we revolt from a mixture of
truth and falsehood, especially where the boundaries
are undistinguished. The quick disgust we feel on a
discovery of this kind, is apt to lead us into an opposite
mistake;—whenever we are required to believe more
than what is probable, we generally end in believing
less, or in entire scepticism. The alterations and
embellishments that have been made on these ancient
Poems have contributed more than anything else to
shake their credit. But let us examine the circumstances which have been chiefly insisted on by the
unbelievers.

First, It is said to be impossible that a people so savage and barbarous as the ancient Celtæ should either entertain generous and tender sentiments, or possess expressive and emphatic language to delineate their feelings and record their exploits. I believe it is generally allowed that the inhabitants of the north of Britain were a branch of the ancient Celtæ whom the very Romans, who called them barbarians (in common with all others who were strangers to the arts conducive to luxury, and to the worship of their deities), allowed to possess exalted notions of liberty, friendship, and generosity, and a sense of probity in their dealings with each other. The clearest way to ascertain the possibility of heroic sentiments being delivered in eloquent language by wandering savages who subsist by hunting, is to trace the manners of people who still exist in a similar state of society. The banks of the *Mohawk* river very lately did, and the borders of the *Huron* and *Oneida* lakes still do afford an apt illustration. There, heroic friendship, exalted notions of probity and honour, the fondest filial and paternal affection, and the most enthusiastic patriotism prevail. There, every chief is an orator, and every orator a poet, if language enriched with glowing imagery, exalted by the noblest conceptions, and modulated into harmonious periods, can be called poetry. The morality, indeed, of these people is not of so mild and amiable a cast as that of the Fingalians. Revenge makes a part of their religion ; the cruelties they commit are not to gratify their inclinations, but to pacify the manes and honour the memory of their departed friends. When that is once performed, they are kind and indulgent, in no common degree, to those whom accident or the chance of war throws under their power.

There is another cause which might operate powerfully to produce a superior refinement of humanity among our ancestors. Women, among uncivilized wandering tribes, are generally in an abject and degraded state, and condemned to the most servile employments. Among the Celtæ this appears not to have been the case. Women possessed considerable influence in society; they were admitted, at a certain age, to councils, and held in reverence, on account of a prophetic spirit with which some individuals were supposed to be endowed. This fact is unquestionably established; and whether their obtaining so high a rank in society, was the cause or the consequence of a greater degree of mildness and humanity in their manners, than is usually found among uncivilized people, the inference is equally just.

The next circumstance which has been urged against the authenticity of the Poems, is, that the language in which they are preserved could not have subsisted for many centuries unaltered. What has altered language, but the invasion and conquest of countries, or the travels of the inhabitants, whom commercial or other pursuits have attracted to foreign countries, and who, returning, bring new customs and foreign languages to the place of their nativity? From the reverence with which people in a state of nature usually regard their ancestors, it is presumable that a man would always call a deer, a fox, a river, or a mountain, by the name his father called it.

Things newly invented or imported would have new names, but that would not change the original form of the language. In a country equally poor and inaccessible, the usual causes of alteration did not occur. It was naturally impregnable, and not worth conquering. Strangers had no motive of curiosity or advantage to visit it; nothing but extreme necessity made the natives emigrate; and when they acquired the language and manners of a civilized country, they were equally unfit and unwilling to live in their own. It is obvious that the language has undergone no material alteration since the establishment of the Monks of *Iona*.

The next impossibility asserted, is, that of preserving an unwritten composition unimpaired for so long a series of ages. People who have long worn spectacles can make little use of their eyes without them. We have so long accustomed ourselves to a certain medium by which knowledge is preserved, and through which it is received, that it is not easy for us to comprehend how others could retain on their memory what ours are unequal to. We have such a number of new images continually passing through our minds, and effacing the old, that we are very inadequate judges of the deep impression which pathos and sublimity might make on a mind open to receive, and at leisure to fix their impressions. Persons still living (1802), remember a woman living in Strathspey, who, though never taught to read, could recite the whole Book of Psalms in the Gaelic translation, merely by hearing it read to her by others. This, to be sure, was the employment and delight of all the leisure hours of a long life; but it is a proof what hold the memory takes when the heart is deeply interested. Dr. Johnson, a name never to be mentioned but with respect and veneration, seems to have erred in his estimation of the faculties of the mind when neither exalted by culture, nor debased by utter neglect. He imputed too much to learning, and did not think that a mind could be informed or enlarged by any other means. He does not appear to have considered that the book of nature lay open to all, and that other books at best contain but the aggregate of human reflection and observation suggested by that great book. People who had abilities made use of them to treasure up in their memories for the delight and instruction of others, what had formerly delighted and instructed themselves. Their bequeathing their most valuable acquirements unimpaired to others was not at all improbable. The errors which crept into written legends were often owing to their being copied over by those who performed merely a task in transcribing them, and felt no interest in the original; but in reciting, or rather chanting poems, where they were well known and highly relished, and where a certain rhyme or cadence was· connected with them, which was broken in upon by the change of a syllable—no great departure from the original words could pass unnoticed—the ear in this case aiding the memory.

　　Supposing that such Poems did once exist, it is not easy to believe that they could be forgotten or neglected by a people whose national vanity was so flattered by them; especially when we consider that every chief retained a bard, whose principal business it was to recite those scriptures of chivalry, for such they were esteemed.

The simplicity of manners, ardent affections, heroic extravagance, and generous contempt of life, which these Poems ascribe to our ancestors, correspond with the description left to us of the ancient Britons in the times of the Druids. Their manners, indeed, strongly marked that period of society which the fables and traditions of various nations have decorated with enthusiastic embellishments, and peopled with heroes and demigods; the time when people were not bound by laws, but, from reverence to their ancestors, held sacred the precepts and customs bequeathed by them, when property was so far ascertained that the courageous might retain what their exertions acquired; yet, so unsettled, that the weak found it necessary to dwell under the shadow of the strong;—when the love of glory predominated over every other passion, because all power, all esteem, all veneration, centered in him who, by uniting courage with generosity, made himself at once beloved and feared;—when the passion of love was a powerful one, because opposed by no other, and exalted by that of glory, every woman being ennobled by the heroes with whom she was allied;—where friendship was a strong, because a beneficial bond—for who loves his friends so well as he who is daily bestowing or receiving assistance and protection? —and lastly, when poetry, the audible and harmonious language of nature, flowed pure from the heart, and was consecrated to its best affections, to reward the successful, or console the suffering hero; to preserve the remembrance of noble actions; to lament the tender lover or faithful friend; and to give the joy of grief to the soul that is purified while it is melted. Such is the age which may be called *the golden one of heroism;* of which every nation delights to preserve the traditions and obscure or exaggerated history; and which intervenes betwixt that of the selfish, solitary savage, whose short life is spent in sudden transitions from violent exertion to gloomy indolence; and that of the civilized inhabitant, who becomes as selfish from the multitude of his wants, as the other from the precariousness of his possessions; adjusting his morality to coercive laws, and regulating his desires by ever-changing fashion. This heroic age is necessarily an illiterate one, the knowledge of letters being always preceded by agriculture and commerce. Civilization and regular polity succeeds so soon to the heroic age (which, after all, is a melancholy and precarious state of life), that it is very difficult to trace the fleeting images of the characters that adorn, or the events that diversify it. What, then, do we owe to the revered personage, at once a poet, a prince, and a hero, who delineated, in unfading colours, a faithful picture of this short, yet interesting interval; who sung the loves, the wars, the woes of his cotemporary heroes, and arrayed them in such truth of character, and beauty of diction, as cannot fail to attract and delight through every age! The frequent recurrence of the same images and incidents may tire and disgust a taste refined to nicety; the style of the translator may perhaps, at times, be justly accused of swelling into tumidity; but wisdom and learning, after having long sat in council upon the nature of poetical excellence, and laid down rules innumerable for attaining it, have, at length, come to this conclusion, that as it is the province of poetry to delight the imagination, and affect the heart, what pleases and affects very many, and continues to please and affect very long, must needs be poetry of no inferior kind, however obvious, or however numerous its blemishes; and daily observation evinces that the most correct and faultless poetry, formed on the purest classical models, if it fails in these great prerequisites, if it can neither fix the attention or affect the heart, sinks into sudden oblivion.

The Translator of Ossian, though he has on many occasions forfeited the praise due to literary integrity, has always rendered the sense of his author in a pleasing, and often in a faithful manner. Many circumstances concurred to lead him into deviations, which, while they adapted his performance more to the popular taste, derogated from the credit of its authenticity, and gave room to those who could not separate what was genuine from what was changed and enlarged, to impeach the whole as an imposture. Mr. Macpherson's early years had been spent among the indigent and illiterate; and when he made a spirited though difficult effort to cultivate those talents which he felt struggling for expansion, his progress in moral improvement and delicacy of sentiment was by no means commensurate with his other attainments. Justly conscious of his abilities, and not unjustly proud of his acquirements, he had not sufficient address, or knowledge of the world, to conceal the opinion he entertained of his own consequence. * * * * He chose his own path, and walked firmly on it, little consulting and less valuing the opinions of others. Hence the liberties he took in enlarging his materials, and the general and vague assertions he made use of to defend the antiquity of the whole collection, as he presented it to the public.

Mr. Macpherson wrote two original poems, which are not without merit, though they were neither formed to please nor to last. The first, entitled *Death*, has many forcible thoughts and striking descriptions. The other, the *Highlander*, has some original ideas and incidents, but is rendered obscure, and sometimes incongruous, by a strange mixture of Grecian and Gothic mythology, and is so strongly marked with the political prejudices in which the Author was educated, that it could not, on that sole account, be well received at the time when it was written. I have seen it in the Author's manuscript only. Two obvious remarks will occur to any one who peruses it with attention :—one, that Mr. Macpherson made no use whatever of the Gaelic fragments, which were then very well known to himself and others, in forming incidents or imagery to this poem ;—the other, that no traces appear in it of that harmonious and flowing diction which prevails in his translation : on the contrary, the sentences are often harshly constructed, and the versification, in general, rugged and uncouth. The progress he had made in the learned languages, enabled him in some degree to form and to improve his poetical taste ; but when he quitted College during the vacation, he only made a transition from Greek to Gaelic, from Homer to Ossian. Dr. Macpherson of *Slate*, whose integrity was equal to his abilities, and whose veracity never was or could be questioned, had, by his learned labours, awakened a spirit of inquiry, and a taste for Gaelic antiquities. These soon became the favourite subject of Mr. James Macpherson's studies,—he delighted in running parallels between the Grecian and Celtic bards, until they became, in a manner, associated in his imagination. Here it may be proper to observe, that the blindness of Ossian, which he has been accused of inventing for this purpose, is alluded to not only in common sayings, but in many Gaelic poems, well known to have existed long previous to his Translation.

Finally, Mr. Macpherson not only resolved to translate and publish the Gaelic fragments of Ossian relative to Fingal's Irish wars, but to enlarge and connect them, so that they should form a continued narrative Poem, which he determined, though strongly dissuaded by a judicious friend, to call Epic, not considering that those poets of nature never did nor ever could produce long, connected narratives. They sat down under the shelter of a hollow rock or an aged tree, and recollected and mused till, as the Psalmist expresses it, " the fire burned;" then they poured out a burst of enthusiasm, and went on till they grew cold or hungry, but never dreamt of resuming the subject. This fire once extinguished could not be rekindled; successive poems might be composed on successive actions, but they had no regular or immediate connection with each other. After the publication of Mr. Macpherson's Fragments, some literary gentlemen in Edinburgh subscribed a sum of money to enable him to make a journey to the Western Highlands and

Islands for the purpose of collecting those larger Poems which he thought proper to call Epic, and which he informed the gentlemen he had reason to believe existed there. This journey afforded him an opportunity also of gaining a more thorough acquaintance with those expressions in the language which were daily becoming obsolete; the purest Gaelic, or what the Highlanders call *fine Gaelic*, being spoken in some of the Islands. This fine Gaelic does not by any means signify a different dialect of the language, but a more elevated style, enriched and varied by a kind of poetical phraseology. The superior classes of every community think more, converse more, and have a more elegant manner of expressing their sentiments than those whose attention is necessarily engaged by their urgent wants. In the Western Isles *gentlemen* still conversed in Gaelic, and this style was still familiar. It may be easily conceived how soon a language will be debased when it ceases to be used except by the mere vulgar.

On the excursion referred to, our Translator was accompanied by a person said to be one of the best Gaelic scholars of his time, who, however, was no otherwise useful to him than as a linguist, being destitute of taste, and even ordinary poetical knowledge, but a man of stubborn integrity, who could have no bias, for he liked his fellow-traveller better than anything except truth. From this worthy and venerable person the principal information here communicated was derived.* The chief acquisition they made in

---

* Mr. Evan Macpherson, by whom Mrs. Grant was instructed in the Gaelic language, appears to be the individual here referred to.

this excursion was a more intimate knowledge of the Ossianic style, which cleared up many obscurities in the former collections, to which, however, much was not added. The collection from which the selection was made was, indeed, a pretty ample one. Something, no doubt, has been added, and much subtracted; and this latter it was necessary to do in justice to the old Bard, to whom his successors had appended many extravagant and grotesque ornaments. These, however, were easily known to be no part of the style of Ossian, which, though bold and figurative is all along distinguished by a dignity, an exquisite pathos, and a sublime and tender melancholy, peculiar to himself. The Translator wisely stripped off these ornaments, and brought the whole poems to the standard of those beautiful and simple ones which he found in their original undebased state. Among these are the Vision of MALVINA, the Death of OSCAR, the Counsel of FINGAL to OSCAR, BERRATHON, and the Courtship of OSSIAN to EVAR ALUINE. It may be easily judged, were there no genuine fragments but these, what the Poet that produced them was capable of, especially when he depicted, with the energy of truth and glow of feeling, those scenes in which he had himself been an actor.

The Translator, with such models before him, was at no loss in forming links to connect the detached parts into a seemly whole. Having fame and profit more in view than tracing the familiar habits and domestic manners of remote times, he threw into

—*See* "Letters from the Mountains," vol. ii., p. 132, Letter dated July 8, 1797, and the note subjoined.—ED.

shade, on some occasions, circumstances that might betray our ancestors to the ridicule of modern fastidiousness ;—such as their rash and sudden quarrels, minute details relative to their hunting, their food and their dogs, their jealousies, and the fatal power which enchanted rings had over their inclinations. These moles and freckles, which might have delighted the virtuoso, as genuine marks of antiquity, would infallibly disgust the common reader. In this respect he might be compared to Susan, when she took such pains in scouring the shield of Scriblerus: he defaced the marks of antiquity, in the hope of procuring the general applause of the gossips who awaited the christening of his work. He was like an architect who should endeavour to adapt a Gothic edifice to the purposes of modern convenience : it might be more elegant, but it would no longer be a genuine Gothic edifice. Thus expanded and embellished, the Translation was published. It happened to be at an unlucky juncture, when the more numerous and clamorous party held the name of Scotchman in detestation, and depreciated, with industrious acrimony every Scotch production, the character of which time had not established. The attack upon Ossian was made upon false grounds, from ignorance of the true and just ones. A violent clamour was raised for the production of these ancient original manuscripts, which never did or could exist. Like a nurse who, being teased by a petulant child to reach him down the moon to play with, assures him he shall have it to-morrow,—Mr. Macpherson, in an evil hour, promised to produce the original manuscripts : and by this pious fraud, injured the credit of those valuable remains. The manuscripts were then eagerly demanded, and the demand variously evaded. Producing a legible manuscript would never do. Yellow parchments of grey antiquity were demanded. To talk of impossibilities to a deaf multitude, predetermined against conviction, was useless. However, it luckily, as he thought, occurred to him to produce a *Leabhar Dearg*, or Red Book, in which a chieftain had caused several of the original fragments to be written down. It was parchment, and it was old; but, upon examination, it shrunk from trial; for I am told it was not three hundred years old; these, however, proved superabundantly that the Translator was not the author of the Poems.

A most formidable adversary now came forth to defy the armies of Fingal.

Dr. Johnson, hardened in prejudice, fortified with incredulity, and covered with the weighty mail of ancient learning (which, however, served only to encumber and retard him in this pursuit), marched heavily on against the *Leabhar Dearg*. Not satisfied with pronouncing the whole an imposture, he pronounced it an easy and flimsy one, and a thing that any one could do with very moderate abilities. He did not leave the Translator the merit of even deceiving agreeably. In short, he said so much on the subject, that he reduced himself to a dilemma like that in which he had involved his opponents. He had said more than he could prove, and, to support the credit of his assertions, he set about looking for proofs where they could not be found. It is probable that his journey to the Hebrides was in a great measure occasioned by his desire to obtain positive proofs of the non-existence of these poems. But the indispensable prerequisite for this inquiry was wanting. He was like a man who should visit a river, without implements for fishing, and declare, upon his return, that there were no fish, because he had caught none. Without understanding the language in which the poems were composed, the evidence of their antiquity, which was entirely local and intrinsic, could not be traced ;—he inquired of country gentlemen, advanced in life, and engrossed by its cares, what they knew of the remains of Ossian? They honestly told him, that they had heard such poems in their youth, but had never thought or inquired about the authenticity of them, or of ascertaining the date of their antiquity ; and that they had never heard them in a connected series. The Highland Presbyterian clergy, who on all other occasions shared in the contempt he averred for that persuasion, seemed to have gained great credit with him, because they showed no extraordinary warmth in defence of these poems, as they appeared in the Translation. He asked of Dr. Macqueen, whether the poems ever existed in the form in which James Macpherson had given them to the world? The Doctor could not, consistently with his wonted probity, say they had, nor did he choose to give such an explanation as would afford a fair pretext for infidelity. The clergy in these remote places were more estimable for the purity of their lives, and the diligence of their evangelical labours, than remarkable for their taste or elegant literature. They rather, from a conscientious motive, maintained a kind of warfare with Bards and Sennachies, such as our more austere divines did with the theatre. Upon the Reformation, they found the taste of the people vitiated by the legends of the monks, and the absurd and extravagant fictions of the latter bards,—and that this acquired passion for the marvellous laid them open to every kind of imposture, and made them less relish the simplicity of those truths in which it was the duty of the clergy to instruct them. It was no wonder, then, that in the indiscriminate war carried on by pious zeal against poetical fiction, these Fragments, rapt in a cloud of adventitious matter, should meet with little favour or indulgence. Yet Dr. Macpherson, whose probity and learning were universally respected, having led the way in elucidating these antiquities, some of the younger clergy of more cultivated taste, admired and studied them. With these, however, Dr. Johnson did not chance to meet; and when he came to Edinburgh, where he met with people abundantly qualified to discuss with him all other points of polite literature, he could not, though he had been open to conviction, obtain any light upon this; a Scotchman, who is not a Highlander, being no better qualified to decide upon it than a native of *London* is to judge of the authenticity of a poem in the Welch language. The Doctor returned hardened in infidelity. The correspondence which succeeded is well known. In this the Doctor had greatly the advantage, from the dignity of his literary character, as well as from the violence with which the current of prejudice ran against his adversary.

Grown quite regardless of his literary character under all this hostility, Mr. Macpherson devoted him-

self to more profitable pursuits, but did not find them
a sufficient consolation for the severity with which he
had been treated by the public, a severity which he
may be said to have, in some measure, justly incurred
by his presumptuous attempt to translate Homer.
Though wealthy, prosperous, and seemingly indifferent
to public applause, the chagrin he felt at having so
mingled fiction with truth, that he could not separate
them with credit to himself, preyed upon his spirits;
and a short time before he died, he ordered the Gaelic
originals of the translated poems to be printed for the
satisfaction of his particular friends.

LAGGAN, OCTOBER, 1802.

LINES WRITTEN IN ONE OF THE DUKE OF ATHOL'S WALKS,
AT BLAIR, IN SUMMER 1796.

[Referred to in Volume II., Letter XXXII., of this Work.]

YOUR jealous walks, great Duke, in vain
  All access would refuse ;
What walls can Highland steps restrain,
  What bars keep out the Muse?
Where'er I go, I bring with me
" That mountain-nymph, sweet Liberty."

Would you engross each breathing sweet
  Yon violent banks exhale ;
Or trees with od'rous blooms replete,
  That scent the enamoured gale?
Alike they smile on you and me,
Like nature and sweet Liberty!

While pleasure's fleeting form you trace
  In Mona's distant isle,

And leave forlorn your native place,
  Where rural beauties smile:
Congenial see them smile for me,
Then do not grudge my Liberty.

Æneas pass'd, with branch of gold,
  The gloomy gates below:
And silver branches, I am told,
  Can smooth your porter's brow;
But wand'ring Highland folks like me,
Can seldom *purchase* Liberty.

While musing by the Tilt I stood,
  And view'd its wand'ring tide,
Uprose a Naiad from the flood,
  And, beckoning, showed its side:
I took the kindly hint with glee
And scrambled hard for Liberty.

Beneath the bridge's bending arch
  My vent'rous steps she led,
Till by yon ancient weeping larch,
  I laid my wearied head:
While birds, methought, on every tree
Rejoicing, hailed my Liberty!

END OF THE SECOND VOLUME.

EDINBURGH :
Printed by THOMAS ALLAN & CO.,
265 High Street.

For EU product safety concerns, contact us at Calle de José Abascal, 56–1°, 28003 Madrid, Spain or eugpsr@cambridge.org.

www.ingramcontent.com/pod-product-compliance
Ingram Content Group UK Ltd.
Pitfield, Milton Keynes, MK11 3LW, UK
UKHW040617240426

470322UK00010B/168